Francis Parkman

The old régime in Canada. France and England in North America.

Part fourth

Vol. 2

Francis Parkman

The old régime in Canada. France and England in North America. Part fourth
Vol. 2

ISBN/EAN: 9783337208356

Printed in Europe, USA, Canada, Australia, Japan

Cover: Foto ©Andreas Hilbeck / pixelio.de

More available books at **www.hansebooks.com**

EDITION DE LUXE.

THE WORKS

OF

FRANCIS PARKMAN.

VOLUME VIII.

Eight Copies of the Edition de Luxe of Francis Parkman's Works have been printed for presentation.

No. *8*

THE OLD RÉGIME IN
CANDA ❧ ❧ ❧ ❧ ❧
FRANCE AND ENGLAND IN
NORTH AMERICA · PART FOURTH
BY FRANCIS PARKMAN ❧ ❧ ❧

IN TWO VOLUMES

VOL. II.

BOSTON ❧ LITTLE BROWN
AND · COMPANY ❧ MDCCCXCVII

Entered according to Act of Congress, in the year 1874, by
FRANCIS PARKMAN,
In the Office of the Librarian of Congress, at Washington.

1893,
BY FRANCIS PARKMAN.

1897,
BY LITTLE, BROWN, AND COMPANY.

University Press:
JOHN WILSON AND SON, CAMBRIDGE, U.S.A.

CONTENTS.

SECTION THIRD,— *Continued.*

THE COLONY AND THE KING.

CHAPTER XV.
1665–1672.
PATERNAL GOVERNMENT.

Talon. — Restriction and Monopoly. — Views of Colbert. — Political Galvanism. — A Father of the People **3**

CHAPTER XVI.
1661–1673.
MARRIAGE AND POPULATION.

Shipment of Emigrants. — Soldier Settlers. — Importation of Wives. — Wedlock. — Summary Methods. — The Mothers of Canada. — Bounties on Marriage. — Celibacy Punished. — Bounties on Children. — Results **11**

CHAPTER XVII.
1665–1672.
THE NEW HOME.

Military Frontier. — The Canadian Settler. — Seignior and Vassal. — Example of Talon. — Plan of Settlement. — Aspect of Canada. — Quebec. — The River Settlements. — Montreal. — The Pioneers **28**

CHAPTER XVIII.

1663–1763.

CANADIAN FEUDALISM.

Transplantation of Feudalism. — Precautions. — Faith and Homage. — The Seignior. — The Censitaire. — Royal Intervention. — The Gentilhomme. — Canadian Noblesse 40

CHAPTER XIX.

1663–1763.

THE RULERS OF CANADA.

Nature of the Government. — The Governor. — The Council. — Courts and Judges. — The Intendant: his Grievances. — Strong Government. — Sedition and Blasphemy. — Royal Bounty. — Defects and Abuses 62

CHAPTER XX.

1663–1763.

TRADE AND INDUSTRY.

Trade in Fetters. — The Huguenot Merchants. — Royal Patronage. — The Fisheries. — Cries for Help. — Agriculture. — Manufactures. — Arts of Ornament. — Finance. — Card Money. — Repudiation. — Imposts. — The Beaver Trade. — The Fair at Montreal. — Contraband Trade. — A Fatal System. — Trouble and Change. — The Coureurs de Bois. — The Forest. — Letter of Carheil 88

CHAPTER XXI.

1663–1702.

THE MISSIONS. — THE BRANDY QUESTION.

The Jesuits and the Iroquois. — Mission Villages. — Michilimackinac. — Father Carheil. — Temperance. — Brandy and the Indians. — Strong Measures. — Disputes. — License and Prohibition. — Views of the King. — Trade and the Jesuits   116

CONTENTS.

CHAPTER XXII.
1663-1763.
PRIESTS AND PEOPLE.

Church and State. — The Bishop and the King. — The King and the Curés. — The New Bishop. — The Canadian Curé. — Ecclesiastical Rule. — Saint-Vallier and Denonville. — Clerical Rigor. — Jesuit and Sulpitian. — Courcelle and Châtelain. — The Récollets. — Heresy and Witchcraft. — Canadian Nuns. — Jeanne Le Ber. — Education. — The Seminary. — Saint Joachim. — Miracles of Saint Anne. — Canadian Schools . . . 132

CHAPTER XXIII.
1640-1763.
MORALS AND MANNERS.

Social Influence of the Troops. — A Petty Tyrant. — Brawls. — Violence and Outlawry. — State of the Population. — Views of Denonville. — Brandy. — Beggary. — The Past and the Present. — Inns. — State of Quebec. — Fires. — The Country Parishes. — Slavery. — Views of La Hontan, — of Hocquart; of Bougainville; of Kalm; of Charlevoix 170

CHAPTER XXIV.
1663-1763.
CANADIAN ABSOLUTISM.

Formation of Canadian Character. — The Rival Colonies. — England and France. — New England. — Characteristics of Race. — Military Qualities. — The Church. — The English Conquest   197

APPENDIX.

A. La Tour and D'Aunay 205
B. The Hermitage of Caen 212
C. Laval and Argenson 217
D. Péronne Dumesnil 220

		PAGE
E.	Laval and Mésy	224
F.	Marriage and Population	229
G.	Château St. Louis	232
H.	Trade and Industry	236
I.	Letter of Father Carheil	242
J.	The Government and the Clergy	248
K.	Canadian Curés. Education. Discipline	256

INDEX 263

LIST OF ILLUSTRATIONS.

VOLUME TWO.

JEAN BAPTISTE COLBERT . . . . *Frontispiece*
    From the original painting by Claude Lefebvre, in the Versailles Gallery.

URSULINE CONVENT, QUEBEC . . . . *Page* 36
    From the painting in the possession of the Order, Quebec.

JEAN GUION BEFORE BOULLÉ . . . . " 44
    Drawn by Orson Lowell.

FRANÇOIS XAVIER DE LAVAL-MONTMORENCY " 132
    From the original painting in Laval University, Quebec.

SAINTE ANNE DU PETIT CAP . . . " 166
    After a photograph from Nature.

HE MADE A JUMP AT THE GUNS, AND TOOK THEM
UNDER HIS ARMS LIKE SO MANY FEATHERS . . " 175
    Drawn by Orson Lowell.

THE OLD RÉGIME IN CANADA.

SECTION THIRD,

Continued.

THE COLONY AND THE KING.

CHAPTER XV.

1665–1672.

PATERNAL GOVERNMENT.

TALON. — RESTRICTION AND MONOPOLY. — VIEWS OF COLBERT. — POLITICAL GALVANISM. — A FATHER OF THE PEOPLE.

TRACY's work was done, and he left Canada with the glittering *noblesse* in his train. Courcelle and Talon remained to rule alone; and now the great experiment was begun. Paternal royalty would try its hand at building up a colony, and Talon was its chosen agent. His appearance did him no justice. The regular contour of his oval face, about which fell to his shoulders a cataract of curls, natural or supposititious; the smooth lines of his well-formed features, brows delicately arched, and a mouth more suggestive of feminine sensibility than of masculine force, — would certainly have misled the disciple of

Lavater.[1] Yet there was no want of manhood in him. He was most happily chosen for the task placed in his hands, and from first to last approved himself a vigorous executive officer. He was a true disciple of Colbert, formed in his school and animated by his spirit.

Being on the spot, he was better able than his master to judge the working of the new order of things. With regard to the company, he writes that it will profit by impoverishing the colony; that its monopolies dishearten the people and paralyze enterprise; that it is thwarting the intentions of the King, who wishes trade to be encouraged; and that if its exclusive privileges are maintained, Canada in ten years will be less populous than now.[2] But Colbert clung to his plan, though he wrote in reply that to satisfy the colonists he had persuaded the company to forego the monopolies for a year.[3] As this proved insufficient, the company was at length forced to give up permanently its right of exclusive trade, still exacting its share of beaver and moose skins. This was its chief source of profit; it begrudged every sou deducted from it for charges of government, and the King was constantly obliged to do at his own cost that which the company should have done. In one point it showed a ceaseless activ-

---

[1] His portrait is at the Hôtel Dieu of Quebec. An engraving from it will be found in the third volume of Shea's Charlevoix.

[2] *Talon à Colbert, 4 Oct., 1665.*

[3] *Colbert à Talon, 5 Avril, 1666.*

ity; and this was the levying of duties, in which it was never known to fail.

Trade, even after its exercise was permitted, was continually vexed by the hand of authority. One of Tracy's first measures had been to issue a decree reducing the price of wheat one half. The council took up the work of regulation, and fixed the price of all imported goods in three several tariffs, — one for Quebec, one for Three Rivers, and one for Montreal.[1] It may well be believed that there was in Canada little capital and little enterprise. Industrially and commercially, the colony was almost dead. Talon set himself to galvanize it; and if one man could have supplied the intelligence and energy of a whole community, the results would have been triumphant.

He had received elaborate instructions, and they indicate an ardent wish for the prosperity of Canada. Colbert had written to him that the true means to strengthen the colony was to "cause justice to reign, establish a good police, protect the inhabitants, discipline them against enemies, and procure for them peace, repose, and plenty."[2] "And as," the minister further says, "the King regards his Canadian subjects, from the highest to the lowest, almost as his own children, and wishes them to enjoy equally with the people of France the mildness and happiness of his reign, the Sieur Talon will study to solace them

---

[1] *Tariff of Prices*, in *N. Y. Colonial Docs.* ix. 36.
[2] *Colbert à Talon*, 5 *Avril*, 1666.

in all things, and encourage them to trade and industry. And, seeing that nothing can better promote this end than entering into the details of their households and of all their little affairs, it will not be amiss that he visit all their settlements one after the other in order to learn their true condition, provide as much as possible for their wants, and, performing the duty of a good head of a family, put them in the way of making some profit." The intendant was also told to encourage fathers to inspire their children with piety, together with "profound love and respect for the royal person of his Majesty."[1]

Talon entered on his work with admirable zeal. Sometimes he used authority, sometimes persuasion, sometimes promises of reward. Sometimes, again, he tried the force of example. Thus he built a ship to show the people how to do it, and rouse them to imitation.[2] Three or four years later, the experiment was repeated. This time it was at the cost of the King, who applied the sum of forty thousand livres[3] to the double purpose of promoting the art of ship-building, and saving the colonists from vagrant habits by giving them employment. Talon wrote that three hundred and fifty men had been supplied that summer with work at the charge of government.[4]

He despatched two engineers to search for coal, lead, iron, copper, and other minerals. Important

[1] *Instruction au Sieur Talon*, 27 *Mars*, 1665.
[2] *Talon à Colbert, Octobre*, 1667; *Colbert à Talon*, 20 *Fév.*, 1668.
[3] *Dépêche de Colbert*, 11 *Fév.*, 1671.
[4] *Talon à Colbert*, 2 *Nov.*, 1671.

discoveries of iron were made; but three generations were destined to pass before the mines were successfully worked.¹ The copper of Lake Superior raised the intendant's hopes for a time, but he was soon forced to the conclusion that it was too remote to be of practical value. He labored vigorously to develop arts and manufactures; made a barrel of tar, and sent it to the King as a specimen; caused some of the colonists to make cloth of the wool of the sheep which the King had sent out; encouraged others to establish a tannery, and also a factory of hats and of shoes. The Sieur Follin was induced by the grant of a monopoly to begin the making of soap and potash.² The people were ordered to grow hemp,³ and urged to gather the nettles of the country as material for cordage; and the Ursulines were supplied with flax and wool, in order that they might teach girls to weave and spin.

Talon was especially anxious to establish trade between Canada and the West Indies; and, to make a beginning, he freighted the vessel he had built with salted cod, salmon, eels, pease, fish-oil, staves, and planks, and sent her thither to exchange her cargo for sugar, which she was in turn to exchange in France for goods suited for the Canadian market.⁴ Another

---

¹ Charlevoix speaks of these mines as having been forgotten for seventy years, and rediscovered in his time. After passing through various hands, they were finally worked on the King's account.

² *Régistre du Conseil Souverain*.

³ Marie de l'Incarnation, *Choix des Lettres de*, 371.

⁴ Le Mercier, *Rel.* 1667, 3; *Dépêches de Talon*.

favorite object with him was the fishery of seals and white porpoises for the sake of their oil; and some of the chief merchants were urged to undertake it, as well as the establishment of stationary cod-fisheries along the Lower St. Lawrence. But, with every encouragement, many years passed before this valuable industry was placed on a firm basis.

Talon saw with concern the huge consumption of wine and brandy among the settlers, costing them, as he wrote to Colbert, a hundred thousand livres a year; and to keep this money in the colony, he declared his intention of building a brewery. The minister approved the plan, not only on economic grounds, but because "the vice of drunkenness would thereafter cause no more scandal by reason of the cold nature of beer, the vapors whereof rarely deprive men of the use of judgment."[1] The brewery was accordingly built, to the great satisfaction of the poorer colonists.

Nor did the active intendant fail to acquit himself of the duty of domiciliary visits, enjoined upon him by the royal instructions, — a point on which he was of one mind with his superiors, for he writes that "those charged in this country with his Majesty's affairs are under a strict obligation to enter into the detail of families."[2] Accordingly, we learn from Mother Juchereau that "he studied with the affection of a father how to succor the poor and cause the

---

[1] *Colbert à Talon*, 20 *Fév.*, 1668.
[2] *Mémoire de* 1667.

colony to grow; entered into the minutest particulars; visited the houses of the inhabitants, and caused them to visit him; learned what crops each one was raising; taught those who had wheat to sell it at a profit, helped those who had none, and encouraged everybody." And Dollier de Casson represents him as visiting in turn every house at Montreal, and giving aid from the King to such as needed it.[1] Horses, cattle, sheep, and other domestic animals were sent out at the royal charge in considerable numbers, and distributed gratuitously, with an order that none of the young should be killed till the country was sufficiently stocked. Large quantities of goods were also sent from the same high quarter. Some of these were distributed as gifts, and the rest bartered for corn to supply the troops. As the intendant perceived that the farmers lost much time in coming from their distant clearings to buy necessaries at Quebec, he caused his agents to furnish them with the King's goods at their own houses, — to the great annoyance of the merchants of Quebec, who complained that their accustomed trade was thus forestalled.[2]

These were not the only cares which occupied the mind of Talon. He tried to open a road across the country to Acadia, — an almost impossible task, in which he and his successors completely failed. Under his auspices, Albanel penetrated to Hudson's

---

[1] *Histoire du Montréal*, A. D. 1666, 1667.
[2] *Talon à Colbert*, 10 *Nov.*, 1670.

Bay, and Saint-Lusson took possession in the King's name of the country of the Upper Lakes. It was Talon, in short, who prepared the way for the remarkable series of explorations described in another work.[1] Again and again he urged upon Colbert and the King a measure from which, had it taken effect, momentous consequences must have sprung. This was the purchase or seizure of New York, — involving the isolation of New England, the subjection of the Iroquois, and the undisputed control of half the continent.

Great as were his opportunities of abusing his trust, it does not appear that he took advantage of them. He held lands and houses in Canada,[2] owned the brewery which he had established, and embarked in various enterprises of productive industry; but, so far as I can discover, he is nowhere accused of making illicit gains, and there is reason to believe that he acquitted himself of his charge with entire fidelity.[3] His health failed in 1668, and for this and other causes he asked for his recall. Colbert granted it with strong expressions of regret; and when, two years later, he resumed the intendancy, the colony seems to have welcomed his return.

[1] La Salle, and the Discovery of the Great West.

[2] In 1682, the Intendant Meules, in a despatch to the minister, makes a statement of Talon's property in Quebec. The chief items are the brewery and a house of some value on the descent of Mountain Street. He owned, also, the valuable seigniory, afterwards barony, Des Islets, in the immediate neighborhood.

[3] Some imputations against him, not of much weight, are, however, made in a memorial of Aubert de la Chesnaye, a merchant of Quebec.

CHAPTER XVI.

1661-1673.

MARRIAGE AND POPULATION.

Shipment of Emigrants. — Soldier Settlers. — Importation of Wives. — Wedlock. — Summary Methods. — The Mothers of Canada. — Bounties on Marriage. — Celibacy Punished. — Bounties on Children. — Results.

The peopling of Canada was due in the main to the King. Before the accession of Louis XIV. the entire population — priests, nuns, traders, and settlers — did not exceed twenty-five hundred;[1] but scarcely had he reached his majority when the shipment of men to the colony was systematically begun. Even in Argenson's time, loads of emigrants sent out by the Crown were landed every year at Quebec. The Sulpitians of Montreal also brought over colonists to people their seigniorial estate; the same was true on a small scale of one or two other proprietors, and once at least the company sent a considerable number: yet the government was the chief agent of emigration. Colbert did the work, and the King paid for it.

[1] Le Clerc, *Établissement de la Foy*, ii. 4.

In 1661, Laval wrote to the cardinals of the Propaganda that during the past two years the King had spent two hundred thousand livres on the colony; that since 1659 he had sent out three hundred men a year; and that he had promised to send an equal number every summer during ten years.[1] These men were sent by squads in merchant-ships, each one of which was required to carry a certain number. In many instances, emigrants were bound on their arrival to enter into the service of colonists already established. In this case the employer paid them wages, and after a term of three years they became settlers themselves.[2]

The destined emigrants were collected by agents in the provinces, conducted to Dieppe or Rochelle, and thence embarked. At first men were sent from Rochelle itself, and its neighborhood; but Laval remonstrated, declaring that he wanted none from that ancient stronghold of heresy.[3] The people of Rochelle, indeed, found no favor in Canada. Another writer describes them as "persons of little conscience, and almost no religion," — adding that the Normans, Percherons, Picards, and peasants of the neighborhood of Paris are docile, industrious, and far more pious. "It is important," he concludes, "in begin-

---

[1] *Lettre de Laval envoyée à Rome*, 21 *Oct.*, 1661 (extract in Faillon from Archives of the Propaganda).

[2] Marie de l'Incarnation, 18 *Août*, 1664. These *engagés* were sometimes also brought over by private persons.

[3] *Colbert à Laval*, 18 *Mars*, 1664.

ning a new colony, to sow good seed."[1] It was, accordingly, from the northwestern provinces that most of the emigrants were drawn.[2] They seem in the main to have been a decent peasantry, though writers who from their position should have been well informed have denounced them in unmeasured terms.[3] Some of them could read and write, and some brought with them a little money.

Talon was constantly begging for more men, till Louis XIV. at length took alarm. Colbert replied to the over-zealous intendant that the King did not

---

[1] *Mémoire de* 1664 (anonymous).

[2] See a paper by Garneau in *Le National* of Quebec, 28 Oct., 1856, embodying the results of research among the papers of the early notaries of Quebec. The chief emigration was from Paris, Normandy, Poitou, Pays d'Aunis, Brittany, and Picardy. Nearly all those from Paris were sent by the King from houses of charity.

[3] "Une foule d'aventuriers, ramassés au hazard en France, presque tous de la lie du peuple, la plupart obérés de dettes ou chargés de crimes," etc. (La Tour, *Vie de Laval*, liv. iv.) "Le vice a obligé la plupart de chercher ce pays comme un asile pour se mettre à couvert de leurs crimes." (Meules, *Dépêche de* 1682.) Meules was intendant in that year. Marie de l'Incarnation, after speaking of the emigrants as of a very mixed character, says that it would have been far better to send a few who were good Christians, rather than so many who give so much trouble. *Lettre du — Octobre*, 1669.

Le Clerc, on the other hand, is emphatic in praise, calling the early colonists "très honnêtes gens, ayant de la probité, de la droiture, et de la religion. . . . L'on a examiné et choisi les habitants, et renvoyé en France les personnes vicieuses." If, he adds, any such were left, "ils effaçaient glorieusement par leur pénitence les taches de leur première condition." Charlevoix is almost as strong in praise as La Tour in censure. Both of them wrote in the next century. We shall have means hereafter of judging between these conflicting statements.

think it expedient to depopulate France in order to people Canada; that he wanted men for his armies; and that the colony must rely chiefly on increase from within. Still the shipments did not cease; and, even while tempering the ardor of his agent, the King gave another proof how much he had the growth of Canada at heart.[1]

The regiment of Carignan-Salières had been ordered home, with the exception of four companies kept in garrison,[2] and a considerable number discharged in order to become settlers. Of those who returned, six companies were a year or two later sent back, discharged in their turn, and converted into colonists. Neither men nor officers were positively constrained to remain in Canada; but the officers were told that if they wished to please his Majesty this was the way to do so; and both they and the men were stimulated by promises and rewards. Fifteen hundred livres were given to La Motte, because he had married in the country and meant to remain there. Six thousand livres were assigned to other officers because they had followed, or were about to follow, La Motte's example; and twelve thousand were set apart to be distributed to the soldiers under similar

---

[1] The King had sent out more emigrants than he had promised, to judge from the census reports during the years 1666, 1667, and 1668. The total population for those years is 3418, 4312, and 5870, respectively. A small part of this growth may be set down to emigration not under government auspices, and a large part to natural increase, — which was enormous at this time, from causes which will soon appear.

[2] *Colbert à Talon*, 20 Fév., 1668.

conditions.[1] Each soldier who consented to remain and settle was promised a grant of land and a hundred livres in money; or, if he preferred it, fifty livres with provisions for a year. This military colonization had a strong and lasting influence on the character of the Canadian people.

But if the colony was to grow from within, the new settlers must have wives. For some years past the Sulpitians had sent out young women for the supply of Montreal; and the King, on a larger scale, continued the benevolent work. Girls for the colony were taken from the hospitals of Paris and of Lyons, which were not so much hospitals for the sick as houses of refuge for the poor. Mother Mary writes in 1665 that a hundred had come that summer, and were nearly all provided with husbands, and that two hundred more were to come next year. The case was urgent, for the demand was great. Complaints, however, were soon heard that women from cities made indifferent partners; and peasant girls, healthy, strong, and accustomed to field-work, were demanded in their place. Peasant girls were therefore sent; but this was not all. Officers as well as men wanted wives; and Talon asked for a consignment of young ladies. His request was promptly answered. In 1667, he writes: "They send us eighty-four girls from Dieppe and twenty-five from Rochelle; among them are fifteen or twenty of pretty good birth; several of them are really *demoiselles*, and tolerably

---

[1] *Colbert à Talon*, 20 Fév., 1668.

well brought up." They complained of neglect and hardship during the voyage. "I shall do what I can to soothe their discontent," adds the intendant; "for if they write to their correspondents at home how ill they have been treated, it would be an obstacle to your plan of sending us next year a number of select young ladies." [1]

Three years later we find him asking for three or four more in behalf of certain bachelor officers. The response surpassed his utmost wishes; and he wrote again: "It is not expedient to send more *demoiselles*. I have had this year fifteen of them, instead of the four I asked for." [2]

As regards peasant girls, the supply rarely equalled the demand. Count Frontenac, Courcelle's successor, complained of the scarcity: "If a hundred and fifty girls and as many servants," he says, "had been sent out this year, they would all have found husbands and masters within a month." [3]

The character of these candidates for matrimony has not escaped the pen of slander. The caustic La Hontan, writing fifteen or twenty years after, draws

[1] "*Des demoiselles bien choisies.*" — *Talon à Colbert*, 27 *Oct.*, 1667.
[2] *Talon à Colbert*, 2 *Nov.*, 1671.
[3] *Frontenac à Colbert*, 2 *Nov.*, 1672. This year only eleven girls had been sent. The scarcity was due to the indiscretion of Talon, who had written to the minister, that, as many of the old settlers had daughters just becoming marriageable, it would be well, in order that they might find husbands, to send no more girls from France at present.

The next year, 1673, the King writes, that, though he is involved in a great war, which needs all his resources, he has nevertheless sent sixty more girls.

the following sketch of the mothers of Canada: "After the regiment of Carignan was disbanded, ships were sent out freighted with girls of indifferent virtue, under the direction of a few pious old duennas, who divided them into three classes. These vestals were, so to speak, piled one on the other in three different halls, where the bridegrooms chose their brides as a butcher chooses his sheep out of the midst of the flock. There was wherewith to content the most fantastical in these three harems; for here were to be seen the tall and the short, the blond and the brown, the plump and the lean; everybody, in short, found a shoe to fit him. At the end of a fortnight not one was left. I am told that the plumpest were taken first, because it was thought that, being less active, they were more likely to keep at home, and that they could resist the winter cold better. Those who wanted a wife applied to the directresses, to whom they were obliged to make known their possessions and means of livelihood before taking from one of the three classes the girl whom they found most to their liking. The marriage was concluded forthwith, with the help of a priest and a notary; and the next day the governor-general caused the couple to be presented with an ox, a cow, a pair of swine, a pair of fowls, two barrels of salted meat, and eleven crowns in money."[1]

[1] La Hontan, *Nouveaux Voyages*, i. 11 (1709). In some of the other editions the same account is given in different words, equally lively and scandalous.

As regards the character of the girls, there can be no doubt that this amusing sketch is, in the main, maliciously untrue. Since the colony began, it had been the practice to send back to France women of the class alluded to by La Hontan, as soon as they became notorious.[1] Those who were not taken from institutions of charity usually belonged to the families of peasants overburdened with children, and glad to find the chance of establishing them.[2] How some of them were obtained appears from a letter of Colbert to Harlay, Archbishop of Rouen. "As in the parishes about Rouen," he writes, "fifty or sixty girls might be found who would be very glad to go to Canada to be married, I beg you to employ your credit and authority with the curés of thirty or forty of these parishes, to try to find in each of them one or two girls disposed to go voluntarily for the sake of a settlement in life."[3]

---

[1] This is the statement of Boucher, a good authority. A case of the sort in 1658 is mentioned in the correspondence of Argenson. Boucher says further, that an assurance of good character was required from the relations or friends of the girl who wished to embark. This refers to a period anterior to 1663, when Boucher wrote his book. Colbert evidently cared for no qualification except the capacity of maternity.

[2] *Témoignage de la Mère du Plessis de Sainte-Hélène* (extract in Faillon).

[3] *Colbert à l'Archevêque de Rouen*, 27 Fév., 1670.

That they were not always destitute may be gathered from a passage in one of Talon's letters: "Entre les filles qu'on fait passer ici il y en a qui ont de légitimes et considérables prétentions aux successions de leurs parents, même entre celles qui sont tirées de l'Hôpital Général." The General Hospital of Paris had recently been established (1656) as a house of refuge for the "Bohemians."

Mistakes nevertheless occurred. "Along with the honest people," complains Mother Mary, "comes a great deal of *canaille* of both sexes, who cause a great deal of scandal."¹ After some of the young women had been married at Quebec, it was found that they had husbands at home. The priests became cautious in tying the matrimonial knot, and Colbert thereupon ordered that each girl should provide herself with a certificate from the curé or magistrate of her parish to the effect that she was free to marry. Nor was the practical intendant unmindful of other precautions to smooth the path to the desired goal. "The girls destined for this country," he writes, "besides being strong and healthy, ought to be entirely free from any natural blemish or anything personally repulsive."²

Thus qualified canonically and physically, the annual consignment of young women was shipped to Quebec, in charge of a matron employed and paid by the King. Her task was not an easy one, for the troop under her care was apt to consist of what

or vagrants of Paris. The royal edict creating it says that "les pauvres mendiants et invalides des deux sexes y seraient enfermés pour estre employés aux manufactures et aultres travaux selon leur pouvoir." They were gathered by force in the streets by a body of special police, called "Archers de l'Hôpital." They resisted at first, and serious riots ensued. In 1662, the General Hospital of Paris contained 6262 paupers. See Clément, *Histoire de Colbert*, 113. Mother de Sainte-Hélène says that the girls sent from this asylum had been there from childhood in charge of nuns.

¹ "Beaucoup de canaille de l'un et l'autre sexe qui causent beaucoup de scandale." — *Lettre du* — *Octobre*, 1669.

² *Talon à Colbert*, 10 *Nov.*, 1670.

Mother Mary in a moment of unwonted levity calls "mixed goods."[1] On one occasion the office was undertaken by the pious widow of Jean Bourdon. Her flock of a hundred and fifty girls, says Mother Mary, "gave her no little trouble on the voyage; for they are of all sorts, and some of them are very rude and hard to manage." Madame Bourdon was not daunted. She not only saw her charge distributed and married, but she continued to receive and care for the subsequent ship-loads as they arrived summer after summer. She was indeed chief among the pious duennas of whom La Hontan irreverently speaks. Marguerite Bourgeoys did the same good offices for the young women sent to Montreal. Here the "King's girls," as they were called, were all lodged together in a house to which the suitors repaired to make their selection. "I was obliged to live there myself," writes the excellent nun, "because families were to be formed;"[2] that is to say, because it was she who superintended these extemporized unions. Meanwhile she taught the girls their catechism, and, more fortunate than Madame Bourdon, inspired them with a confidence and affection which they retained long after.

[1] "Une marchandise mêlée." — *Lettre du* — 1668. In that year, 1668, the King spent 40,000 livres in the shipment of men and girls. In 1669, a hundred and fifty girls were sent; in 1670, a hundred and sixty-five; and Talon asks for a hundred and fifty or two hundred more to supply the soldiers who had got ready their houses and clearings, and were now prepared to marry. The total number of girls sent from 1665 to 1673, inclusive, was about a thousand.

[2] Extract in Faillon, *Colonie Française*, iii. 214.

At Quebec, where the matrimonial market was on a larger scale, a more ample bazaar was needed. That the girls were assorted into three classes, each penned up for selection in a separate hall, is a statement probable enough in itself, but resting on no better authority than that of La Hontan. Be this as it may, they were submitted together to the inspection of the suitor; and the awkward young peasant or the rugged soldier of Carignan was required to choose a bride without delay from among the anxious candidates. They, on their part, were permitted to reject any applicant who displeased them; and the first question, we are told, which most of them asked was whether the suitor had a house and a farm.

Great as was the call for wives, it was thought prudent to stimulate it. The new settler was at once enticed and driven into wedlock. Bounties were offered on early marriages. Twenty livres were given to each youth who married before the age of twenty, and to each girl who married before the age of sixteen.[1] This, which was called the "King's gift," was exclusive of the dowry given by him to every girl brought over by his orders. The dowry varied greatly in form and value; but, according to Mother Mary, it was sometimes a house with provisions for eight months. More often it was fifty livres in household supplies, besides a barrel or two of salted meat. The royal solicitude extended also

[1] *Arrêt du Conseil d'État du Roy* (see *Édits et Ordonnances*, i. 67).

to the children of colonists already established. "I pray you," writes Colbert to Talon, "to commend it to the consideration of the whole people, that their prosperity, their subsistence, and all that is dear to them depend on a general resolution, never to be departed from, to marry youths at eighteen or nineteen years and girls at fourteen or fifteen; since abundance can never come to them except through the abundance of men."[1] This counsel was followed by appropriate action. Any father of a family who, without showing good cause, neglected to marry his children when they had reached the ages of twenty and sixteen was fined;[2] and each father thus delinquent was required to present himself every six months to the local authorities to declare what reason, if any, he had for such delay.[3] Orders were issued, a little before the arrival of the yearly ships from France, that all single men should marry within a fortnight after the landing of the prospective brides. No mercy was shown to the obdurate bachelor. Talon issued an order forbidding unmarried men to hunt, fish, trade with the Indians, or go into the woods under any pretence whatsoever.[4] In

---

[1] *Colbert à Talon*, 20 Fév., 1668.

[2] *Arrêts du Conseil d'État*, 1669 (cited by Faillon); *Arrêt du Conseil d'État*, 1670 (see *Édits et Ordonnances*, i. 67); *Ordonnance du Roy*, 5 Avril, 1669. See Clément, *Instructions, etc. de Colbert*, iii. 2me Partie, 657.

[3] *Régistre du Conseil Souverain*.

[4] *Talon au Ministre*, 10 Oct., 1670. Colbert highly approves this order. Faillon found a case of its enforcement among the ancient records of Montreal. In December, 1670, François Le Noir, an

short, they were made as miserable as possible. Colbert goes further. He writes to the intendant, "Those who may seem to have absolutely renounced marriage should be made to bear additional burdens, and be excluded from all honors; it would be well even to add some marks of infamy."[1] The success of these measures was complete. "No sooner," says Mother Mary, "have the vessels arrived than the young men go to get wives; and, by reason of the great number, they are married by thirties at a time." Throughout the length and breadth of Canada, Hymen, if not Cupid, was whipped into a frenzy of activity. Dollier de Casson tells us of a widow who was married afresh before her late husband was buried.[2]

Nor was the fatherly care of the King confined to the humbler classes of his colonists. He wished to form a Canadian *noblesse*, to which end early mar-

---

inhabitant of La Chine, was summoned before the judge, because, though a single man, he had traded with Indians at his own house. He confessed the fact, but protested that he would marry within three weeks after the arrival of the vessels from France, or, failing to do so, that he would give a hundred and fifty livres to the church of Montreal, and an equal sum to the hospital. On this condition he was allowed to trade, but was still forbidden to go into the woods. The next year he kept his word, and married Marie Magdeleine Charbonnier, late of Paris.

The prohibition to go into the woods was probably intended to prevent the bachelor from finding a temporary Indian substitute for a French wife.

[1] "Il serait à propos de leur augmenter les charges, de les priver de tous honneurs, même d'y ajouter quelque marque d'infamie." *Lettre du 20 Fév.,* 1668.

[2] *Histoire du Montréal,* A. D. 1671, 1672.

riages were thought needful among officers and others of the better sort. The progress of such marriages was carefully watched and reported by the intendant. We have seen the reward bestowed upon La Motte for taking to himself a wife, and the money set apart for the brother officers who imitated him. In his despatch of October, 1667, the intendant announces that two captains are already married to two damsels of the country; that a lieutenant has espoused a daughter of the governor of Three Rivers; and that "four ensigns are in treaty with their mistresses, and are already half engaged."[1] The paternal care of government, one would think, could scarcely go further.

It did, however, go further. Bounties were offered on children. The King, in council, passed a decree "that in future all inhabitants of the said country of Canada who shall have living children to the number of ten, born in lawful wedlock, not being priests, monks, or nuns, shall each be paid out of the moneys sent by his Majesty to the said country a pension of three hundred livres a year, and those who shall have twelve children, a pension of four hundred livres; and that, to this effect, they shall be required to declare the number of their children every year in

---

[1] "Quatre enseignes sont en pourparler avec leurs maîtresses et sont déjà à demi engagés." (*Dépêche du* 27 *Oct.*, 1667.) The lieutenant was René Gaultier de Varennes, who on the 26th September, 1667, married Marie Bochart, daughter of the governor of Three Rivers, aged twelve years. One of the children of this marriage was Varennes de la Vérendrye, whose son discovered the Rocky Mountains.

the months of June or July to the intendant of justice, police, and finance, established in the said country, who, having verified the same, shall order the payment of said pensions, one-half in cash, and the other half at the end of each year."[1] This was applicable to all. Colbert had before offered a reward, intended specially for the better class, of twelve hundred livres to those who had fifteen children, and eight hundred to those who had ten.

These wise encouragements, as the worthy Faillon calls them, were crowned with the desired result. A despatch of Talon in 1670 informs the minister that most of the young women sent out last summer are pregnant already; and in 1671 he announces that from six hundred to seven hundred children have been born in the colony during the year, — a prodigious number in view of the small population. The climate was supposed to be particularly favorable to the health of women, which is somewhat surprising in view of recent American experience. "The first reflection I have to make," says Dollier de Casson, "is on the advantage that women have in this place [Montreal] over men; for though the cold is very wholesome to both sexes, it is incomparably

---

[1] *Édits et Ordonnances*, i. 67. It was thought at this time that the Indians, mingled with the French, might become a valuable part of the population. The reproductive qualities of Indian women, therefore, became an object of Talon's attention, and he reports that they impair their fertility by nursing their children longer than is necessary; "but," he adds, "this obstacle to the speedy building up of the colony can be overcome by a police regulation." *Mémoire sur l'État Présent du Canada*, 1667.

more so to the female, who is almost immortal here." Her fecundity matched her longevity, and was the admiration of Talon and his successors, accustomed as they were to the scanty families of France.

Why with this great natural increase joined to an immigration which, though greatly diminishing, did not entirely cease, was there not a corresponding increase in the population of the colony? Why, more than half a century after the King took Canada in charge, did the census show a total of less than twenty-five thousand souls? The reasons will appear hereafter.

It is a peculiarity of Canadian immigration, at this its most flourishing epoch, that it was mainly an immigration of single men and single women. The cases in which entire families came over were comparatively few.[1] The new settler was found by the King, sent over by the King, and supplied by the

---

[1] The principal emigration of families seems to have been in 1669, when, at the urgency of Talon, then in France, a considerable number were sent out. In the earlier period the emigration of families was, relatively, much greater. Thus, in 1634, the physician Giffard brought over seven to people his seigniory of Beauport. Before 1663, when the King took the colony in hand, the emigrants were for the most part apprenticed laborers.

The zeal with which the King entered into the work of stocking his colony is shown by numberless passages in his letters, and those of his minister. "The end and the rule of all your conduct," says Colbert to the intendant Bouteroue, "should be the increase of the colony; and on this point you should never be satisfied, but labor without ceasing to find every imaginable expedient for preserving the inhabitants, attracting new ones, and multiplying them by marriage." — *Instruction pour M. Bouteroue*, 1668.

King with a wife, a farm, and sometimes with a house. Well did Louis XIV. earn the title of Father of New France. But the royal zeal was spasmodic. The King was diverted to other cares; and soon after the outbreak of the Dutch war in 1672 the regular despatch of emigrants to Canada wellnigh ceased, — though the practice of disbanding soldiers in the colony, giving them lands, and turning them into settlers, was continued in some degree, even to the last.

CHAPTER XVII.

1665-1672.

THE NEW HOME.

Military Frontier. — The Canadian Settler. — Seignior and Vassal. — Example of Talon. — Plan of Settlement. — Aspect of Canada. — Quebec. — The River Settlements. — Montreal. — The Pioneers.

We have seen the settler landed and married; let us follow him to his new home. At the end of Talon's administration, the head of the colony — that is to say, the island of Montreal and the borders of the Richelieu — was the seat of a peculiar colonization, the chief object of which was to protect the rest of Canada against Iroquois incursions. The lands along the Richelieu, from its mouth to a point above Chambly, were divided in large seigniorial grants among several officers of the regiment of Carignan, who in their turn granted out the land to the soldiers, reserving a sufficient portion as their own. The officer thus became a kind of feudal chief, and the whole settlement a permanent military cantonment admirably suited to the object in view. The disbanded soldier was practically a soldier still, but he was also a farmer and a landholder.

Talon had recommended this plan as being in accordance with the example of the Romans. "The practice of that politic and martial people," he wrote, "may, in my opinion, be wisely adopted in a country a thousand leagues distant from its monarch. And as the peace and harmony of peoples depend above all things on their fidelity to their sovereign, our first kings, better statesmen than is commonly supposed, introduced into newly conquered countries men of war, of approved trust, in order at once to hold the inhabitants to their duty within, and repel the enemy from without."[1]

The troops were accordingly discharged, and settled not alone on the Richelieu, but also along the St. Lawrence, between Lake St. Peter and Montreal, as well as at some other points. The Sulpitians, feudal owners of Montreal, adopted a similar policy, and surrounded their island with a border of fiefs large and small, granted partly to officers and partly to humbler settlers, bold, hardy, and practised in bush-fighting. Thus a line of sentinels was posted around their entire shore, ready to give the alarm whenever an enemy appeared. About Quebec the settlements, covered as they were by those above, were for the most part of a more pacific character.

To return to the Richelieu. The towns and villages which have since grown upon its banks and along the adjacent shores of the St. Lawrence owe their names to these officers of Carignan, ancient

[1] *Projets de Réglemens*, 1667 (see *Édits et Ordonnances*, ii. 29).

lords of the soil, — Sorel, Chambly, Saint Ours, Contrecœur, Varennes, Verchères. Yet let it not be supposed that villages sprang up at once. The military seignior, valiant and poor as Walter the Penniless, was in no condition to work such magic. His personal possessions usually consisted of little but his sword and the money which the King had paid him for marrying a wife. A domain varying from half a league to six leagues in front on the river, and from half a league to two leagues in depth, had been freely given him. When he had distributed a part of it in allotments to the soldiers, a variety of tasks awaited him, — to clear and cultivate his land; to build his seigniorial mansion, often a log hut; to build a fort; to build a chapel; and to build a mill. To do all this at once was impossible. Chambly, the chief proprietor on the Richelieu, was better able than the others to meet the exigency. He built himself a good house, where, with cattle and sheep furnished by the King, he lived in reasonable comfort.[1] The King's fort, close at hand, spared him and his tenants the necessity of building one for themselves, and furnished, no doubt, a mill, a chapel, and a chaplain. His brother officers, Sorel excepted, were less fortunate. They and their tenants were forced to provide defence as well as shelter. Their houses were all built together, and surrounded by a palisade, so as to form a little fortified village. The

---

[1] *Frontenac au Ministre*, 2 *Nov.*, 1672. Marie de l'Incarnation speaks of these officers on the Richelieu as *très honnêtes gens*.

ever-active benevolence of the King had aided them in the task, for the soldiers were still maintained by him while clearing the lands and building the houses destined to be their own; nor was it till this work was done that the provident government despatched them to Quebec with orders to bring back wives. The settler, thus lodged and wedded, was required on his part to aid in clearing lands for those who should come after him.[1]

It was chiefly in the more exposed parts of the colony that the houses were gathered together in palisaded villages, thus forcing the settler to walk or paddle some distance to his farm. He naturally preferred to build when he could on the front of his farm itself, near the river, which supplied the place of a road. As the grants of land were very narrow, his house was not far from that of his next neighbor; and thus a line of dwellings was ranged along the shore, forming what in local language was called a *côte*, — a use of the word peculiar to Canada, where it still prevails.

The impoverished seignior rarely built a chapel. Most of the early Canadian churches were built with

[1] "Sa Majesté semble prétendre faire la dépense entière pour former le commencement des habitations par l'abattis du bois, la culture et semence de deux arpens de terre, l'avance de quelques farines aux familles venantes," etc. (*Projets de Réglemens*, 1667.) This applied to civil and military settlers alike. The established settler was allowed four years to clear two arpents of land for a new-comer. The soldiers were maintained by the King during a year, while preparing their farms and houses. Talon asks that two years more be given them. *Talon au Roy*, 10 *Nov.*, 1670.

funds furnished by the seminaries of Quebec or of Montreal, aided by contributions of material and labor from the parishioners.[1] Meanwhile mass was said in some house of the neighborhood by a missionary priest, paddling his canoe from village to village, or from *côte* to *côte*.

The mill was an object of the last importance. It was built of stone and pierced with loopholes, to serve as a blockhouse in case of attack. The great mill at Montreal was one of the chief defences of the place. It was at once the duty and the right of the seignior to supply his tenants, or rather vassals, with this essential requisite; and they on their part were required to grind their grain at his mill, leaving the fourteenth part in payment. But for many years there was not a seigniory in Canada where this fraction would pay the wages of a miller; and, except the ecclesiastical corporations, there were few seigniors who could pay the cost of building. The first settlers were usually forced to grind for themselves after the tedious fashion of the Indians.

Talon, in his capacity of counsellor, friend, and father to all Canada, arranged the new settlements near Quebec in the manner which he judged best, and which he meant to serve as an example to the rest of the colony. It was his aim to concentrate population around this point, so that, should an enemy appear, the sound of a cannon-shot from the Château St. Louis might summon a numerous body

---

[1] La Tour, *Vie de Laval*, chap. x.

of defenders to this the common point of rendezvous.¹ He bought a tract of land near Quebec, laid it out, and settled it as a model seigniory, hoping, as he says, to kindle a spirit of emulation among the new-made seigniors to whom he had granted lands from the King. He also laid out at the royal cost three villages in the immediate neighborhood, planning them with great care, and peopling them partly with families newly arrived, partly with soldiers, and partly with old settlers, in order that the new-comers might take lessons from the experience of these veterans. That each village might be complete in itself, he furnished it as well as he could with the needful carpenter, mason, blacksmith, and shoemaker. These inland villages, called respectively Bourg Royal, Bourg la Reine, and Bourg Talon, did not prove very thrifty.² Wherever the settlers were allowed to choose for themselves, they ranged their dwellings along the watercourses. With the exception of Talon's villages, one could have seen nearly every house in Canada, by paddling a canoe up the St. Lawrence and the Richelieu. The settlements formed long thin lines on the edges of the rivers, — a convenient arrangement, but one very unfavorable to defence, to ecclesiastical control, and to strong government. The King soon discovered this; and repeated orders were sent to concentrate the inhab-

---

[1] *Projets de Réglemens*, 1667.

[2] In 1672 the King, as a mark of honor, attached these villages to Talon's seigniory. See Documents on Seigniorial Tenure.

itants and form Canada into villages, instead of *côtes*. To do so would have involved a general revocation of grants and abandonment of houses and clearings, — a measure too arbitrary and too wasteful, even for Louis XIV., and one extremely difficult to enforce. Canada persisted in attenuating herself, and the royal will was foiled.

As you ascended the St. Lawrence, the first harboring place of civilization was Tadoussac, at the mouth of the Saguenay, where the company had its trading station, where its agents ruled supreme, and where, in early summer, all was alive with canoes and wigwams, and troops of Montagnais savages, bringing their furs to market. Leave Tadoussac behind, and, embarked in a sail-boat or a canoe, follow the northern coast. Far on the left, twenty miles away, the southern shore lies pale and dim, and mountain ranges wave their faint outline along the sky. You pass the beetling rocks of Mal Bay, a solitude but for the bark hut of some wandering Indian beneath the cliff, the Eboulements with their wild romantic gorge and foaming waterfalls, and the Bay of St. Paul with its broad valley and its woody mountains, rich with hidden stores of iron. Vast piles of savage verdure border the mighty stream, till at length the mountain of Cape Tourmente upheaves its huge bulk from the bosom of the water, shadowed by lowering clouds, and dark with forests. Just beyond, begin the settlements of Laval's vast seigniory of Beaupré, which had not been forgotten in the distribution of emigrants, and which, in 1667, contained more inhabitants than Quebec itself.[1] The ribbon of rich meadow land that borders that beautiful shore was yellow with wheat in harvest time; and on the woody slopes behind, the frequent clearings and the solid little dwellings of logs continued for a long distance to relieve the sameness of the forest. After passing the cataract of Montmorenci, there was another settlement, much smaller, at Beauport, the seigniory of the ex-physician Giffard, one of the earliest proprietors in Canada. The neighboring shores of the Island of Orleans were also edged with houses and clearings. The promontory of Quebec now towered full in sight, crowned with church, fort, château, convents, and seminary. There was little else on the rock. Priests, nuns, government officials, and soldiers were the denizens of the Upper Town; while commerce and the trades were cabined along the strand beneath.[2] From the gallery of the château, you might toss a pebble far down on their shingled roofs. In the midst of them was the magazine of the company, with its two round towers and two projecting wings. It was here that

[1] The census of 1667 gives to Quebec only 448 souls; Côte de Beaupré, 656; Beauport, 123; Island of Orleans, 529; other settlements included under the government of Quebec, 1,011; Côte de Lauzon (south shore), 113; Trois Rivières and its dependencies, 666; Montreal, 766. Both Beaupré and Isle d'Orleans belonged at this time to the bishop.

[2] According to Juchereau, there were seventy houses at Quebec about the time of Tracy's arrival.

all the beaver-skins of the colony were collected, assorted, and shipped for France. The so-called Château St. Louis was an indifferent wooden structure planted on a site truly superb, — above the Lower Town, above the river, above the ships, gazing abroad on a majestic panorama of waters, forests, and mountains.[1] Behind it was the area of the fort, of which it formed one side. The governor lived in the château, and soldiers were on guard night and day in the fort. At some little distance was the convent of the Ursulines, ugly but substantial,[2] where Mother Mary of the Incarnation ruled her pupils and her nuns; and a little farther on, towards the right, was the Hôtel Dieu. Between them were the massive buildings of the Jesuits, then as now facing the principal square. At one side was their church, newly finished; and opposite, across the square, stood and still stands the great church of Notre Dame. Behind the church was Laval's seminary, with the extensive enclosures belonging to it. The *sénéchaussée* or court-house, the tavern of one Jacques Boisdon on the square near the church, and a few houses along the line of what is now St. Louis Street comprised nearly all the civil part of the Upper Town. The ecclesiastical buildings were of stone, and the church of Notre Dame and the Jesuit

---

[1] In 1660, an exact inventory was taken of the contents of the fort and château, — a beggarly account of rubbish. The château was then a long low building roofed with shingles.

[2] There is an engraving of it in Abbé Casgrain's interesting *Vie de Marie de l'Incarnation*. It was burned in 1686.

Ursuline Convent.

College were marvels of size and solidity in view of the poverty and weakness of the colony.[1]

Proceeding upward along the north shore of the St. Lawrence, one found a cluster of houses at Cap Rouge, and, farther on, the frequent rude beginnings of a seigniory. The settlements thickened on approaching Three Rivers, a fur-trading hamlet enclosed with a square palisade. Above this place, a line of incipient seigniories bordered the river, most of them granted to officers, — Laubia, a captain; Labadie, a sergeant; Moras, an ensign; Berthier, a captain; Randin, an ensign; La Valterie, a lieutenant.[2] Under their auspices, settlers, military and civilian, were ranging themselves along the shore, and ugly gaps in the forest thickly set with stumps bore witness to their toils. These settlements rapidly extended, till in a few years a chain of houses and clearings reached with little interruption from Quebec to Montreal. Such was the fruit of Tracy's chastisement of the Mohawks, and the influx of immigrants that followed.

As you approached Montreal, the fortified mill

---

[1] The first stone of Notre Dame de Quebec was laid in September, 1647, and the first mass was said in it on the 24th of December, 1650. The side walls still remain as part of the present structure. The Jesuit College was also begun in 1647. The walls and roof were finished in 1649. The church connected with it, since destroyed, was begun in 1666. See *Journal des Jésuites*.

[2] See Documents on the Seigniorial Tenure; Abstracts of Titles. Most of these grants, like those on the Richelieu, were made by Talon in 1672; but the land had, in many cases, been occupied and cleared in anticipation of the title.

built by the Sulpitians at Point aux Trembles towered above the woods; and soon after the newly built chapel of the Infant Jesus. More settlements followed, till at length the great fortified mill of Montreal rose in sight; then the long row of compact wooden houses, the Hôtel Dieu, and the rough masonry of the Seminary of St. Sulpice. Beyond the town, the clearings continued at intervals till you reached Lake St. Louis, where young Cavelier de la Salle had laid out his seigniory of La Chine, and abandoned it to begin his hard career of western exploration. Above the island of Montreal, the wilderness was broken only by a solitary trading station on the neighboring Isle Pérot.

Now cross Lake St. Louis, shoot the rapids of La Chine, and follow the southern shore downward. Here the seigniories of Longueuil, Boucherville, Varennes, Verchères, and Contrecœur were already begun. From the fort of Sorel one could visit the military seigniories along the Richelieu or descend towards Quebec, passing on the way those of Lussaudière, Becancour, Lotbinière, and others still in a shapeless infancy. Even far below Quebec, at St. Anne de la Pocatière, River Ouelle, and other points, cabins and clearings greeted the eye of the passing canoeman.

For a year or two the settler's initiation was a rough one; but when he had a few acres under tillage he could support himself and his family on the produce, aided by hunting, if he knew how to use a gun, and by the bountiful profusion of eels which the St. Lawrence never failed to yield in their season, and which, smoked or salted, supplied his larder for months. In winter he hewed timber, sawed planks, or split shingles for the market of Quebec, obtaining in return such necessaries as he required. With thrift and hard work he was sure of comfort at last; but the former habits of the military settlers and of many of the others were not favorable to a routine of dogged industry. The sameness and solitude of their new life often became insufferable; nor, married as they had been, was the domestic hearth likely to supply much consolation. Yet, thrifty or not, they multiplied apace. "A poor man," says Mother Mary, "will have eight children and more, who run about in winter with bare heads and bare feet, and a little jacket on their backs, live on nothing but bread and eels, and on that grow fat and stout." With such treatment the weaker sort died, but the strong survived; and out of this rugged nursing sprang the hardy Canadian race of bush-rangers and bush-fighters.

CHAPTER XVIII.

1663-1763.

CANADIAN FEUDALISM.

TRANSPLANTATION OF FEUDALISM. — PRECAUTIONS. — FAITH AND HOMAGE. — THE SEIGNIOR. — THE CENSITAIRE. — ROYAL INTERVENTION. — THE GENTILHOMME. — CANADIAN NOBLESSE.

CANADIAN society was beginning to form itself, and at its base was the feudal tenure. European feudalism was the indigenous and natural growth of political and social conditions which preceded it. Canadian feudalism was an offshoot of the feudalism of France, modified by the lapse of centuries, and further modified by the royal will.

In France, as in the rest of Europe, the system had lost its vitality. The warrior-nobles who placed Hugh Capet on the throne, and began the feudal monarchy, formed an aristocratic republic; and the King was one of their number, whom they chose to be their chief. But through the struggles and vicissitudes of many succeeding reigns royalty had waxed and oligarchy had waned. The fact had changed, and the theory had changed with it. The King, once powerless among a host of turbulent nobles, was now a king indeed. Once a chief, because his equals had made him so, he was now the anointed of the Lord. This triumph of royalty had culminated in Louis XIV. The stormy energies and bold individualism of the old feudal nobles had ceased to exist. They who had held his predecessors in awe had become his obsequious servants. He no longer feared his nobles: he prized them as gorgeous decorations of his court and satellites of his royal person.

It was Richelieu who first planted feudalism in Canada.[1] The King would preserve it there, because with its teeth drawn he was fond of it; and because, as the feudal tenure prevailed in Old France, it was natural that it should prevail also in the New. But he continued as Richelieu had begun, and moulded it to the form that pleased him. Nothing was left which could threaten his absolute and undivided authority over the colony. In France, a multitude of privileges and prescriptions still clung, despite its fall, about the ancient ruling class. Few of these were allowed to cross the Atlantic, while the old lingering abuses, which had made the system odious, were at the same time lopped away. Thus retrenched, Canadian feudalism was made to serve a double end, — to produce a faint and harmless reflection of French aristocracy, and simply and practically to supply agencies for distributing land among the settlers.

[1] By the charter of the Company of the Hundred Associates, 1627.

The nature of the precautions which it was held to require appear in the plan of administration which Talon and Tracy laid before the minister. They urge that, in view of the distance from France, special care ought to be taken to prevent changes and revolutions, aristocratic or otherwise, in the colony, whereby in time sovereign jurisdictions might grow up, as formerly occurred in various parts of France.[1] And in respect to grants already made an inquiry was ordered, to ascertain "if seigniors in distributing lands to their vassals have exacted any conditions injurious to the rights of the Crown and the subjection due solely to the King." In the same view the seignior was denied any voice whatever in the direction of government; and it is scarcely necessary to say that the essential feature of feudalism in the day of its vitality, the requirement of military service by the lord from the vassal, was utterly unknown in Canada. The royal governor called out the militia whenever he saw fit, and set over it what officers he pleased.

The seignior was usually the immediate vassal of the Crown, from which he had received his land gratuitously. In a few cases he made grants to other seigniors inferior in the feudal scale, and they, his vassals, granted in turn to their vassals, — the *habitants*, or cultivators of the soil.[2] Sometimes the

[1] *Projet de Règlement fait par MM. de Tracy et Talon pour la justice et la distribution des terres du Canada*, Jan. 24, 1667.

[2] Most of the seigniories of Canada were simple fiefs; but there were some exceptions. In 1671, the King, as a mark of honor to

habitant held directly of the Crown, in which case there was no step between the highest and lowest degrees of the feudal scale. The seignior held by the tenure of faith and homage, the *habitant* by the inferior tenure *en censive*. Faith and homage were rendered to the Crown or other feudal superior whenever the seigniory changed hands, or, in the case of seigniories held by corporations, after long stated intervals. The following is an example, drawn from the early days of the colony, of the performance of this ceremony by the owner of a fief to the seignior who had granted it to him. It is that of Jean Guion, vassal of Giffard, seignior of Beauport.

The act recounts how, in presence of a notary, Guion presented himself at the principal door of the manor-house of Beauport; how, having knocked, one Boullé, farmer of Giffard, opened the door, and in reply to Guion's question if the seignior was at home, replied that he was not, but that he, Boullé, was empowered to receive acknowledgments of faith and homage from the vassals in his name. "After the which reply," proceeds the act, "the said Guion, being at the principal door, placed himself on his

---

Talon, erected his seigniory Des Islets into a barony; and it was soon afterwards made an earldom, *comté*. In 1676, the seigniory of St. Laurent, on the island of Orleans, once the property of Laval, and then belonging to François Berthelot, councillor of the King, was erected into an earldom. In 1681, the seigniory of Portneuf, belonging to Réné Robineau, chevalier, was made a barony. In 1700, three seigniories on the south side of the St. Lawrence were united into the barony of Longueuil. (See Papers on the Feudal Tenure in Canada, Abstract of Titles.)

knees on the ground, with head bare, and without sword or spurs, and said three times these words: ' Monsieur de Beauport, Monsieur de Beauport, Monsieur de Beauport! I bring you the faith and homage which I am bound to bring you on account of my fief Du Buisson, which I hold as a man of faith of your seigniory of Beauport, declaring that I offer to pay my seigniorial and feudal dues in their season, and demanding of you to accept me in faith and homage as aforesaid.' "[1]

The following instance is the more common one of a seignior holding directly of the Crown. It is widely separated from the first in point of time, having occurred a year after the army of Wolfe entered Quebec.

Philippe Noël had lately died, and Jean Noël, his son, inherited his seigniory of Tilly and Bonsecours. To make the title good, faith and homage must be renewed. Jean Noël was under the bitter necessity of rendering this duty to General Murray, governor for the King of Great Britain. The form is the same as in the case of Guion, more than a century before. Noël repairs to the Government House at Quebec, and knocks at the door. A servant opens it. Noël asks if the governor is there. The servant replies that he is. Murray, informed of the visitor's object, comes to the door, and Noël then and there, "without sword or spurs, with bare head,

---

[1] Ferland, *Notes sur les Registres de Notre Dame de Québec*, 65. This was a *fief en roture*, as distinguished from a *fief noble*, to which judicial powers and other privileges were attached.

*Jean **Guion** before *Boullé*.*

and one knee on the ground," repeats the acknowledgment of faith and homage for his seigniory. He was compelled, however, to add a detested innovation, — the oath of fidelity to his Britannic Majesty, coupled with a pledge to keep his vassals in obedience to the new sovereign.[1]

The seignior was a proprietor holding that relation to the feudal superior which, in its pristine character, has been truly described as servile in form, proud and bold in spirit. But in Canada this bold spirit was very far from being strengthened by the changes which the policy of the Crown had introduced into the system. The reservation of mines and minerals, oaks for the royal navy, roadways, and a site (if needed) for royal forts and magazines, had in it nothing extraordinary. The great difference between the position of the Canadian seignior and that of the vassal proprietor of the Middle Ages lay in the extent and nature of the control which the Crown and its officers held over him. A decree of the King, an edict of the council, or an ordinance of the intendant, might at any moment change old conditions, impose new ones, interfere between the lord of the manor and his grantees, and modify or annul his bargains, past or present. He was never sure whether or not the government would let him alone; and against its most arbitrary intervention he had no remedy.

One condition was imposed on him which may be

---

[1] See the act in *Observations de Sir L. H. Lafontaine, Bart., sur la Tenure Seigneuriale*, 217, note.

said to form the distinctive feature of Canadian feudalism, — that of clearing his land within a limited time on pain of forfeiting it. The object was the excellent one of preventing the lands of the colony from lying waste. As the seignior was often the penniless owner of a domain three or four leagues wide and proportionably deep, he could not clear it all himself, and was therefore under the necessity of placing the greater part in the hands of those who could. But he was forbidden to sell any part of it which he had not cleared. He must grant it without price, on condition of a small perpetual rent; and this brings us to the cultivator of the soil, the *censitaire*, the broad base of the feudal pyramid.[1]

The tenure *en censive*, by which the *censitaire* held of the seignior, consisted in the obligation to make

---

[1] The greater part of the grants made by the old Company of New France were resumed by the Crown for neglect to occupy and improve the land, which was granted out anew under the administration of Talon. The most remarkable of these forfeited grants is that of the vast domain of La Citière, large enough for a kingdom. Lauson, afterwards governor, had obtained it from the company, but had failed to improve it. Two or three sub-grants which he had made from it were held valid; the rest was reunited to the royal domain. On repeated occasions at later dates, negligent seigniors were threatened with the loss of half or the whole of their land, and various cases are recorded in which the threat took effect. In 1741, an ordinance of the governor and intendant reunited to the royal domain seventeen seigniories at one stroke; but the former owners were told that if within a year they cleared and settled a reasonable part of the forfeited estates, the titles should be restored to them. (*Édits et Ordonnances*, ii. 555.) In the case of the *habitant* or *censitaire*, forfeitures for neglect to improve the land and live on it are very numerous.

annual payments in money, produce, or both. In Canada these payments, known as *cens et rente*, were strangely diverse in amount and kind; but in all the early period of the colony they were almost ludicrously small. A common charge at Montreal was half a sou and half a pint of wheat for each arpent. The rate usually fluctuated in the early times between half a sou and two sous; so that a farm of a hundred and sixty arpents would pay from four to sixteen francs, of which a part would be in money and the rest in live capons, wheat, eggs, or all three together, in pursuance of contracts as amusing in their precision as they are bewildering in their variety. Live capons, estimated at twenty sous each, though sometimes not worth ten, form a conspicuous feature in these agreements; so that on payday the seignior's barnyard presented an animated scene. Later in the history of the colony grants were at somewhat higher rates. Payment was commonly made on St. Martin's day, when there was a general muster of tenants at the seigniorial mansion, with a prodigious consumption of tobacco and a corresponding retail of neighborhood gossip, joined to the outcries of the captive fowls bundled together for delivery, with legs tied, but throats at full liberty.

A more considerable but a very uncertain source of income to the seignior were the *lods et ventes*, or mutation fines. The land of the *censitaire* passed freely to his heirs; but if he sold it, a twelfth part of the purchase-money must be paid to the seignior. The seignior, on his part, was equally liable to pay a mutation fine to his feudal superior if he sold his seigniory; and for him the amount was larger, — being a *quint*, or a fifth of the price received, of which, however, the greater part was deducted for immediate payment. This heavy charge, constituting as it did a tax on all improvements, was a principal cause of the abolition of the feudal tenure in 1854.

The obligation of clearing his land and living on it was laid on seignior and *censitaire* alike; but the latter was under a variety of other obligations to the former, partly imposed by custom and partly established by agreement when the grant was made. To grind his grain at the seignior's mill, bake his bread in the seignior's oven, work for him one or more days in the year, and give him one fish in every eleven, for the privilege of fishing in the river before his farm, — these were the most annoying of the conditions to which the *censitaire* was liable. Few of them were enforced with much regularity. That of baking in the seignior's oven was rarely carried into effect, though occasionally used for purposes of extortion. It is here that the royal government appears in its true character, so far as concerns its relations with Canada, — that of a well-meaning despotism. It continually intervened between *censitaire* and seignior, on the principle that "as his Majesty gives the land for nothing, he can make what conditions he pleases, and change them when he pleases."[1]

These interventions were usually favorable to the *censitaire*. On one occasion an intendant reported to the minister, that in his opinion all rents ought to be reduced to one sou and one live capon for every arpent of front, equal in most cases to forty superficial arpents.[2] Everything, he remarks, ought to be brought down to the level of the first grants "made in days of innocence," — a happy period which he does not attempt to define. The minister replies that the diversity of the rent is, in fact, vexatious, and that for his part he is disposed to abolish it altogether.[3] Neither he nor the intendant gives the slightest hint of any compensation to the seignior.

Though these radical measures were not executed, many changes were decreed from time to time in the relations between seignior and *censitaire*, — sometimes as a simple act of sovereign power, and sometimes on the ground that the grants had been made with conditions not recognized by the *Coutume de Paris*. This was the code of law assigned to Canada; but most of the contracts between seignior and *censitaire* had been agreed upon in good faith by men who knew as much of the *Coutume de Paris* as of the Capitularies of Charlemagne, and their conditions

---

[1] This doctrine is laid down in a letter of the Marquis de Beauharnois, governor, to the minister, 1734.
[2] *Lettre de Raudot, père, au Ministre*, 10 *Nov.*, 1707.
[3] *Lettre de Pontchartrain à Raudot, père*, 13 *Juin*, 1708.

had remained in force unchallenged for generations. These interventions of government sometimes contradicted one another, and often proved a dead letter. They are more or less active through the whole period of the French rule.

The seignior had judicial powers, which, however, were carefully curbed and controlled. His jurisdiction, when exercised at all, extended in most cases only to trivial causes. He very rarely had a prison, and seems never to have abused it. The dignity of a seigniorial gallows with *high justice* or jurisdiction over heinous offences was granted only in three or four instances.[1]

Four arpents in front by forty in depth were the ordinary dimensions of a grant *en censive*. These ribbons of land, nearly a mile and a half long, with one end on the river and the other on the uplands behind, usually combined the advantages of meadows for cultivation, and forests for timber and firewood. So long as the *censitaire* brought in on Saint Martin's day his yearly capons and his yearly handful of copper, his title against the seignior was perfect. There are farms in Canada which have passed from father to son for two hundred years. The condition of the cultivator was incomparably better than that of the French peasant, crushed by taxes, and oppressed by feudal burdens far heavier than those of Canada.

---

[1] Baronies and *comtés* were empowered to set up gallows and pillories, to which the arms of the owner were affixed. See, for example, the edict creating the Barony des Islets.

In fact, the Canadian settler scorned the name of peasant, and then, as now, was always called the *habitant*. The government held him in wardship, watched over him, interfered with him, but did not oppress him or allow others to oppress him. Canada was not governed to the profit of a class; and if the King wished to create a Canadian *noblesse*, he took care that it should not bear hard on the country.[1]

Under a genuine feudalism, the ownership of land conferred nobility; but all this was changed. The King and not the soil was now the parent of honor. France swarmed with landless nobles, while *roturier* land-holders grew daily more numerous. In Canada half the seigniories were in *roturier* or plebeian hands, and in course of time some of them came into possession of persons on very humble degrees of the social scale. A seigniory could be bought and sold, and a trader or a thrifty *habitant* might, and often did, become the buyer.[2] If the Canadian noble

[1] On the seigniorial tenure, I have examined the entire mass of papers printed at the time when the question of its abolition was under discussion. A great deal of legal research and learning was then devoted to the subject. The argument of Mr. Dunkin in behalf of the seigniors, and the observations of Judge Lafontaine are especially instructive, as is also the collected correspondence of the governors and intendants with the central government on matters relating to the seigniorial system.

[2] In 1712, the engineer Catalogne made a very long and elaborate report on the condition of Canada, with a full account of all the seigniorial estates. Of ninety-one seigniories, fiefs, and baronies, described by him, ten belonged to merchants, twelve to husbandmen, and two to masters of small river craft. The rest belonged to religious corporations, members of the council, judges, officials of the Crown, widows, and discharged officers or their sons.

was always a seignior, it is far from being true that the Canadian seignior was always a noble.

In France, it will be remembered, nobility did not in itself imply a title. Besides its titled leaders, it had its rank and file, numerous enough to form a considerable army. Under the later Bourbons, the penniless young nobles were, in fact, enrolled into regiments, — turbulent, difficult to control, obeying officers of high rank, but scorning all others, and conspicuous by a fiery and impetuous valor which on more than one occasion turned the tide of victory. The *gentilhomme*, or untitled noble, had a distinctive character of his own, — gallant, punctilious, vain; skilled in social and sometimes in literary and artistic accomplishments, but usually ignorant of most things except the handling of his rapier. Yet there were striking exceptions; and to say of him, as has been said, that "he knew nothing but how to get himself killed," is hardly just to a body which has produced some of the best writers and thinkers of France. Sometimes the origin of his nobility was lost in the mists of time; sometimes he owed it to a patent from the King. In either case, the line of demarcation between him and the classes below him was perfectly distinct; and in this lies an essential difference between the French *noblesse* and the English gentry, a class not separated from others by a definite barrier. The French *noblesse*, unlike the English gentry, constituted a caste.

The *gentilhomme* had no vocation for emigrating.

He liked the army and he liked the court. If he could not be of it, it was something to live in its shadow. The life of a backwoods settler had no charm for him. He was not used to labor; and he could not trade, at least in retail, without becoming liable to forfeit his nobility. When Talon came to Canada, there were but four noble families in the colony.[1] Young nobles in abundance came out with Tracy; but they went home with him. Where, then, should be found the material of a Canadian *noblesse?* First, in the regiment of Carignan, of which most of the officers were *gentilshommes;* secondly, in the issue of patents of nobility to a few of the more prominent colonists. Tracy asked for four such patents; Talon asked for five more;[2] and such requests were repeated at intervals by succeeding governors and intendants, in behalf of those who had gained their favor by merit or otherwise. Money smoothed the path to advancement, so far had *noblesse* already fallen from its old estate. Thus Jacques Le Ber, the merchant, who had long kept a shop at Montreal, got himself made a "gentleman" for six thousand livres.[3]

All Canada soon became infatuated with *noblesse;*

---

[1] Talon, *Mémoire sur l'Etat présent du Canada,* 1667. The families of Repentigny, Tilly, Potherie, and Ailleboust appear to be meant.

[2] Tracy's request was in behalf of Bourdon, Boucher, Auteuil, and Juchereau. Talon's was in behalf of Godefroy, Le Moyne, Denis, Amiot, and Couillard.

[3] Faillon, *Vie de Mademoiselle Le Ber,* 325.

and country and town, merchant and seignior, vied with each other for the quality of *gentilhomme*. If they could not get it, they often pretended to have it, and aped its ways with the zeal of Monsieur Jourdain himself. "Everybody here," writes the intendant Meules, "calls himself *Esquire*, and ends with thinking himself a gentleman." Successive intendants repeat this complaint. The case was worst with *roturiers* who had acquired seigniories. Thus Noël Langlois was a good carpenter till he became owner of a seigniory, on which he grew lazy and affected to play the gentleman. The real *gentilshommes*, as well as the spurious, had their full share of official stricture. The governor Denonville speaks of them thus: "Several of them have come out this year with their wives, who are very much cast down; but they play the fine lady, nevertheless. I had much rather see good peasants; it would be a pleasure to me to give aid to such, knowing, as I should, that within two years their families would have the means of living at ease; for it is certain that a peasant who can and will work is well off in this country, while our nobles with nothing to do can never be anything but beggars. Still they ought not to be driven off or abandoned. The question is how to maintain them."[1]

The intendant Duchesneau writes to the same effect: "Many of our *gentilshommes*, officers, and other owners of seigniories, lead what in France is

[1] *Lettre de Denonville au Ministre*, 10 Nov., 1686.

called the life of a country gentleman, and spend most of their time in hunting and fishing. As their requirements in food and clothing are greater than those of the simple *habitants*, and as they do not devote themselves to improving their land, they mix themselves up in trade, run in debt on all hands, incite their young *habitants* to range the woods, and send their own children there to trade for furs in the Indian villages and in the depths of the forest, in spite of the prohibition of his Majesty. Yet, with all this, they are in miserable poverty."[1]

Their condition, indeed, was often deplorable. "It is pitiful," says the intendant Champigny, "to see their children, of which they have great numbers, passing all summer with nothing on them but a shirt, and their wives and daughters working in the fields."[2] In another letter he asks aid from the King for Repentigny with his thirteen children, and for Tilly with his fifteen. "We must give them some corn at once," he says, "or they will starve."[3] These were two of the original four noble families of Canada. The family of Ailleboust, another of the four, is described as equally destitute. "Pride and sloth," says the same intendant, "are the great faults of the people of Canada, and especially of the nobles and those who pretend to be such. I pray you grant

[1] *Lettre de Duchesneau au Ministre*, 10 *Nov.*, 1679.
[2] *Lettre de Champigny au Ministre*, 26 *Août*, 1687.
[3] *Ibid.*, 6 *Nov.*, 1687.

no more letters of nobility, unless you want to multiply beggars."[1]

The governor Denonville is still more emphatic: "Above all things, Monseigneur, permit me to say that the nobles of this new country are everything that is most beggarly, and that to increase their number is to increase the number of do-nothings. A new country requires hard workers, who will handle the axe and mattock. The sons of our councillors are no more industrious than the nobles; and their only resource is to take to the woods, trade a little with the Indians, and, for the most part, fall into the disorders of which I have had the honor to inform you. I shall use all possible means to induce them to engage in regular commerce; but as our nobles and councillors are all very poor and weighed down with debt, they could not get credit for a single crown piece."[2] "Two days ago," he writes in another letter, "Monsieur de Saint-Ours, a gentleman of Dauphiny, came to me to ask leave to go back to France in search of bread. He says that he will put his ten children into the charge of any who will give them a living, and that he himself will go into the army again. His wife and he are in despair; and yet they do what they can. I have seen two of his girls reaping grain and holding the plough. Other families are in the same condition. They

---

[1] *Mémoire instructif sur le Canada, joint à la lettre de M. de Champigny du 10 Mai,* 1691.

[2] *Lettre de Denonville au Ministre,* 13 *Nov.,* 1685.

come to me with tears in their eyes. All our married officers are beggars; and I entreat you to send them aid. There is need that the King should provide support for their children, or else they will be tempted to go over to the English."[1] Again he writes that the sons of the councillor D'Amours have been arrested as *coureurs de bois*, or outlaws in the bush; and that if the minister does not do something to help them, there is danger that all the sons of the *noblesse*, real or pretended, will turn bandits, since they have no other means of living.

The King, dispenser of charity for all Canada, came promptly to the rescue. He granted an alms of a hundred crowns to each family, coupled with a warning to the recipients of his bounty that "their misery proceeds from their ambition to live as persons of quality and without labor."[2] At the same time, the minister announced that no more letters of nobility would be granted in Canada; adding, "to relieve the country of some of the children of those who are really noble, I send you [the governor] six commissions of *Gardes de la Marine*, and recommend you to take care not to give them to any who are not actually *gentilshommes*." The *Garde de la Marine* answered to the midshipman of the English or American service. As the six commissions could

---

[1] *Lettre de Denonville au Ministre*, 10 *Nov.*, 1686. (Condensed in the translation.)

[2] Abstract of Denonville's Letters, and of the Minister's Answers, in *N. Y. Colonial Docs.*, ix. 317, 318.

bring little relief to the crowd of needy youths, it was further ordained that sons of nobles or persons living as such should be enrolled into companies at eight sous a day for those who should best conduct themselves, and six sous a day for the others. Nobles in Canada were also permitted to trade, even at retail, without derogating from their rank.[1]

They had already assumed this right, without waiting for the royal license; but thus far it had profited them little. The *gentilhomme* was not a good shopkeeper, nor, as a rule, was the shopkeeper's vocation very lucrative in Canada. The domestic trade of the colony was small; and all trade was exposed to such vicissitudes from the intervention of intendants, ministers, and councils, that at one time it was almost banished. At best, it was carried on under conditions auspicious to a favored few and withering to the rest. Even when most willing to work, the position of the *gentilhomme* was a painful one. Unless he could gain a post under the Crown, which was rarely the case, he was as complete a political cipher as the meanest *habitant*. His rents were practically nothing, and he had no capital to improve his seigniorial estate. By a peasant's work he could gain a peasant's living, and this was all. The prospect was not inspiring. His long initiation of misery was the natural result of his position and surroundings; and it is no matter of wonder that he threw himself into the only field of action

[1] *Lettre de Meules au Ministre*, 1685.

which in time of peace was open to him. It was trade, but trade seasoned by adventure and ennobled by danger, defiant of edict and ordinance, outlawed, conducted in arms among forests and savages; in short, it was the Western fur-trade. The tyro was likely to fail in it at first, but time and experience formed him to the work. On the Great Lakes, in the wastes of the Northwest, on the Mississippi and the plains beyond, we find the roving *gentilhomme*, chief of a gang of bush-rangers, often his own *habitants*, — sometimes proscribed by the government, sometimes leagued in contraband traffic with its highest officials; a hardy vidette of civilization, tracing unknown streams, piercing unknown forests, trading, fighting, negotiating, and building forts. Again we find him on the shores of Acadia or Maine, surrounded by Indian retainers, a menace and a terror to the neighboring English colonist. Saint-Castin, Du Lhut, La Durantaye, La Salle, La Mothe-Cadillac, Iberville, Bienville, La Vérendrye, are names that stand conspicuous on the page of half-savage romance that refreshes the hard and practical annals of American colonization. But a more substantial debt is due to their memory. It was they, and such as they, who discovered the Ohio, explored the Mississippi to its mouth, discovered the Rocky Mountains, and founded Detroit, St. Louis, and New Orleans.

Even in his earliest day, the *gentilhomme* was not always in the evil plight where we have found him.

There were a few exceptions to the general misery, and the chief among them is that of the Le Moynes of Montreal. Charles Le Moyne, son of an innkeeper of Dieppe and founder of a family the most truly eminent in Canada, was a man of sterling qualities who had been long enough in the colony to learn how to live there.[1] Others learned the same lesson at a later day, adapted themselves to soil and situation, took root, grew, and became more Canadian than French. As population increased, their seigniories began to yield appreciable returns, and their reserved domains became worth cultivating. A future dawned upon them; they saw in hope their names, their seigniorial estates, their manor-houses, their tenantry, passing to their children and their children's children. The beggared noble of the early time became a sturdy country gentleman, — poor, but not wretched; ignorant of books, except possibly a few scraps of rusty Latin picked up in a Jesuit school; hardy as the hardiest woodsman, yet never forgetting his quality of *gentilhomme;* scrupulously wearing its badge, the sword, and copying as well as he could the fashions of the court, which glowed on his vision across the sea in all the effulgence of

---

[1] Berthelot, proprietor of the *comté* of St. Laurent, and Robineau, of the barony of Portneuf, may also be mentioned as exceptionally prosperous. Of the younger Charles Le Moyne, afterwards Baron de Longueuil, Frontenac the governor says, " son fort et sa maison nous donnent une idée des châteaux de France fortifiez." His fort was of stone and flanked with four towers. It was nearly opposite Montreal, on the south shore.

Versailles, and beamed with reflected ray from the Château of Quebec. He was at home among his tenants, at home among the Indians, and never more at home than when, a gun in his hand and a crucifix on his breast, he took the war-path with a crew of painted savages and Frenchmen almost as wild, and pounced like a lynx from the forest on some lonely farm or outlying hamlet of New England. How New England hated him, let her records tell. The reddest blood-streaks on her old annals mark the track of the Canadian *gentilhomme*.

CHAPTER XIX.

1663-1763.

THE RULERS OF CANADA.

Nature of the Government. — The Governor. — The Council. — Courts and Judges. — The Intendant: his Grievances. — Strong Government. — Sedition and Blasphemy. — Royal Bounty. — Defects and Abuses.

The government of Canada was formed in its chief features after the government of a French province. Throughout France the past and the present stood side by side. The kingdom had a double administration; or, rather, the shadow of the old administration and the substance of the new. The government of provinces had long been held by the high nobles, often kindred to the Crown; and hence, in former times, great perils had arisen, amounting during the civil wars to the danger of dismemberment. The high nobles were still governors of provinces; but here, as elsewhere, they had ceased to be dangerous. Titles, honors, and ceremonial they had in abundance; but they were deprived of real power. Close beside them was the royal intendant, an obscure figure, lost amid the vain-glories of the feudal sunset, but in the name of the King holding the reins of government. —

a check and a spy on his gorgeous colleague. He was the King's agent; of modest birth, springing from the legal class; owing his present to the King, and dependent on him for his future; learned in the law and trained to administration. It was by such instruments that the powerful centralization of the monarchy enforced itself throughout the kingdom, and, penetrating beneath the crust of old prescriptions, supplanted without seeming to supplant them. The courtier noble looked down in the pride of rank on the busy man in black at his side; but this man in black, with the troop of officials at his beck, controlled finance, the royal courts, public works, and all the administrative business of the province.

The governor-general and the intendant of Canada answered to those of a French province. The governor, excepting in the earliest period of the colony, was a military noble, — in most cases bearing a title and sometimes of high rank. The intendant, as in France, was usually drawn from the *gens de robe*, or legal class.[1] The mutual relations of the two officers were modified by the circumstances about them. The governor was superior in rank to the intendant; he commanded the troops, conducted relations with foreign colonies and Indian tribes, and took precedence on all occasions of ceremony. Unlike a

---

[1] The governor was styled in his commission, *Gouverneur et Lieutenant-Général en Canada, Acadie, Isle de Terreneuve, et autres pays de la France Septentrionale;* and the intendant, *Intendant de la Justice, Police, et Finances en Canada, Acadie, Terreneuve, et autres pays de la France Septentrionale.*

provincial governor in France, he had great and substantial power. The King and the minister, his sole masters, were a thousand leagues distant, and he controlled the whole military force. If he abused his position, there was no remedy but in appeal to the court, which alone could hold him in check. There were local governors at Montreal and Three Rivers; but their power was carefully curbed, and they were forbidden to fine or imprison any person without authority from Quebec.[1]

The intendant was virtually a spy on the governor-general, of whose proceedings and of everything else that took place he was required to make report. Every year he wrote to the minister of state one, two, three, or four letters, often forty or fifty pages long, filled with the secrets of the colony, political and personal, great and small, set forth with a minuteness often interesting, often instructive, and often excessively tedious.[2] The governor, too, wrote letters of pitiless length; and each of the colleagues was jealous of the letters of the other. In truth, their relations to each other were so critical, and perfect harmony so rare, that they might almost be described as natural enemies. The court, it is certain, did not

---

[1] The Sulpitian seigniors of Montreal claimed the right of appointing their own local governor. This was denied by the court, and the excellent Sulpitian governor, Maisonneuve, was removed by De Tracy, to die in patient obscurity at Paris. Some concessions were afterwards made in favor of the Sulpitian claims.

[2] I have carefully read about two thousand pages of these letters.

desire their perfect accord; nor, on the other hand, did it wish them to quarrel: it aimed to keep them on such terms that, without deranging the machinery of administration, each should be a check on the other.[1]

The governor, the intendant, and the supreme council or court were absolute masters of Canada under the pleasure of the King. Legislative, judicial, and executive power, all centred in them. We have seen already the very unpromising beginnings of the supreme council. It had consisted at first of the governor, the bishop, and five councillors chosen by them. The intendant was soon added, to form the ruling triumvirate; but the appointment of the councillors, the occasion of so many quarrels, was afterwards exercised by the King himself.[2] Even the name of the council underwent a change in the interest of his autocracy, and he commanded that it should no longer be called the *Supreme*, but only the *Superior* Council. The same change had just been imposed on all the high tribunals of France.[3] Under the shadow of the *fleur-de-lis*, the King alone was to be supreme.

[1] The governor and intendant made frequent appeals to the court to settle questions arising between them. Several of these appeals are preserved. The King wrote replies on the margin of the paper, but they were usually too curt and general to satisfy either party.

[2] *Déclaration du Roi du 16 Juin*, 1703. Appointments were made by the King many years earlier. As they were always made on the recommendation of the governor and intendant, the practical effect of the change was merely to exclude the bishop from a share in them. The West India Company made the nominations during the ten years of its ascendancy.

[3] Cheruel, *Administration Monarchique en France*, ii. 100.

In 1675 the number of councillors was increased to seven, and in 1703 it was again increased to twelve; but the character of the council or court remained the same. It issued decrees for the civil, commercial, and financial government of the colony, and gave judgment in civil and criminal causes according to the royal ordinances and the *Coutume de Paris*. It exercised also the function of registration borrowed from the parliament of Paris. That body, it will be remembered, had no analogy whatever with the English parliament. Its ordinary functions were not legislative, but judicial; and it was composed of judges hereditary under certain conditions. Nevertheless, it had long acted as a check on the royal power through its right of registration. No royal edict had the force of law till entered upon its books, and this custom had so deep a root in the monarchical constitution of France, that even Louis XIV., in the flush of his power, did not attempt to abolish it. He did better; he ordered his decrees to be registered, and the humbled parliament submissively obeyed. In like manner all edicts, ordinances, or declarations relating to Canada were entered on the registers of the superior council at Quebec. The order of registration was commonly affixed to the edict or other mandate, and nobody dreamed of disobeying it.[1]

---

[1] Many general edicts relating to the whole kingdom are also registered on the books of the council; but the practice in this respect was by no means uniform.

The council or court had its attorney-general, who heard complaints, and brought them before the tribunal if he thought necessary; its secretary, who kept its registers, and its *huissiers* or attendant officers. It sat once a week; and, though it was the highest court of appeal, it exercised at first original jurisdiction in very trivial cases.[1] It was empowered to establish subordinate courts or judges throughout the colony. Besides these, there was a judge appointed by the King for each of the three districts into which Canada was divided, — those of Quebec, Three Rivers, and Montreal. To each of the three royal judges were joined a clerk and an attorney-general, under the supervision and control of the attorney-general of the superior court, to which tribunal appeal lay from all the subordinate jurisdictions. The jurisdiction of the seigniors within their own limits has already been mentioned. They were entitled by the terms of their grants to the exercise of "high, middle, and low justice;" but most of them were practically restricted to the last of the three, — that is, to petty disputes between the *habitants*, involving not more than sixty sous, or offences for which the fine did not exceed ten sous.[2] Thus limited, their judgments were often useful in saving

---

[1] See the *Registres du Conseil Supérieur*, preserved at Quebec. Between 1663 and 1673 are a multitude of judgments on matters great and small, — from murder, rape, and infanticide, down to petty nuisances, misbehavior of servants, and disputes about the price of a sow.

[2] Doutre et Lareau, *Histoire du Droit Canadien*, 135.

time, trouble, and money to the disputants. The corporate seigniors of Montreal long continued to hold a feudal court in form, with attorney-general, clerk, and *huissier;* but very few other seigniors were in a condition to imitate them. Added to all these tribunals was the bishop's court at Quebec, to try causes held to be within the province of the Church.

The office of judge in Canada was no sinecure. The people were of a litigious disposition, — partly from their Norman blood; partly, perhaps, from the idleness of the long and tedious winter, which gave full leisure for gossip and quarrel; and partly from the very imperfect manner in which titles had been drawn and the boundaries of grants marked out, whence ensued disputes without end between neighbor and neighbor.

"I will not say," writes the satirical La Hontan, "that Justice is more chaste and disinterested here than in France; but, at least, if she is sold, she is sold cheaper. We do not pass through the clutches of advocates, the talons of attorneys, and the claws of clerks. These vermin do not infest Canada yet. Everybody pleads his own cause. Our Themis is prompt, and she does not bristle with fees, costs, and charges. The judges have only four hundred francs a year, — a great temptation to look for law in the bottom of the suitor's purse. Four hundred francs! Not enough to buy a cap and gown; so these gentry never wear them."[1]

Thus far La Hontan. Now let us hear the King

---

[1] La Hontan, i. 21 (ed. 1705). In some editions, the above is expressed in different language.

himself. "The greatest disorder which has hitherto existed in Canada," writes Louis XIV. to the intendant Meules, "has come from the small degree of liberty which the officers of justice have had in the discharge of their duties, by reason of the violence to which they have been subjected, and the part they have been obliged to take in the continual quarrels between the governor and the intendant; insomuch that justice having been administered by cabal and animosity, the inhabitants have hitherto been far from the tranquillity and repose which cannot be found in a place where everybody is compelled to take side with one party or another."[1]

Nevertheless, on ordinary local questions between the *habitants*, justice seems to have been administered on the whole fairly; and judges of all grades often interposed in their personal capacity to bring parties to an agreement without a trial. From head to foot, the government kept its attitude of paternity.

Beyond and above all the regular tribunals, beyond and above the council itself, was the independent jurisdiction lodged in the person of the King's man, the intendant. His commission empowered him, if he saw fit, to call any cause whatever before himself for judgment; and he judged exclusively the cases which concerned the King, and those involving the relations of seignior and vassal.[2] He appointed sub-

[1] *Instruction du Roy pour le Sieur de Meules*, 1682.
[2] See the commissions of various intendants, in *Édits et Ordonnances*, iii.

ordinate judges, from whom there was appeal to him; but from his decisions, as well as from those of the superior council, there was no appeal but to the King in his council of state.

On any Monday morning one would have found the superior council in session in the antechamber of the governor's apartment, at the Château St. Louis. The members sat at a round table. At the head was the governor, with the bishop on his right, and the intendant on his left. The councillors sat in the order of their appointment, and the attorney-general also had his place at the board. As La Hontan says, they were not in judicial robes, but in their ordinary dress, and all but the bishop wore swords.[1] The want of the cap and gown greatly disturbed the intendant Meules; and he begs the minister to consider how important it is that the councillors, in order to inspire respect, should appear in public in long black robes, which on occasions of ceremony they should exchange for robes of red. He thinks that the principal persons of the colony would thus be induced to train up their children to so enviable a dignity; "and," he concludes, "as none of the councillors can afford to buy red robes, I hope that the King will vouchsafe to send out nine such. As for the black robes, they can furnish those themselves."[2] The King did not respond, and the nine robes never arrived.

[1] Compare La Potherie, i. 260; and La Tour, *Vie de Laval*, liv. vii.
[2] *Meules au Ministre*, 28 Sept., 1685.

The official dignity of the council was sometimes exposed to trials against which even red gowns might have proved an insufficient protection. The same intendant urges that the tribunal ought to be provided immediately with a house of its own. "It is not decent," he says, "that it should sit in the governor's antechamber any longer. His guards and valets make such a noise that we cannot hear one another speak. I have continually to tell them to keep quiet, which causes them to make a thousand jokes at the councillors as they pass in and out."[1] As the governor and the council were often on ill terms, the official head of the colony could not always be trusted to keep his attendants on their good behavior. The minister listened to the complaint of Meules, and adopted his suggestion that the government should buy the old brewery of Talon, — a large structure of mingled timber and masonry on the banks of the St. Charles. It was at an easy distance from the château; passing the Hôtel Dieu and descending the rock, one reached it by a walk of a few minutes. It was accordingly repaired, partly rebuilt, and fitted up to serve the double purpose of a lodging for the intendant and a court-house. Henceforth the transformed brewery was known as the Palace of the Intendant, or the Palace of Justice; and here the council and inferior courts long continued to hold their sessions.

Some of these inferior courts appear to have needed

[1] *Meules au Ministre,* 12 *Nov.*, 1684.

a lodging quite as much as the council. The watchful Meules informs the minister that the royal judge for the district of Quebec was accustomed in winter, with a view to saving fuel, to hear causes and pronounce judgment by his own fireside, in the midst of his children, whose gambols disturbed the even distribution of justice.[1]

The superior council was not a very harmonious body. As its three chiefs — the man of the sword, the man of the church, and the man of the law — were often at variance, the councillors attached themselves to one party or the other, and hot disputes sometimes ensued. The intendant, though but third in rank, presided at the sessions, took votes, pronounced judgment, signed papers, and called special meetings. This matter of the presidency was for some time a source of contention between him and the governor, till the question was set at rest by a decree of the King.

The intendants in their reports to the minister do not paint the council in flattering colors. One of them complains that the councillors, being busy with their farms, neglect their official duties. Another says that they are all more or less in trade. A third calls them uneducated persons of slight account, allied to the chief families and chief merchants in Canada, in whose interest they make laws; and he adds, that, as a year and a half or even two years usually elapse before the answer to a complaint is

[1] *Meules au Ministre*, 12 Nov., 1684.

received from France, they take advantage of this long interval to the injury of the King's service.[1] These and other similar charges betray the continual friction between the several branches of the government.

The councillors were rarely changed, and they usually held office for life. In a few cases the King granted to the son of a councillor yet living the right of succeeding his father when the charge should become vacant.[2] It was a post of honor and not of profit, at least of direct profit. The salaries were very small, and coupled with a prohibition to receive fees.

Judging solely by the terms of his commission, the intendant was the ruling power in the colony. He controlled all expenditure of public money, and not only presided at the council, but was clothed in his own person with independent legislative as well as judicial power. He was authorized to issue ordinances having the force of law whenever he thought necessary, and, in the words of his commission, "to order everything as he shall see just and proper."[3] He was directed to be present at councils of war, though war was the special province of his colleague,

---

[1] *Meules au Ministre*, 12 *Nov.*, 1684.

[2] A son of Amours was named in his father's lifetime to succeed him, as was also a son of the attorney-general Auteuil. There are several other cases. A son of Tilly, to whom the right of succeeding his father had been granted, asks leave to sell it to the merchant La Chesnaye.

[3] Commissions of Bouteroue, Duchesneau, Meules, etc.

and to protect soldiers and all others from official extortion and abuse; that is, to protect them from the governor. Yet there were practical difficulties in the way of his apparent power. The King, his master, was far away; but official jealousy was busy around him, and his patience was sometimes put to the proof. Thus the royal judge of Quebec had fallen into irregularities. "I can do nothing with him," writes the intendant; "he keeps on good terms with the governor and council, and sets me at naught." The governor had, as he thought, treated him amiss. "You have told me," he writes to the minister, "to bear everything from him and report to you;" and he proceeds to recount his grievances. Again, "the attorney-general is bold to insolence, and needs to be repressed. The King's interposition is necessary." He modestly adds that the intendant is the only man in Canada whom his Majesty can trust, and that he ought to have more power.[1]

These were far from being his only troubles. The enormous powers with which his commission clothed him were sometimes retrenched by contradictory instructions from the King;[2] for this government, not of laws but of arbitrary will, is marked by frequent inconsistencies. When he quarrelled with the governor, and the governor chanced to have strong

---

[1] *Meules au Ministre*, 12 *Nov.*, 1684.

[2] Thus, Meules is flatly forbidden to compel litigants to bring causes before him (*Instruction pour le Sieur de Meules*, 1682); and this prohibition is nearly of the same date with the commission in which the power to do so is expressly given him.

friends at court, his position became truly pitiable. He was berated as an imperious master berates an offending servant. "Your last letter is full of nothing but complaints." "You have exceeded your authority." "Study to know yourself, and to understand clearly the difference there is between a governor and an intendant." "Since you failed to comprehend the difference between you and the officer who represents the King's person, you are in danger of being often condemned, or rather of being recalled; for his Majesty cannot endure so many petty complaints, founded on nothing but a certain *quasi* equality between the governor and you, which you assume, but which does not exist." "Meddle with nothing beyond your functions." "Take good care to tell me nothing but the truth." "You ask too many favors for your adherents." "You must not spend more than you have authority to spend, or it will be taken out of your pay." In short, there are several letters from the minister Colbert to his colonial man-of-all-work, which, from beginning to end, are one continued scold.[1]

The luckless intendant was liable to be held to account for the action of natural laws. "If the population does not increase in proportion to the pains I take," writes the King to Duchesneau, "you are to lay the blame on yourself for not having exe-

[1] The above examples are all taken from the letters of Colbert to the intendant Duchesneau. It is an extreme case, but other intendants are occasionally treated with scarcely more ceremony.

cuted my principal order [to promote marriages], and for having failed in the principal object for which I sent you to Canada."[1]

A great number of ordinances of intendants are preserved. They were usually read to the people at the doors of churches after mass, or sometimes by the curé from his pulpit. They relate to a great variety of subjects, — regulation of inns and markets, poaching, preservation of game, sale of brandy, rent of pews, stray hogs, mad dogs, tithes, matrimonial quarrels, fast driving, wards and guardians, weights and measures, nuisances, value of coinage, trespass on lands, building churches, observance of Sunday, preservation of timber, seignior and vassal, settlement of boundaries, and many other matters. If a curé with some of his parishioners reported that his church or his house needed repair or rebuilding, the intendant issued an ordinance requiring all the inhabitants of the parish, "both those who have consented and those who have not consented," to contribute materials and labor, on pain of fine or other penalty.[2] The militia captain of the *côte* was to direct the work and see that each parishioner did his due part, which was determined by the extent of his farm; so, too, if the *grand voyer*, an officer charged with the superintendence of highways, reported that a new road was wanted or that an old

---

[1] *Le Roi à Duchesneau*, 11 Juin, 1680.

[2] See, among many examples, the ordinance of 24th December, 1715. *Edits et Ordonnances*, ii. 443.

one needed mending, an ordinance of the intendant set the whole neighborhood at work upon it, directed, as in the other case, by the captain of militia. If children were left fatherless, the intendant ordered the curé of the parish to assemble their relations or friends for the choice of a guardian. If a *censitaire* did not clear his land and live on it, the intendant took it from him and gave it back to the seignior.[1]

Chimney-sweeping having been neglected at Quebec, the intendant commands all householders promptly to do their duty in this respect, and at the same time fixes the pay of the sweep at six sous a chimney. Another order forbids quarrelling in church. Another assigns pews in due order of precedence to the seignior, the captain of militia, and the wardens. The intendant Raudot, who seems to have been inspired even more than the others with the spirit of paternal intervention, issued a mandate to the effect, that, whereas the people of Montreal raise too many horses, which prevents them from raising cattle and sheep, "being therein ignorant of their true interest. . . . Now, therefore, we command that each inhabitant of the *côtes* of this government shall hereafter own no more than two horses, or mares, and one foal, — the same to take effect after the sowing-season of the ensuing year, 1710, giving them time to rid themselves of their horses in excess of said number, after which they will be required to

---

[1] Compare the numerous ordinances printed in the second and third volumes of *Édits et Ordonnances*.

kill any of such excess that may remain in their possession."¹ Many other ordinances, if not equally preposterous, are equally stringent; such, for example, as that of the intendant Bigot, in which, with a view of promoting agriculture, and protecting the morals of the farmers by saving them from the temptations of cities, he proclaims to them: "We prohibit and forbid you to remove to this town [Quebec] under any pretext whatever, without our permission in writing, on pain of being expelled and sent back to your farms, your furniture and goods confiscated, and a fine of fifty livres laid on you for the benefit of the hospitals. And, furthermore, we forbid all inhabitants of the city to let houses or rooms to persons coming from the country, on pain of a fine of a hundred livres, also applicable to the hospitals."² At about the same time a royal edict, designed to prevent the undue subdivision of farms, forbade the country people, except such as were authorized to live in villages, to build a house or barn on any piece of land less than one and a half arpents wide and thirty arpents long;³ while a subsequent ordinance of the intendant commands the immediate demolition of certain houses built in contravention of the edict.⁴

The spirit of absolutism is everywhere apparent. "It is of very great consequence," writes the intendant Meules, "that the people should not be left at

---

[1] *Édits et Ordonnances*, ii. 273.   [2] *Ibid.*, ii. 399.
[3] *Ibid.*, i. 585.   [4] *Ibid.*, ii. 400.

liberty to speak their minds."[1] Hence public meetings were jealously restricted. Even those held by parishioners under the eye of the curé to estimate the cost of a new church seem to have required a special license from the intendant. During a number of years a meeting of the principal inhabitants of Quebec was called in spring and autumn by the council to discuss the price and quality of bread, the supply of firewood, and other similar matters. The council commissioned two of its members to preside at these meetings, and on hearing their report took what action it thought best. Thus, after the meeting held in February, 1686, it issued a decree, in which, after a long and formal preamble, it solemnly ordained "that besides white-bread and light brown-bread, all bakers shall hereafter make dark brown-bread whenever the same shall be required."[2] Such assemblies, so controlled, could scarcely, one would think, wound the tenderest susceptibilities of authority; yet there was evident distrust of them, and after a few years this modest shred of self-government is seen no more. The syndic, too, that functionary whom the people of the towns were at first allowed to choose, under the eye of the authorities, was conjured out of existence by a word from the King. Seignior, *censitaire*, and citizen were prostrate alike

---

[1] "Il ne laisse pas d'être de très grande conséquence de ne pas laisser la liberté au peuple de dire son sentiment." — *Meules au Ministre*, 1685.

[2] *Édits et Ordonnances*, ii. 112.

in flat subjection to the royal will. They were not free even to go home to France. No inhabitant of Canada, man or woman, could do so without leave; and several intendants express their belief that without this precaution there would soon be a falling off in the population.

In 1671 the council issued a curious decree. One Paul Dupuy had been heard to say that there is nothing like righting one's self, and that when the English cut off the head of Charles I. they did a good thing, with other discourse to the like effect. The council declared him guilty of speaking ill of royalty in the person of the King of England, and uttering words tending to sedition. He was condemned to be dragged from prison by the public executioner, and led in his shirt, with a rope about his neck and a torch in his hand, to the gate of the Château St. Louis, there to beg pardon of the King; thence to the pillory of the Lower Town to be branded with a *fleur-de-lis* on the cheek, and set in the stocks for half an hour; then to be led back to prison, and put in irons "till the information against him shall be completed."[1]

If irreverence to royalty was thus rigorously chastised, irreverence to God was threatened with still sharper penalties. Louis XIV., ever haunted with the fear of the Devil, sought protection against him by his famous edict against swearing, duly registered on the books of the council at Quebec. "It is our

---

[1] *Jugements et Délibérations du Conseil Supérieur.*

will and pleasure," says this pious mandate, "that all persons convicted of profane swearing or blaspheming the name of God, the most Holy Virgin his mother, or the saints, be condemned for the first offence to a pecuniary fine according to their possessions and the greatness and enormity of the oath and blasphemy; and if those thus punished repeat the said oaths, then for the second, third, and fourth time they shall be condemned to a double, triple, and quadruple fine; and for the fifth time, they shall be set in the pillory on Sunday or other festival days, there to remain from eight in the morning till one in the afternoon, exposed to all sorts of opprobrium and abuse, and be condemned besides to a heavy fine; and for the sixth time, they shall be led to the pillory, and there have the upper lip cut with a hot iron; and for the seventh time, they shall be led to the pillory and have the lower lip cut; and if, by reason of obstinacy and inveterate bad habit, they continue after all these punishments to utter the said oaths and blasphemies, it is our will and command that they have the tongue completely cut out, so that thereafter they cannot utter them again."[1] All those who should hear anybody swear were further required to report the fact to the nearest judge within twenty-four hours, on pain of fine.

This is far from being the only instance in which the temporal power lends aid to the spiritual.

---

[1] *Édit du Roy contre les Jureurs et Blasphémateurs, du 30me Juillet,* 1666. See *Édits et Ordonnances,* i. 62.

Among other cases, the following is worth mentioning: Louis Gaboury, an inhabitant of the island of Orleans, charged with eating meat in Lent without asking leave of the priest, was condemned by the local judge to be tied three hours to a stake in public, and then led to the door of the chapel, there on his knees, with head bare and hands clasped, to ask pardon of God and the King. The culprit appealed to the council, which revoked the sentence and imposed only a fine.[1]

The due subordination of households had its share of attention. Servants who deserted their masters were to be set in the pillory for the first offence, and whipped and branded for the second; while any person harboring them was to pay a fine of twenty francs.[2] On the other hand, nobody was allowed to employ a servant without a license.[3]

In case of heinous charges, torture of the accused was permitted under the French law; and it was sometimes practised in Canada. Condemned murderers and felons were occasionally tortured before being strangled; and the dead body, enclosed in a kind of iron cage, was left hanging for months at the top of Cape Diamond, a terror to children and a warning to evil-doers. Yet, on the whole, Canadian justice, tried by the standard of the time, was neither vindictive nor cruel.

---

[1] Doutre et Lareau, *Histoire du Droit Canadien*, 163.
[2] *Règlement de Police*, 1676.
[3] *Édits et Ordonnances*, ii. 53.

In reading the voluminous correspondence of governors and intendants, the minister and the King, nothing is more apparent than the interest with which, in the early part of his reign, Louis XIV. regarded his colony. One of the faults of his rule is the excess of his benevolence; for not only did he give money to support parish priests, build churches, and aid the seminary, the Ursulines, the missions, and the hospitals; but he established a fund destined, among other objects, to relieve indigent persons, subsidized nearly every branch of trade and industry, and in other instances did for the colonists what they would far better have learned to do for themselves.

Meanwhile, the officers of government were far from suffering from an excess of royal beneficence. La Hontan says that the local governor of Three Rivers would die of hunger if, besides his pay, he did not gain something by trade with the Indians; and that Perrot, local governor of Montreal, with one thousand crowns of salary, traded to such purpose that in a few years he made fifty thousand crowns. This trade, it may be observed, was in violation of the royal edicts. The pay of the governor-general varied from time to time. When La Potherie wrote, it was twelve thousand francs a year, besides three thousand which he received in his capacity of local governor of Quebec.[1] This would hardly tempt a

[1] In 1674, the governor-general received 20,718 francs, out of which he was to pay 8,718 to his guard of twenty men and officers.

Frenchman of rank to expatriate himself; and yet some at least of the governors came out to the colony for the express purpose of mending their fortunes. Indeed, the higher nobility could scarcely, in time of peace, have other motives for going there; the court and the army were their element, and to be elsewhere was banishment. We shall see hereafter by what means they sought compensation for their exile in Canadian forests.

Loud complaints sometimes found their way to Versailles. A memorial addressed to the regent duke of Orleans, immediately after the King's death, declares that the ministers of state, who have been the real managers of the colony, have made their creatures and relations governors and intendants, and set them free from all responsibility. High colonial officers, pursues the writer, come home rich, while the colony languishes almost to perishing.[1] As for lesser offices, they were multiplied to satisfy needy retainers, till lean and starving Canada was covered

---

(*Ordonnance du Roy*, 1675.) Yet in 1677, in the *État de la Dépense que le Roy veut et ordonne estre faite*, etc., the total pay of the governor-general is set down at 3,000 francs, and so also in 1681, 1682, and 1687. The local governor of Montreal was to have 1,800 francs, and the governor of Three Rivers 1,200. It is clear, however, that this *État de dépense* is not complete, as there is no provision for the intendant. The first councillor received 500 francs, and the rest 300 francs each, equal in Canadian money to 400. An ordinance of 1676 gives the intendant 12,000 francs. It is tolerably clear that the provision of 3,000 francs for the governor-general was meant only to apply to his capacity of local governor of Quebec.

[1] *Mémoire addressé au Régent*, 1715.

with official leeches, sucking, in famished desperation, at her bloodless veins.

The whole system of administration centred in the King, who, to borrow the formula of his edicts, "in the fulness of our power and our certain knowledge," was supposed to direct the whole machine, from its highest functions to its pettiest intervention in private affairs. That this theory, like all extreme theories of government, was an illusion, is no fault of Louis XIV. Hard-working monarch as he was, he spared no pains to guide his distant colony in the paths of prosperity. The prolix letters of governors and intendants were carefully studied; and many of the replies, signed by the royal hand, enter into details of surprising minuteness. That the King himself wrote these letters is incredible; but in the early part of his reign he certainly directed and controlled them. At a later time, when more absorbing interests engrossed him, he could no longer study in person the long-winded despatches of his Canadian officers. They were usually addressed to the minister of state, who caused abstracts to be made from them for the King's use, and perhaps for his own.[1] The minister, or the minister's secretary, could suppress or color as he or those who influenced him saw fit.

In the latter half of his too long reign, when cares, calamities, and humiliations were thickening around the King, another influence was added to make the

[1] Many of these abstracts are still preserved in the Archives of the Marine and Colonies.

theoretical supremacy of his royal will more than ever a mockery. That prince of annalists, Saint-Simon, has painted Louis XIV. ruling his realm from the bedchamber of Madame de Maintenon, — seated with his minister at a small table beside the fire, the King in an arm-chair, the minister on a stool, with his bag of papers on a second stool near him. In another arm-chair, at another table on the other side of the fire, sat the sedate favorite, busy to all appearance with a book or a piece of tapestry, but listening to everything that passed. "She rarely spoke," says Saint-Simon, "except when the King asked her opinion, which he often did; and then she answered with great deliberation and gravity. She never, or very rarely, showed a partiality for any measure, still less for any person; but she had an understanding with the minister, who never dared do otherwise than she wished. Whenever any favor or appointment was in question, the business was settled between them beforehand. She would send to the minister that she wanted to speak to him, and he did not dare bring the matter on the carpet till he had received her orders." Saint-Simon next recounts the subtle methods by which Maintenon and the minister, her tool, beguiled the King to do their will, while never doubting that he was doing his own. "He thought," concludes the annalist, "that it was he alone who disposed of all appointments; while in reality he disposed of very few indeed, except on the rare occasions when he had taken a fancy to somebody, or when somebody whom he wanted to favor had spoken to him in behalf of somebody else."[1]

Add to all this the rarity of communication with the distant colony. The ships from France arrived at Quebec in July, August, or September, and returned in November. The machine of Canadian government, wound up once a year, was expected to run unaided at least a twelvemonth. Indeed, it was often left to itself for two years, such was sometimes the tardiness of the overburdened government in answering the despatches of its colonial agents. It is no matter of surprise that a writer well versed in its affairs calls Canada the "country of abuses."[2]

---

[1] *Mémoires du Duc de Saint-Simon*, xiii. 38, 39 (Cheruel, 1857). Saint-Simon, notwithstanding the independence of his character and his violent prejudices, held a high position at court; and his acute and careful observation, joined to his familiar acquaintance with ministers and other functionaries, both in and out of office, gives a rare value to his matchless portraitures, and makes him indispensable to the annalist of his time.

[2] *État présent du Canada*, 1758.

CHAPTER XX.

1663–1763.

TRADE AND INDUSTRY.

Trade in Fetters. — The Huguenot Merchants. — Royal Patronage. — The Fisheries. — Cries for Help. — Agriculture. — Manufactures. — Arts of Ornament. — Finance. — Card Money. — Repudiation. — Imposts. — The Beaver Trade. — The Fair at Montreal. — Contraband Trade. — A Fatal System. — Trouble and Change. — The Coureurs de Bois. — The Forest. — Letter of Carheil.

We have seen the head of the colony, its guiding intellect and will: it remains to observe its organs of nutrition. Whatever they might have been under a different treatment, they were perverted and enfeebled by the regimen to which they were subjected.

The spirit of restriction and monopoly had ruled from the beginning. The old governor Lauson, seignior for a while of a great part of the colony, held that Montreal had no right to trade directly with France, but must draw all her supplies from Quebec;[1] and this preposterous claim was revived in the time of Mézy. The successive companies to whose hands the colony was consigned had a baneful effect on

---

[1] Faillon, *Colonie Française*, ii. 244.

individual enterprise. In 1674 the charter of the West India Company was revoked, and trade was declared open to all subjects of the King; yet commerce was still condemned to wear the ball and chain. New restrictions were imposed, meant for good, but resulting in evil. Merchants not resident in the colony were forbidden all trade, direct or indirect, with the Indians.[1] They were also forbidden to sell any goods at retail except in August, September, and October;[2] to trade anywhere in Canada above Quebec, and to sell clothing or domestic articles ready made. This last restriction was designed to develop colonial industry. No person, resident or not, could trade with the English colonies, or go thither without a special passport, and rigid examination by the military authorities.[3] Foreign trade of any kind was stiffly prohibited. In 1719, after a new company had engrossed the beaver-trade, its agents were empowered to enter all houses in Canada, whether ecclesiastical or secular, and search them for foreign goods, which when found were publicly burned.[4] In the next year the royal council ordered that vessels engaged in foreign trade should be captured by force of arms, like pirates, and confiscated along with their cargoes;[5] while anybody having an article of foreign manufacture in his possession was subjected to a heavy fine.[6]

[1] *Règlement de Police*, 1676. Art. xl.
[2] *Édits et Ordonnances*, ii. 100.　　[3] *Ibid.*, i. 489.
[4] *Ibid.*, i. 402.　　[5] *Ibid.*, i. 425.　　[6] *Ibid.*, i. 505.

Attempts were made to fix the exact amount of profit which merchants from France should be allowed to make in the colony; one of the first acts of the superior council was to order them to bring their invoices immediately before that body, which thereupon affixed prices to each article. The merchant who sold and the purchaser who bought above this tariff were alike condemned to heavy penalties; and so, too, was the merchant who chose to keep his goods rather than sell them at the price ordained.[1] Resident merchants, on the other hand, were favored to the utmost: they could sell at what price they saw fit; and, according to La Hontan, they made great profit by the sale of laces, ribbons, watches, jewels, and similar superfluities to the poor but extravagant colonists.

A considerable number of the non-resident merchants were Huguenots, for most of the importations were from the old Huguenot city of Rochelle. No favor was shown them; they were held under rigid restraint, and forbidden to exercise their religion, or to remain in the colony during winter without special license.[2] This sometimes bore very hard upon them. The governor, Denonville, an ardent Catholic, states the case of one Bernon, who had done great service to the colony, and whom La Hontan mentions as the principal French merchant in the Canadian trade. "It is a pity," says Denonville, "that he

[1] *Édits et Ordonnances*, ii. 17, 19.
[2] *Règlement de Police*, 1676. Art. xxxvii.

cannot be converted. As he is a Huguenot, the bishop wants me to order him home this autumn, — which I have done, though he carries on a large business, and a great deal of money remains due to him here."[1]

For a long time the ships from France went home empty, except a favored few which carried furs, or occasionally a load of dried pease or of timber. Payment was made in money when there was any in Canada, or in bills of exchange. The colony, drawing everything from France and returning little besides beaver-skins, remained under a load of debt. French merchants were discouraged, and shipments from France languished. As for the trade with the West Indies, which Talon had tried by precept and example to build up, the intendant reports in 1680 that it had nearly ceased; though six years later it grew again to the modest proportions of three vessels loaded with wheat.[2]

The besetting evil of trade and industry in Canada was the habit they contracted, and were encouraged to contract, of depending on the direct aid of government. Not a new enterprise was set on foot without a petition to the King to lend a helping hand. Sometimes the petition was sent through the governor, sometimes through the intendant; and it was rarely refused. Denonville writes that the merchants

---

[1] *Denonville au Ministre*, 1685.
[2] *Ibid.*, 1686. The year before, about 18,000 *minots* of grain were sent hither. In 1736 the shipments reached 80,000 *minots*.

of Quebec, by a combined effort, had sent a vessel of sixty tons to France with colonial produce; and he asks that the royal commissaries at Rochefort be instructed to buy the whole cargo, in order to encourage so deserving an enterprise. One Hazeur set up a saw-mill at Mal Bay. Finding a large stock of planks and timber on his hands, he begs the King to send two vessels to carry them to France; and the King accordingly did so. A similar request was made in behalf of another saw-mill at St. Paul's Bay. Denonville announces that one Riverin wishes to embark in the whale and cod fishery, and that though strong in zeal he is weak in resources. The minister replies that he is to be encouraged, and that his Majesty will favorably consider his enterprise.[1] Various gifts were soon after made him. He now took to himself a partner, the Sieur Chalons; whereupon the governor writes to ask the minister's protection for them. "The Basques," he says, "formerly carried on this fishery, but some monopoly or other put a stop to it." The remedy he proposes is homœopathic. He asks another monopoly for the two partners. Louis Joliet, the discoverer of the Missis-

---

[1] The interest felt by the King in these matters is shown in a letter signed by his hand in which he enters with considerable detail into the plans of Riverin. (*Le Roy à Denonville et Champigny*, 1 *Mai*, 1689.) He afterwards ordered boats, harpooners, and cordage to be sent him, for which he was to pay at his convenience. Four years later he complains that, though Riverin had been often helped, his fisheries were of slight account. "Let him take care," pursues the King, "that he does not use his enterprises as a pretext to obtain favors." *Mémoire du Roy à Frontenac et Champigny*, 1693.

sippi, made a fishing-station on the island of Anticosti; and he begs help from the King, on the ground that his fishery will furnish a good and useful employment to young men. The Sieur Vitry wished to begin a fishery of white porpoises, and he begs the King to give him two thousand pounds of cod-line and two thousand pounds of one and two inch rope. His request was granted, on which he asked for five hundred livres. The money was given him; and the next year he asked to have the gift renewed.[1]

The King was very anxious to develop the fisheries of the colony. "His Majesty," writes the minister, "wishes you to induce the inhabitants to unite with the merchants for this object, and to incite them by all sorts of means to overcome their natural laziness, since there is no other way of saving them from the misery in which they now are."[2] "I wish," says the zealous Denonville, "that fisheries could be well established to give employment to our young men, and prevent them from running wild in the woods;" and he adds mournfully, "they [the fisheries] are

---

[1] All the above examples are drawn from the correspondence of the governor and intendant with the minister, between 1680 and 1699, together with a memorial of Hazeur and another of Riverin, addressed to the minister.

Vitry's porpoise-fishing appears to have ended in failure. In 1707 the intendant Raudot granted the porpoise-fishery of the seigniory of Rivière Ouelle to six of the *habitants*. This fishery is carried on here successfully at the present day. A very interesting account of it was published in the *Opinion Publique*, 1873, by my friend Abbé Casgrain, whose family residence is the seigniorial mansion of Rivière Ouelle.

[2] *Mémoire pour Denonville et Champigny*, 8 Mars, 1688.

enriching Boston at our expense." "They are our true mines," urges the intendant Meules; "but the English of Boston have got possession of those of Acadia, which belong to us, and we ought to prevent it." It was not prevented; and the Canadian fisheries, like other branches of Canadian industry, remained in a state of almost hopeless languor.[1]

The government applied various stimulants. One of these, proposed by the intendant Duchesneau, is characteristic. He advises the formation of a company which should have the exclusive right of exporting fish; but which on its part should be required to take, at a fixed price, all that the inhabitants should bring them. This notable plan did not find favor with the King.[2] It was practised, however, in the case of beaver-skins, and also in that of wood-ashes. The farmers of the revenue were required to take this last commodity at a fixed price, on their own risk, and in any quantity offered. They remonstrated, saying that it was unsalable, — adding, that, if the inhabitants would but take the trouble to turn it into

[1] The Canadian fisheries must not be confounded with the French fisheries of Newfoundland, which were prosperous, but were carried on wholly from French ports.

In a memorial addressed by the partners Chalons and Riverin to the minister Seignelay, they say: "Baston [Boston] et toute sa colonie nous donne un exemple qui fait honte à nostre nation, puisqu'elle s'augmente tous les jours par cette pesche (*de la morue*) qu'elle fait la plus grande partie sur nos costes pendant que les François ne s'occupent à rien." Meules urges that the King should undertake the fishing business himself, since his subjects cannot or will not.

[2] *Ministre à Duchesneau*, 15 *Mai*, 1678.

potash, it might be possible to find a market for it. The King released them entirely, coupling his order to that effect with a eulogy of free-trade.[1]

In all departments of industry the appeals for help are endless. Governors and intendants are so many sturdy beggars for the languishing colony. "Send us money to build storehouses, to which the *habitants* can bring their produce and receive goods from the government in exchange." "Send us a teacher to make sailors of our young men: it is a pity the colony should remain in such a state for want of instruction for youth."[2] "We want a surgeon: there is none in Canada who can set a bone."[3] "Send us some tilers, brick-makers, and potters."[4] "Send us iron-workers to work our mines."[5] "It is to be wished that his Majesty would send us all sorts of artisans, especially potters and glass-workers."[6] "Our Canadians need aid and instruction in their fisheries; they need pilots."[7]

In 1688 the intendant reported that Canada was entirely without either pilots or sailors; and as late as 1712 the engineer Catalogne informed the government, that, though the St. Lawrence was dangerous, a pilot was rarely to be had. "There ought to be

---

[1] *Le Roy à Duchesneau*, 11 *Juin*, 1680.
[2] *Mémoire à Monseigneur le Marquis de Seignelay, présenté par les Sieurs Chalons et Riverin*, 1686.
[3] *Champigny au Ministre*, 1688.
[4] *Ibid.*
[5] *Denonville au Ministre*, 1686.
[6] *Mémoire de Catalogne*, 1712.
[7] *Denonville au Ministre*, 1685.

trade with the West Indies and other places," urges another writer. "Everybody says it is best, but nobody will undertake it. Our merchants are too poor, or else are engrossed by the fur-trade."[1]

The languor of commerce made agriculture languish. "It is of no use now," writes Meules, in 1682, "to raise any crops except what each family wants for itself." In vain the government sent out seeds for distribution; in vain intendants lectured the farmers, and lavished well-meant advice. Tillage remained careless and slovenly. "If," says the all-observing Catalogne, "the soil were not better cultivated in Europe than here, three-fourths of the people would starve." He complains that the festivals of the Church are so numerous that not ninety working-days are left during the whole working season. The people, he says, ought to be compelled to build granaries to store their crops, instead of selling them in autumn for almost nothing, and every *habitant* should be required to keep two or three sheep. The intendant Champigny calls for seed of hemp and flax, and promises to visit the farms, and show the people the lands best suited for their culture. He thinks that favors should be granted to those who raise hemp and flax as well as to those who marry. Denonville is of opinion that each *habitant* should be compelled to raise a little hemp every year, and that the King should then buy it of him at a high price.[2]

[1] *Mémoire de Chalons et Riverin présenté au Marquis de Seignelay.*
[2] *Denonville au Ministre,* 13 *Nov.*, 1685.

It will be well, he says, to make use of severity, while at the same time holding out a hope of gain; and he begs that weavers be sent out to teach the women and girls, who spend the winter in idleness, how to weave and spin. Weaving and spinning, however, as well as the culture of hemp and flax, were neglected till 1705, when the loss of a ship laden with goods for the colony gave the spur to home industry; and Madame de Repentigny set the example of making a kind of coarse blanket of nettle and linden bark.[1]

The jealousy of colonial manufactures shown by England appears but rarely in the relations of France with Canada. According to its light, the French government usually did its best to stimulate Canadian industry, with what results we have just seen. There was afterwards some improvement. In 1714 the intendant Bégon reported that coarse fabrics of wool and linen were made; that the sisters of the congregation wove cloth for their own habits as good as the same stuffs in France; that black cloth was made for priests, and blue cloth for the pupils of the colleges. The inhabitants, he says, have been taught these arts by necessity. They were naturally adroit at handiwork of all kinds; and during the last half-century of the French rule, when the population had settled into comparative stability, many of the mechanic arts were practised with success, notwithstanding the assertion of the Abbé La Tour that everything but

[1] *Beauharnois et Raudot au Ministre*, 1705.

bread and meat had still to be brought from France. This change may be said to date from the peace of Utrecht, or a few years before it. At that time one Duplessis had a new vessel on the stocks. Catalogne, who states the fact, calls it the beginning of ship-building in Canada, — evidently ignorant that Talon had made a fruitless beginning more than forty years before.

Of the arts of ornament not much could have been expected; but, strangely enough, they were in somewhat better condition than the useful arts. The nuns of the Hôtel-Dieu made artificial flowers for altars and shrines, under the direction of Mother Juchereau;[1] and the boys of the seminary were taught to make carvings in wood for the decoration of churches.[2] Pierre, son of the merchant Le Ber, had a turn for painting, and made religious pictures, described as very indifferent.[3] His sister Jeanne, an enthusiastic devotee, made embroideries for vestments and altars, and her work was much admired.

The colonial finances were not prosperous. In the absence of coin, beaver-skins long served as currency. In 1669 the council declared wheat a legal tender, at four francs the *minot* or three French bushels;[4] and, five years later, all creditors were ordered to receive moose-skins in payment at the market rate.[5] Coin would not remain in the colony: if the company or

---

[1] Juchereau, *Hist. de l'Hôtel-Dieu*, 244.   [2] *Abeille*, ii. 13.
[3] Faillon, *Vie de Mlle. Le Ber*, 331.   [4] *Edits et Ord.*, ii. 47.
[5] *Ibid.*, ii. 55.

the King sent any thither, it went back in the returning ships. The government devised a remedy. A coinage was ordered for Canada one-fourth less in value than that of France. Thus the Canadian livre or franc was worth, in reality, fifteen sous instead of twenty.[1] This shallow expedient produced only a nominal rise of prices, and coin fled the colony as before. Trade was carried on for a time by means of negotiable notes, payable in furs, goods, or farm produce. In 1685 the intendant Meules issued a card currency. He had no money to pay the soldiers, "and not knowing," he informs the minister, "to what saint to make my vows, the idea occurred to me of putting in circulation notes made of cards, each cut into four pieces; and I have issued an ordinance commanding the inhabitants to receive them in payment."[2] The cards were common playing-cards, and each piece was stamped with a *fleur-de-lis* and a crown, and signed by the governor, the intendant, and the clerk of the treasury at Quebec.[3] The example of Meules found ready imitation. Governors and intendants made card-money whenever they saw fit; and, being worthless everywhere but in Canada, it showed no disposition to escape the colony. It was declared convertible not into coin, but into bills of exchange; and this conversion could only take place at brief specified periods. "The currency used

[1] This device was of very early date. See Boucher, *Hist. Véritable*, chap. xiv.
[2] *Meules au Ministre*, 24 Sept., 1685.
[3] *Mémoire addressé au Régent*, 1715.

in Canada," says a writer in the last years of the French rule, "has no value as a representative of money. It is the sign of a sign."[1] It was card representing paper, and this paper was very often dishonored. In 1714 the amount of card rubbish had risen to two million livres. Confidence was lost, and trade was half dead. The minister Ponchartrain came to the rescue, and promised to redeem it at half its nominal value. The holders preferred to lose half rather than the whole, and accepted the terms. A few of the cards were redeemed at the rate named; then the government broke faith, and payment ceased. "This afflicting news," says a writer of the time, "was brought out by the vessel which sailed from France last July."

In 1717 the government made another proposal, and the cards were converted into bills of exchange. At the same time a new issue was made, which it was declared should be the last.[2] This issue was promptly redeemed; but twelve years later another followed it. In the interval, a certain quantity of coin circulated in the colony; but it underwent fluctuations through the intervention of government, and within eight years at least four edicts were issued affecting its value.[3] Then came more promises to pay, till, in the last bitter years of its existence, the colony floundered in drifts of worthless paper.

One characteristic grievance was added to the

---

[1] *Considérations sur l'État du Canada*, 1758.
[2] *Édits et Ordonnances*, i. 370.   [3] *Ibid.*, 400, 432, 436, 484.

countless woes of Canadian commerce. The government was so jealous of popular meetings of all kinds, that for a long time it forbade merchants to meet together for discussing their affairs; and it was not till 1717 that the establishment of a *bourse*, or exchange, was permitted at Quebec and Montreal.[1]

In respect of taxation, Canada, as compared with France, had no reason to complain. If the King permitted governors and intendants to make card-money, he permitted nobody to impose taxes but himself. The Canadians paid no direct civil tax, except in a few instances where temporary and local assessments were ordered for special objects. It was the fur-trade on which the chief burden fell. One-fourth of the beaver-skins, and one-tenth of the moose-hides belonged to the King; and wine, brandy, and tobacco contributed a duty of ten per cent. During a long course of years these were the only imposts. The King also retained the exclusive right of the fur-trade at Tadoussac. A vast tract of wilderness extending from St. Paul's Bay to a point eighty leagues down the St. Lawrence, and stretching indefinitely northward towards Hudson's Bay, formed a sort of royal preserve, whence every settler was rigidly excluded. The farmers of the revenue had their trading-houses at Tadoussac, whither the northern tribes, until war, pestilence, and brandy consumed them, brought every summer a large quantity of furs.

[1] Doutre et Lareau, *Hist. du Droit Canadien*, 254.

When, in 1674, the West India Company, to whom these imposts had been granted, was extinguished, the King resumed possession of them. The various duties, along with the trade of Tadoussac, were now farmed out to one Oudiette and his associates, who paid the Crown three hundred and fifty thousand livres for their privilege.[1]

We come now to a trade far more important than all the others together, one which absorbed the enterprise of the colony, drained the life-sap from other branches of commerce, and, even more than a vicious system of government, kept them in a state of chronic debility, — the hardy, adventurous, lawless, fascinating fur-trade. In the eighteenth century, Canada exported a moderate quantity of timber, wheat, the herb called ginseng, and a few other commodities; but from first to last she lived chiefly on beaver-skins. The government tried without ceasing to control and regulate this traffic; but it never succeeded. It aimed, above all things, to bring the trade home to the colonists; to prevent them from

[1] The annual return to the King from the *ferme du Canada* was, for some years, 119,000 francs (livres). Out of this were paid from 35,000 to 40,000 francs a year for "ordinary charges." The governor, intendant, and all troops, except the small garrisons of Quebec, Montreal, and Three Rivers, were paid from other sources. There was a time when the balance must have been in the King's favor; but profit soon changed to loss, owing partly to wars, partly to the confusion into which the beaver-trade soon fell. "His Majesty," writes the minister to the governor in 1698, "may soon grow tired of a colony which, far from yielding him any profit, costs him immense sums every year."

going to the Indians, and induce the Indians to come to them. To this end a great annual fair was established by order of the King at Montreal. Thither every summer a host of savages came down from the lakes in their bark canoes. A place was assigned them at a little distance from the town. They landed, drew up their canoes in a line on the bank, took out their packs of beaver-skins, set up their wigwams, slung their kettles, and encamped for the night. On the next day there was a grand council on the common, between St. Paul Street and the river. Speeches of compliment were made amid a solemn smoking of pipes. The governor-general was usually present, seated in an arm-chair, while the visitors formed a ring about him, ranged in the order of their tribes. On the next day the trade began in the same place. Merchants of high and low degree brought up their goods from Quebec, and every inhabitant of Montreal, of any substance, sought a share in the profit. Their booths were set along the palisades of the town, and each had an interpreter, to whom he usually promised a certain portion of his gains. The scene abounded in those contrasts — not always edifying, but always picturesque — which mark the whole course of French-Canadian history. Here was a throng of Indians armed with bows and arrows, war-clubs, or the cheap guns of the trade, — some of them being completely naked, except for the feathers on their heads and the paint on their faces; French bush-rangers tricked out with savage finery; merchants and *habitants* in their coarse and plain attire, and the grave priests of St. Sulpice robed in black. Order and sobriety were their watchwords; but the wild gathering was beyond their control. The prohibition to sell brandy could rarely be enforced; and the fair ended at times in a pandemonium of drunken frenzy. The rapacity of trade, and the license of savages and *coureurs de bois*, had completely transformed the pious settlement.

A similar fair was established at Three Rivers, for the Algonquin tribes north of that place. These yearly markets did not fully answer the desired object. There was a constant tendency among the inhabitants of Canada to form settlements above Montreal, in order to intercept the Indians on their way down, drench them with brandy, and get their furs from them at low rates in advance of the fair. Such settlements were forbidden, but not prevented. The audacious "squatter" defied edict and ordinance and the fury of drunken savages, and boldly planted himself in the path of the descending trade. Nor is this a matter of surprise; for he was usually the secret agent of some high colonial officer, — an intendant, the local governor, or the governor-general, who often used his power to enforce the law against others, and to violate it himself.

This was not all; for the more youthful and vigorous part of the male population soon began to escape into the woods, and trade with the Indians far beyond the limits of the remotest settlements.

Here, too, many of them were in league with the authorities, who denounced the abuse while secretly favoring the portion of it in which they themselves were interested. The home government, unable to prevent the evil, tried to regulate it. Licenses were issued for the forest-trade.[1] Their number was limited to twenty-five, and the privileges which they conferred varied at different periods. In La Hontan's time, each license authorized the departure of two canoes loaded with goods. One canoe only was afterwards allowed, bearing three men with about four hundred pounds of freight. The licenses were sometimes sold for the profit of government; but many were given to widows of officers and other needy persons, to the hospitals, or to favorites and retainers of the governor. Those who could not themselves use them sold them to merchants or *voyageurs*, at a price varying from a thousand to eighteen hundred francs. They were valid for a year and a half; and each canoeman had a share in the profits, which, if no accident happened, were very large. The license system was several times suppressed and renewed again; but, like the fair at Montreal, it failed completely to answer its purpose, and restrain the young men of Canada from a general exodus into the wilderness.[2]

The most characteristic features of the Canadian

---

[1] *Ordres du Roy au sujet de la Traite du Canada*, 1681.

[2] Before me is one of these licenses, signed by the governor Denonville. A condition of carrying no brandy is appended to it.

fur-trade still remain to be seen. Oudiette and his associates were not only charged with collecting the revenue, but were also vested with an exclusive right of transporting all the beaver-skins of the colony to France. On their part they were compelled to receive all beaver-skins brought to their magazines, and, after deducting the fourth belonging to the King, to pay for the rest at a fixed price. This price was graduated to the different qualities of the fur; but the average cost to the collectors was a little more than three francs a pound. The inhabitants could barter their furs with merchants; but the merchants must bring them all to the magazines of Oudiette, who paid in receipts convertible into bills of exchange. He soon found himself burdened with such a mass of beaver-skins that the market was completely glutted. The French hatters refused to take them all; and for the part which they consented to take they paid chiefly in hats, which Oudiette was not allowed to sell in France, but only in the French West Indies, where few people wanted them. An unlucky fashion of small hats diminished the consumption of fur and increased his embarrassments, as did also a practice common among the hatters of mixing rabbit fur with the beaver. In his extremity he bethought him of setting up a hat factory for himself, under the name of a certain licensed hatter, thinking thereby to alarm his customers into buying his stock.[1] The other hatters rose in wrath, and

[1] *Mémoire touchant le Commerce du Canada*, 1687.

petitioned the minister. The new factory was suppressed, and Oudiette soon became bankrupt. Another company of farmers of the revenue took his place with similar results. The action of the law of supply and demand was completely arrested by the peremptory edict which, with a view to the prosperity of the colony and the profit of the King, required the company to take every beaver-skin offered.

All Canada, thinking itself sure of its price, rushed into the beaver-trade, and the accumulation of unsalable furs became more and more suffocating. The farmers of the revenue could not meet their engagements. Their bills of exchange were unpaid, and Canada was filled with distress and consternation. In 1700 a change of system was ordered. The monopoly of exporting beaver was placed in the hands of a company formed of the chief inhabitants of Canada. Some of them hesitated to take the risk; but the government was not to be trifled with, and the minister, Pouchartrain, wrote in terms so peremptory, and so menacing to the recusants, that, in the words of a writer of the time, he "shut everybody's mouth." About a hundred and fifty merchants accordingly subscribed to the stock of the new company, and immediately petitioned the King for a ship and a loan of seven hundred thousand francs. They were required to take off the hands of the farmers of the revenue an accumulation of more than six hundred thousand pounds of beaver, for which, however, they were to pay but half its usual price.

The market of France absolutely refused it, and the directors of the new company saw no better course than to burn three-fourths of the troublesome and perishable commodity; nor was this the first resort to this strange expedient. One cannot repress a feeling of indignation at the fate of the interesting and unfortunate animals uselessly sacrificed to a false economic system. In order to rid themselves of what remained, the directors begged the King to issue a decree, requiring all hatters to put at least three ounces of genuine beaver-fur into each hat.

All was in vain. The affairs of the company fell into a confusion which was aggravated by the bad faith of some of its chief members. In 1707 it was succeeded by another company, to whose magazines every *habitant* or merchant was ordered to bring every beaver-skin in his possession within forty-eight hours; and the company, like its predecessors, was required to receive it, and pay for it in written promises. Again the market was overwhelmed with a surfeit of beaver. Again the bills of exchange were unpaid, and all was confusion and distress. Among the memorials and petitions to which this state of things gave birth, there is one conspicuous by the presence of good sense and the absence of self-interest. The writer proposes that there should be no more monopoly, but that everybody should be free to buy beaver-skins and send them to France, subject only to a moderate duty of entry. The proposal was not accepted. In 1721 the monopoly of exporting beaver-skins was given to the new West India Company; but this time it was provided that the government should direct from time to time, according to the capacities of the market, the quantity of furs which the company should be forced to receive.[1]

Out of the beaver-trade rose a huge evil, baneful to the growth and the morals of Canada. All that was most active and vigorous in the colony took to the woods, and escaped from the control of intendants, councils, and priests, to the savage freedom of the wilderness. Not only were the possible profits great; but, in the pursuit of them, there was a fascinating element of adventure and danger. The bush-rangers, or *coureurs de bois*, were to the King an object of horror. They defeated his plans for the increase of the population, and shocked his native instinct of discipline and order. Edict after edict was directed against them; and more than once the colony presented the extraordinary spectacle of the greater part of its young men turned into forest out-

---

[1] On the fur-trade the documents consulted are very numerous. The following are the most important: *Mémoire sur ce qui concerne le Commerce du Castor et ses dépendances*, 1715; *Mémoire concernant le Commerce de Traite entre les François et les Sauvages*, 1691; *Mémoire sur le Canada addressé au Régent*, 1715; *Mémoire sur les Affaires de Canada dans leur Estat présent*, 1696; *Mémoire des Négotiants de la Rochelle qui font Commerce en Canada sur la Proposition de ne plus recevoir les Castors et d'engager les Habitants à la Culture des Terres et Pesche de la Molue*, 1696; *Mémoire du Sr. Riverin sur la Traite et la Ferme du Castor*, 1696; *Mémoire touchant le Commerce du Canada*, 1687, etc.

laws. But severity was dangerous. The offenders might be driven over to the English, or converted into a lawless banditti, — renegades of civilization and the faith. Therefore, clemency alternated with rigor, and declarations of amnesty with edicts of proscription. Neither threats nor blandishments were of much avail. We hear of seigniories abandoned; farms turning again into forests; wives and children left in destitution. The exodus of the *coureurs de bois* would take, at times, the character of an organized movement. The famous Du Lhut is said to have made a general combination of the young men of Canada to follow him into the woods. Their plan was to be absent four years, in order that the edicts against them might have time to relent. The intendant Duchesneau reported that eight hundred men out of a population of less than ten thousand souls had vanished from sight in the immensity of a boundless wilderness. Whereupon the King ordered that any person going into the woods without a license should be whipped and branded for the first offence, and sent for life to the galleys for the second.[1] The order was more easily given than enforced. "I must not conceal from you, Monseigneur," again writes Duchesneau, "that the disobedience of the *coureurs de bois* has reached such a point that everybody boldly contravenes the King's interdictions; that there is no longer any concealment; and that parties

[1] *Le Roy à Frontenac*, 30 Avril, 1681. On another occasion, it was ordered that any person thus offending should suffer death.

are collected with astonishing insolence to go and trade in the Indian country. I have done all in my power to prevent this evil, which may cause the ruin of the colony. I have enacted ordinances against the *coureurs de bois;* against the merchants who furnish them with goods; against the gentlemen and others who harbor them; and even against those who have any knowledge of them, and will not inform the local judges. All has been in vain; inasmuch as some of the most considerable families are interested with them, and the governor lets them go on and even shares their profits."[1] "You are aware, Monseigneur," writes Denonville, some years later, "that the *coureurs de bois* are a great evil, but you are not aware how great this evil is. It deprives the country of its effective men; makes them indocile, debauched, and incapable of discipline, and turns them into pretended nobles, — wearing the sword and decked out with lace, both they and their relations, who all affect to be gentlemen and ladies. As for cultivating the soil, they will not hear of it. This, along with the scattered condition of the settlements, causes their children to be as unruly as Indians, being brought up in the same manner. Not that there are not some very good people here, but they are in a minority."[2] In another despatch he enlarges on their vagabond and lawless ways, their indiffer-

---

[1] *N. Y. Colonial Docs.*, ix. 131.
[2] Denonville, *Mémoire sur l'Estat des Affaires de la Nouvelle France.*

ence to marriage, and the mischief caused by their example; describes how, on their return from the woods, they swagger like lords, spend all their gains in dress and drunken revelry, and despise the peasants, whose daughters they will not deign to marry, though they are peasants themselves.

It was a curious scene when a party of *coureurs de bois* returned from their rovings. Montreal was their harboring place, and they conducted themselves much like the crew of a man-of-war paid off after a long voyage. As long as their beaver-skins lasted, they set no bounds to their riot. Every house in the place, we are told, was turned into a drinking-shop. The new-comers were bedizened with a strange mixture of French and Indian finery; while some of them, with instincts more thoroughly savage, stalked about the streets as naked as a Pottawattamie or a Sioux. The clamor of tongues was prodigious, and gambling and drinking filled the day and the night. When at last they were sober again, they sought absolution for their sins; nor could the priests venture to bear too hard on their unruly penitents, lest they should break wholly with the Church and dispense thenceforth with her sacraments.

Under such leaders as Du Lhut, the *coureurs de bois* built forts of palisades at various points throughout the West and Northwest. They had a post of this sort at Detroit some time before its permanent settlement, as well as others on Lake Superior and in the valley of the Mississippi. They occupied them as long as it suited their purposes, and then abandoned them to the next comer. Michilimackinac was, however, their chief resort; and thence they would set out, two or three together, to roam for hundreds of miles through the endless mesh-work of interlocking lakes and rivers which seams the northern wilderness.

No wonder that a year or two of bush-ranging spoiled them for civilization. Though not a very valuable member of society, and though a thorn in the side of princes and rulers, the *coureur de bois* had his uses, at least from an artistic point of view; and his strange figure, sometimes brutally savage, but oftener marked with the lines of a dare-devil courage, and a reckless, thoughtless gayety, will always be joined to the memories of that grand world of woods which the nineteenth century is fast civilizing out of existence. At least, he is picturesque, and with his red-skin companion serves to animate forest scenery. Perhaps he could sometimes feel, without knowing that he felt them, the charms of the savage nature that had adopted him. Rude as he was, her voice may not always have been meaningless for one who knew her haunts so well, — deep recesses where, veiled in foliage, some wild shy rivulet steals with timid music through breathless caves of verdure; gulfs where feathered crags rise like castle walls, where the noonday sun pierces with keen rays athwart the torrent, and the mossed arms of fallen pines cast wavering shadows on the illumined foam;

pools of liquid crystal turned emerald in the reflected green of impending woods; rocks on whose rugged front the gleam of sunlit waters dances in quivering light; ancient trees hurled headlong by the storm, to dam the raging stream with their forlorn and savage ruin; or the stern depths of immemorial forests, dim and silent as a cavern, columned with innumerable trunks, each like an Atlas upholding its world of leaves, and sweating perpetual moisture down its dark and channelled rind, — some strong in youth, some grisly with decrepit age, nightmares of strange distortion, gnarled and knotted with wens and goitres; roots intertwined beneath like serpents petrified in an agony of contorted strife; green and glistening mosses carpeting the rough ground, mantling the rocks, turning pulpy stumps to mounds of verdure, and swathing fallen trunks as, bent in the impotence of rottenness, they lie outstretched over knoll and hollow, like mouldering reptiles of the primeval world, while around, and on and through them, springs the young growth that battens on their decay, — the forest devouring its own dead; or, to turn from its funereal shade to the light and life of the open woodland, the sheen of sparkling lakes, and mountains basking in the glory of the summer noon, flecked by the shadows of passing clouds that sail on snowy wings across the transparent azure.[1]

[1] An adverse French critic gives as his opinion that the sketch of the primeval wilderness on the preceding page is drawn from fancy, and not from observation. It is, however, copied in every

Yet it would be false coloring to paint the half-savage *coureur de bois* as a romantic lover of Nature. He liked the woods because they emancipated him from restraint. He liked the lounging ease of the camp-fire, and the license of Indian villages. His life has a dark and ugly side, which is nowhere drawn more strongly than in a letter written by the Jesuit Carheil to the intendant Champigny. It was at a time when some of the outlying forest posts, originally either missions or transient stations of *coureurs de bois*, had received regular garrisons. Carheil writes from Michilimackinac, and describes the state of things around him like one whom long familiarity with them had stripped of every illusion.[1]

But here, for the present, we pause; for the father touches on other matters than the *coureurs de bois*, and we reserve him and his letter for the next chapter.

particular, without exception, from a virgin forest in a deep moist valley by the upper waters of the little river Pemigewasset in northern New Hampshire, where I spent a summer afternoon a few days before the passage was written.

[1] See the letter in Appendix I.

CHAPTER XXI.

1663-1702.

THE MISSIONS. — THE BRANDY QUESTION.

THE JESUITS AND THE IROQUOIS. — MISSION VILLAGES. — MICHILIMACKINAC. — FATHER CARHEIL. — TEMPERANCE. — BRANDY AND THE INDIANS. — STRONG MEASURES. — DISPUTES. — LICENSE AND PROHIBITION. — VIEWS OF THE KING. — TRADE AND THE JESUITS.

For a year or two after De Tracy had chastised the Mohawks, and humbled the other Iroquois nations, all was rose-color on the side of that dreaded confederacy. The Jesuits, defiant as usual of hardship and death, had begun their ruined missions anew. Bruyas took the Mission of the Martyrs among the Mohawks; Milet, that of Saint Francis Xavier, among the Oneidas; Lamberville, that of Saint John the Baptist among the Onondagas; Carheil, that of Saint Joseph among the Cayugas; and Raffeix and Julien Garnier shared between them the three missions of the Senecas. The Iroquois, after their punishment, were in a frame of mind so hopeful that the fathers imagined for a moment that they were all on the point of accepting the faith. This was a consummation earnestly to be wished, not only from a religious, but also from a political, point of view. The complete conversion of the Iroquois meant their estrangement from the heretic English and Dutch, and their firm alliance with the French. It meant safety for Canada, and it insured for her the fur-trade of the interior freed from English rivalry. Hence the importance of these missions, and hence their double character. While the Jesuit toiled to convert his savage hosts, he watched them at the same time with the eye of a shrewd political agent; reported at Quebec the result of his observations, and by every means in his power sought to alienate them from England, and attach them to France.

Their simple conversion, by placing them wholly under his influence, would have outweighed in political value all other agencies combined; but the flattering hopes of the earlier years soon vanished. Some petty successes against other tribes so elated the Iroquois that they ceased to care for French alliance or French priests. Then a few petty reverses would dash their spirits, and dispose them again to listen to Jesuit counsels. Every success of a war-party was a loss to the faith, and every reverse was a gain. Meanwhile a more repulsive or a more critical existence than that of a Jesuit father in an Iroquois town is scarcely conceivable. The torture of prisoners turned into a horrible festivity for the whole tribe; foul and crazy orgies in which, as the priest thought, the powers of darkness took a special delight; drunken riots, the work of Dutch brandy, when he was forced to seek refuge from death in his chapel, — a sanctuary which superstitious fear withheld the Indians from violating, — these, and a thousand disgusts and miseries, filled the record of his days; and he bore them all in patience. Not only were the early Canadian Jesuits men of an intense religious zeal, but they were also men who lived not for themselves but for their Order. Their faults were many and great, but the grandeur of their self-devotion towers conspicuous over all.

At Caughnawaga, near Montreal, may still be seen the remnants of a mission of converted Iroquois, whom the Jesuits induced to leave the temptations of their native towns and settle here, under the wing of the Church. They served as a bulwark against the English, and sometimes did good service in time of war. At Sillery, near Quebec, a band of Abenakis, escaping from the neighborhood of the English towards the close of Philip's War, formed another mission of similar character. The Sulpitians had a third at the foot of the mountain of Montreal, where two massive stone-towers of the fortified Indian town are standing to this day. All these converted savages, as well as those of Lorette and other missions far and near, were used as allies in war, and launched in scalping-parties against the border settlements of New England.

Not only the Sulpitians, but also the seminary priests of Quebec, the Récollets, and even the

Capuchins, had missions more or less important, and more or less permanent. But the Jesuits stood always in the van of religious and political propagandism; and all the forest tribes felt their influence, from Acadia and Maine to the plains beyond the Mississippi. Next in importance to their Iroquois missions were those among the Algonquins of the northern lakes. Here was the grand domain of the beaver-trade; and the chief woes of the missionary sprang not from the Indians, but from his own countrymen. Beaver-skins had produced an effect akin to that of gold in our own day, and the deepest recesses of the wilderness were invaded by eager seekers after gain.

The focus of the evil was at Father Marquette's old mission of Michilimackinac. First, year after year came a riotous invasion of *coureurs de bois*, and then a garrison followed to crown the mischief. Discipline was very weak at these advanced posts, and, to eke out their pay, the soldiers were allowed to trade, — brandy, whether permitted or interdicted, being the chief article of barter. Father Étienne Carheil was driven almost to despair; and he wrote to the intendant, his fast friend and former pupil, the long letter already mentioned. "Our missions," he says, "are reduced to such extremity that we can no longer maintain them against the infinity of disorder, brutality, violence, injustice, impiety, impurity, insolence, scorn, and insult, which the deplorable and infamous traffic in brandy has spread universally among the

Indians of these parts. . . . In the despair in which we are plunged, nothing remains for us but to abandon them to the brandy-sellers as a domain of drunkenness and debauchery." He complains bitterly of the officers in command of the fort, who, he says, far from repressing disorders, encourage them by their example, and are even worse than their subordinates, "insomuch that all our Indian villages are so many taverns for drunkenness and Sodoms for iniquity, which we shall be forced to leave to the just wrath and vengeance of God." He insists that the garrisons are entirely useless, as they have only four occupations, — first, to keep open liquor-shops for crowds of drunken Indians; secondly, to roam from place to place, carrying goods and brandy under the orders of the commandant, who shares their profits; thirdly, to gamble day and night; fourthly, to "turn the fort into a place which I am ashamed to call by its right name;" and he describes, with a curious amplitude of detail, the swarms of Indian girls who are hired to make it their resort. "Such, Monseigneur, are the only employments of the soldiers maintained here so many years. If this can be called doing the King service, I admit that such service is done for him here now, and has always been done for him here; but I never saw any other done in my life." He further declares that the commandants oppose and malign the missionaries, while of the presents which the King sends up the country for distribution to the Indians, they, the Indians, get nothing but a little tobacco, and the officer keeps the rest for himself.[1]

From the misconduct of officers and soldiers, the father passes to that of the *coureurs de bois* and licensed traders; and here he is equally severe. He dilates on the evils which result from permitting the colonists to go to the Indians instead of requiring the Indians to come to the settlements. "It serves only to rob the country of all its young men, weaken families, deprive wives of their husbands, sisters of their brothers, and parents of their children; expose the voyagers to a hundred dangers of body and soul; involve them in a multitude of expenses, some necessary, some useless, and some criminal; accustom them to do no work, and at last disgust them with it forever; make them live in constant idleness, unfit them completely for any trade, and render them useless to themselves, their families, and the public. But it is less as regards the body than as regards the soul that this traffic of the French among the savages is infinitely hurtful. It carries them far away from churches, separates them from priests and nuns, and severs them from all instruction, all exercise of

[1] Of the officers in command at Michilimackinac while Carheil was there, he partially excepts La Durantaye from his strictures, but bears very hard on La Mothe-Cadillac, who hated the Jesuits and was hated by them in turn. La Mothe, on his part, writes that "the missionaries wish to be masters wherever they are, and cannot tolerate anybody above themselves." (*N. Y. Colonial Docs.*, ix. 587.) For much more emphatic expressions of his views concerning them, see two letters from him, translated in Sheldon's *Early History of Michigan*.

religion, and all spiritual aid. It sends them into places wild and almost inaccessible, through a thousand perils by land and water, to carry on by base, abject, and shameful means a trade which would much better be carried on at Montreal."

But in the complete transfer of the trade to Montreal, Father Carheil sees insuperable difficulties; and he proceeds to suggest, as the last and best resort, that garrisons and officers should be withdrawn, and licenses abolished; that discreet and virtuous persons should be chosen to take charge of all the trade of the upper country; that these persons should be in perfect sympathy and correspondence with the Jesuits; and that the trade should be carried on at the missions of the Jesuits and in their presence.[1]

This letter brings us again face to face with the brandy question, of which we have seen something already in the quarrel between Avaugour and the bishop. In the summer of 1648 there was held at the mission of Sillery a temperance meeting, — the first in all probability on this continent. The drum beat after mass, and the Indians gathered at the summons. Then an Algonquin chief, a zealous convert of the Jesuits, proclaimed to the crowd a late edict of the governor imposing penalties for drunkenness, and, in his own name and that of the other

---

[1] *Lettre du Père Étienne Carheil de la Compagnie de Jésus à l'Intendant Champigny, Michilimackinac, 30 Août, 1702 (Archives Nationales),* Appendix I.

chiefs, exhorted them to abstinence, declaring that all drunkards should be handed over to the French for punishment. Father Jerome Lalemant looked on delighted. "It was," he says, "the finest public act of jurisdiction exercised among the Indians since I have been in this country. From the beginning of the world they have all thought themselves as great lords, the one as the other, and never before submitted to their chiefs any further than they chose to do so."[1]

There was great need of reform; for a demon of drunkenness seemed to possess these unhappy tribes. Nevertheless, with all their rage for brandy, they sometimes showed in regard to it a self-control quite admirable in its way. When at a fair, a council, or a friendly visit, their entertainers regaled them with rations of the coveted liquor, so prudently measured out that they could not be the worse for it, they would unite their several portions in a common stock, which they would then divide among a few of their number, — thus enabling them to attain that complete intoxication which, in their view, was the true end of all drinking. The objects of this singular benevolence were expected to requite it in kind on some future occasion.

A drunken Indian, with weapons within reach, was very dangerous, and all prudent persons kept out of his way. This greatly pleased him; for, seeing everybody run before him, he fancied himself a great chief,

[1] Lalemant, *Relation*, 1648, p. 43.

and howled and swung his tomahawk with redoubled fury. If, as often happened, he maimed or murdered some wretch not nimble enough to escape, his countrymen absolved him from all guilt, and blamed only the brandy. Hence, if an Indian wished to take a safe revenge on some personal enemy, he would pretend to be drunk; and not only murders but other crimes were often committed by false claimants to the bacchanalian privilege.

In the eyes of the missionaries, brandy was a fiend with all crimes and miseries in his train; and, in fact, nothing earthly could better deserve the epithet infernal than an Indian town in the height of a drunken debauch. The orgies never ceased till the bottom of the barrel was reached. Then came repentance, despair, wailing, and bitter invective against the white men, the cause of all the woe. In the name of the public good, of humanity, and above all of religion, the bishop and the Jesuits denounced the fatal traffic.

Their case was a strong one; but so was the case of their opponents. There was real and imminent danger that the thirsty savages, if refused brandy by the French, would seek it from the Dutch and English of New York. It was the most potent lure and the most killing bait. Wherever it was found, thither the Indians and their beaver-skins were sure to go, and the interests of the fur-trade, vital to the colony, were bound up with it. Nor was this all, for the merchants and the civil powers insisted that religion and the saving of souls were bound up with it no less; since, to repel the Indians from the Catholic French, and attract them to the heretic English, was to turn them from ways of grace to ways of perdition.[1] The argument, no doubt, was dashed largely with hypocrisy in those who used it; but it was one which the priests were greatly perplexed to answer.

In former days, when Canada was not yet transformed from a mission to a colony, the Jesuits entered with a high hand on the work of reform. It fared hard with the culprit caught in the act of selling brandy to Indians. They led him, after the sermon, to the door of the church; where, kneeling on the pavement, partially stript and bearing in his hand the penitential torch, he underwent a vigorous flagellation, laid on by Father Le Mercier himself, after the fashion formerly practised in the case of refractory school-boys.[2] Bishop Laval not only discharged against the offenders volleys of wholesale excommunication, but he made of the offence a "reserved case;" that is, a case in which the power of granting absolution was reserved to himself alone. This produced great commotion, and a violent conflict between religious scruples and a passion for gain. The bishop and the Jesuits stood inflexible; while their

---

[1] "Ce commerce est absolument nécessaire pour attirer les sauvages dans les colonies françoises, et par ce moyen leur donner les premières teintures de la foy." — *Mémoire de Colbert, joint à sa lettre à Duchesneau du* 24 *Mai*, 1678.

[2] *Mémoire de Dumesnil*, 1671.

opponents added bitterness to the quarrel by charging them with permitting certain favored persons to sell brandy, unpunished, and even covertly selling it themselves.[1]

Appeal was made to the King, who — with his Jesuit confessor, guardian of his conscience on one side, and Colbert, guardian of his worldly interests on the other — stood in some perplexity. The case was referred to the fathers of the Sorbonne; and they, after solemn discussion, pronounced the selling of brandy to Indians a mortal sin.[2] It was next referred to an assembly of the chief merchants and inhabitants of Canada, held under the eye of the governor, intendant, and council, in the Château St.

---

[1] *Lettre de Charles Aubert de la Chesnaye*, 24 Oct., 1693. After speaking of the excessive rigor of the bishop, he adds: "L'on dit, et il est vrai, que dans ces temps si fâcheux, sous pretexte de pauvreté dans les familles, certaines gens avoient permission d'en traiter, je crois toujours avec la réserve de ne pas enivrer." Dumesnil, *Mémoire de* 1671, says that Laval excommunicated all brandy-sellers, " à l'exception, néanmoins, de quelques particuliers qu'il voulait favoriser." He says further that the bishop and the Jesuit Ragueneau had a clerk whom they employed at 500 francs a year to trade with the Indians, paying them in liquors for their furs; and that for a time the ecclesiastics had this trade to themselves, their severities having deterred most others from venturing into it. La Salle, *Mémoire de* 1678, declares that, " Ils [les Jésuites] refusent l'absolution à ceux qui ne veulent pas promettre de n'en plus vendre, et s'ils meurent en cet état, ils les privent de la sépulture ecclésiastique: au contraire, ils se permettent à eux mesmes sans aucune difficulté ce mesme trafic, quoyque toute sorte de trafic soit interdite à tous les ecclésiastiques par les ordonnances du Roy et par une bulle expresse du Pape." I give these assertions as I find them, and for what they are worth.

[2] *Délibération de la Sorbonne sur la Traite des Boissons*, 8 Mars, 1675.

Louis. Each was directed to state his views in writing. The great majority were for unrestricted trade in brandy; a few were for a limited and guarded trade; and two or three declared for prohibition.[1] Decrees of prohibition were passed from time to time, but they were unavailing. They were revoked, renewed, and revoked again. They were, in fact, worse than useless; for their chief effect was to turn traders and *coureurs de bois* into troops of audacious contrabandists. Attempts were made to limit the brandy-trade to the settlements, and exclude it from the forest country, where its regulation was impossible; but these attempts, like the others, were of little avail. It is worthy of notice that when brandy was forbidden everywhere else, it was permitted in the trade of Tadoussac, carried on for the profit of government.[2]

In spite of the Sorbonne, in spite of Père La Chaise, and of the Archbishop of Paris, whom he also consulted, the King was never at heart a prohibitionist.[3] His Canadian revenue was drawn from the fur-trade; and the singular argument of the partisans of brandy, that its attractions were needed

---

[1] *Procès-verbal de l'Assemblée tenue au Château de St. Louis de Québec, le 26 Oct., 1676, et jours suivants.*

[2] *Lettre de Charles Aubert de la Chesnaye,* 24 *Oct.,* 1683. In the course of the quarrel, a severe law passed by the General Court of Massachusetts against the sale of liquors to Indians was several times urged as an example to be imitated. A copy of it was sent to the minister, and is still preserved in the Archives of the Marine and Colonies.

[3] See, among other evidence, *Mémoire sur la Traite des Boissons,* 1678.

to keep the Indians from contact with heresy, served admirably to salve his conscience. Bigot as he was, he distrusted the Bishop of Quebec, the great champion of the anti-liquor movement. His own letters, as well as those of his minister, prove that he saw, or thought that he saw, motives for the crusade very different from those inscribed on its banners. He wrote to Saint-Vallier, Laval's successor in the bishopric, that the brandy-trade was very useful to the kingdom of France; that it should be regulated, but not prevented; that the consciences of his subjects must not be disturbed by denunciations of it as a sin; and that "it is well that you [the bishop] should take care that the zeal of the ecclesiastics is not excited by personal interests and passions."[1] Perhaps he alludes to the spirit of encroachment and domination which he and his minister in secret instructions to their officers often impute to the bishop and the clergy; or perhaps he may have in mind other accusations which had reached him from time to time during many years, and of which the following from the pen of the most noted of Canadian governors will serve as an example. Count Frontenac declares that the Jesuits greatly exaggerate the disorders caused by brandy, and that they easily convince persons "who do not know the interested motives which have led them to harp continually on this string for more than forty years. . . . They have long wished to have the fur-trade entirely

---

[1] *Le Roy à Saint-Vallier*, 7 *Avril*, 1691.

to themselves, and to keep out of sight the trade which they have always carried on in the woods, and which they are carrying on there now." [1]

TRADE OF THE JESUITS. — As I have observed in a former volume, the charge against the Jesuits of trading in beaver-skins dates from the beginning of the colony. In the private journal of Father Jerome Lalemant, their superior, occurs the following curious passage, under date of November, 1645: *Pour la traite des castors. Le 15 de Nov. le bruit estant qu'on s'en alloit icy publier la defense qui auoit esté publiée aux Trois Riuieres que pas vn n'eut à traiter auec les sauuages, le P. Vimont demanda à Mons. des Chastelets commis general si nous serions de pire condition soubs eux que soubs Messieurs de la Compagnie. La conclusion fut que non et que cela iroit pour nous à l'ordinaire, mais que nous le fissions doucement.*" (*Journal des Jésuites.*) Two years after, on the request of Lalemant, the governor Montmagny, and his destined successor Ailleboust, gave the Jesuits a certificate to the effect that " les pères de la compagnie de Jésus sont innocents de la calomnie qui leur a été imputée, et *ce qu'ils en ont fait a été pour le bien de la communauté et pour un bon sujet.*" This leaves it to be inferred that they actually traded, though with good intentions. In 1661, in reply to similar " calumnies," the Jesuits made by proxy a declaration before the council, stating, " que les dits Révérends Pères Jésuites n'ont fait jamais aucune profession de vendre et n'ont jamais rien vendu, *mais seulement que les marchandises qu'ils donnent aux particuliers ne sont que pour avoir leurs nécessités.*" This is an admission in a thin disguise. The word *nécessités* is of very elastic interpretation. In a memoir of Talon, 1667, he mentions, " la traite de pelleteries qu'on assure qu'ils [*les Jésuites*] font aux Outaouacks et au Cap de la Madeleine ; ce que je ne sais pas de science certaine."

That which Talon did not know with certainty is made reasonably clear for us by a line in the private journal of

---

[1] *Frontenac au Ministre*, 29 Oct., 1676.

Father Le Mercier, who writes under date of 17 August, 1665, "Le Père Frémin remonte supérieur au Cap de la Magdeleine, ou le temporel est en bon estat. *Comme il est delivré de tout soin d'aucune traite,* il doit s'appliquer à l'instruction tant des Montagnets que des Algonquins." Father Charles Albanel was charged, under Frémin, with the affairs of the mission, including doubtless the temporal interests, to the prosperity of which Father Le Mercier alludes, and the cares of trade from which Father Frémin was delivered. Cavelier de la Salle declared in 1678, "Le père Arbanelle [*Albanel*] jésuite a traité au Cap [*de la Madeleine*] pour 700 pistoles de peaux d'orignaux et de castors; luy mesme me l'a dit en 1667. Il vend le pain, le vin, le bled, le lard, et il tient magazin au Cap aussi bien que le frère Joseph à Québec. Ce frère gagne 500 pour 100 sur tous les peuples. Ils [*les Jésuites*] ont bâti leur collège en partie de leur traite et en partie de l'emprunt." La Salle further says that Frémin, being reported to have made enormous profits, "ce père répondit au gouverneur (*qui lui en avait fait des plaintes*) par un billet que luy a conservé, que c'estoit une calomnie que ce grand gain prétendu; puisque tout ce qui se passoit par ses mains ne pouvoit produire par an que quatre mille de revenant bon, tous frais faits, sans comprendre les gages des domestiques." La Salle gives also many other particulars, especially relating to Michilimackinac, where, as he says, the Jesuits had a large stock of beaver-skins. According to Péronne Dumesnil, *Mémoire de* 1671, the Jesuits had at that time more than 20,000 francs a year, — partly from trade and partly from charitable contributions of their friends in France.

The King repeatedly forbade the Jesuits and other ecclesiastics in Canada to carry on trade. On one occasion he threatened strong measures should they continue to disobey him. (*Le Roi à Frontenac,* 28 *Avril,* 1677.) In the same year the minister wrote to the intendant Duchesneau: "Vous ne sauriez apporter trop de precautions pour abolir entièrement la constume que les Ecclesiastiques seculiers et reguliers avaient pris de traitter ou de faire traitter leurs valets," 18 *Avril,* 1677.

The Jesuits entered also into other branches of trade and

industry with a vigor and address which the inhabitants of Canada might have emulated with advantage. They were successful fishers of eels. In 1646 their eel-pots at Sillery are said to have yielded no less than forty thousand eels, some of which they sold at the modest price of thirty sous a hundred. (Ferland, *Notes sur les Registres de N. D. de Québec*, 82.) The members of the Order were exempted from payment of duties, and in 1674 they were specially empowered to construct mills, including sugar-mills, and keep slaves, apprentices, and hired servants. *Droit Canadien*, 180.

CHAPTER XXII.

1663–1763.

PRIESTS AND PEOPLE.

CHURCH AND STATE. — THE BISHOP AND THE KING. — THE KING AND THE CURÉS. — THE NEW BISHOP.— THE CANADIAN CURÉ. — ECCLESIASTICAL RULE. — SAINT-VALLIER AND DENONVILLE. — CLERICAL RIGOR. — JESUIT AND SULPITIAN. — COURCELLE AND CHÂTELAIN. — THE RÉCOLLETS. — HERESY AND WITCHCRAFT. — CANADIAN NUNS. — JEANNE LE BER. — EDUCATION. — THE SEMINARY. — SAINT JOACHIM. — MIRACLES OF SAINT ANNE. — CANADIAN SCHOOLS.

WHEN Laval and the Jesuits procured the recall of Mézy, they achieved a seeming triumph; yet it was but a defeat in disguise. While ordering home the obnoxious governor, the King and Colbert made a practical assertion of their power too strong to be resisted. A vice-regal officer, a governor, an intendant, and a regiment of soldiers were silent but convincing proofs that the mission days of Canada were over, and the dream of a theocracy dispelled forever. The ecclesiastics read the signs of the times, and for a while seemed to accept the situation.

The King on his part, in vindicating the civil power, had shown a studious regard to the sensibilities of the bishop and his allies. The lieutenant-

François Xavier de Laval-Montmorency.

general Tracy, a zealous devotee, and the intendant Talon, who at least professed to be one, were not men to offend the clerical party needlessly. In the choice of Courcelle, the governor, a little less caution had been shown. His chief business was to fight the Iroquois, for which he was well fitted; but he presently showed signs of a willingness to fight the Jesuits also. The colonists liked him for his lively and impulsive speech; but the priests were of a different mind, and so, too, was his colleague Talon, — a prudent person, who studied the amenities of life, and knew how to pursue his ends with temper and moderation. On the subject of the clergy he and the governor substantially agreed, but the ebullitions of the one and the smooth discretion of the other were mutually repugnant to both. Talon complained of his colleague's impetuosity; and Colbert directed him to use his best efforts to keep Courcelle within bounds, and prevent him from publicly finding fault with the bishop and the Jesuits.[1] Next we find the minister writing to Courcelle himself to soothe his ruffled temper, and enjoining him to act discreetly, "because," said Colbert, "as the colony grows, the King's authority will grow with it, and the authority of the priests will be brought back in time within lawful bounds."[2]

Meanwhile, Talon had been ordered to observe carefully the conduct of the bishop and the Jesuits,

---

[1] *Colbert à Talon*, 20 *Fév.*, 1668.
[2] *Colbert à Courcelle*, 19 *Mai*, 1669.

"who," says the minister, "have hitherto nominated governors for the King, and used every means to procure the recall of those chosen without their participation;[1] filled offices with their adherents, and tolerated no secular priests except those of one mind with them."[2] Talon, therefore, under the veil of a reverent courtesy, sharply watched them. They paid courtesy with courtesy, and the intendant wrote home to his master that he saw nothing amiss in them. He quickly changed his mind. "I should have had less trouble and more praise," he writes in the next year, "if I had been willing to leave the power of the Church where I found it."[3] "It is easy," he says again, "to incur the ill-will of the Jesuits if one does not accept all their opinions and abandon one's self to their direction even in temporal matters; for their encroachments extend to affairs of police, which concern only the civil magistrate," — and he recommends that one or two of them be sent home as disturbers of the peace.[4] They, on their part, changed attitude towards both him and the governor. One of them, Father Bardy, less discreet than the rest, is said to have preached a sermon against them at Quebec, in which he likened them to a pair of toadstools springing up in a night, — adding that a good remedy would soon be found, and

---

[1] *Instruction au Sieur Talon.*
[2] *Mémoire pour M. de Tracy.*
[3] *Talon au Ministre*, 13 Nov., 1666.
[4] *Talon, Mémoire de* 1667.

that Courcelle would have to run home like other governors before him.[1]

Tracy escaped clerical attacks. He was extremely careful not to provoke them; and one of his first acts was to restore to the council the bishop's adherents whom Mézy had expelled.[2] And if, on the one hand, he was too pious to quarrel with the bishop, so, on the other, the bishop was too prudent to invite collision with a man of his rank and influence.

After all, the dispute between the civil and ecclesiastical powers was not fundamental. Each had need of the other; both rested on authority, and they differed only as to the boundary lines of their respective shares in it. Yet the dispute of boundaries was a serious one, and it remained a source of bitterness for many years. The King, though rigidly Catholic, was not yet sunk in the slough of bigotry into which Maintenon and the Jesuits succeeded at last in plunging him. He had conceived a distrust of Laval, and his jealousy of his royal authority disposed him to listen to the anti-clerical counsels of his minister. How needful they both thought it to prune the exuberant growth of clerical power, and how cautiously they set themselves to do so, their letters attest again and again. "The bishop," writes Colbert, "assumes a domination far beyond that of

---

[1] La Salle, *Mémoire de* 1678. This sermon was preached on the 12th of March, 1667.

[2] A curious account of his relations with Laval is given in a letter of La Mothe-Cadillac, 28 September, 1694.

other bishops throughout the Christian world, and particularly in the kingdom of France."[1] "It is the will of his Majesty that you confine him and the Jesuits within just bounds, and let none of them overstep these bounds in any manner whatsoever. Consider this as a matter of the greatest importance, and one to which you cannot give too much attention."[2] "But," the prudent minister elsewhere writes, "it is of the greatest consequence that the bishop and the Jesuits do not perceive that the intendant blames their conduct."[3]

It was to the same intendant that Colbert wrote, "it is necessary to diminish as much as possible the excessive number of priests, monks, and nuns in Canada." Yet in the very next year, and on the advice of Talon, he himself sent four more to the colony. His motive was plain. He meant that they should serve as a counterpoise to the Jesuits.[4] They were mendicant friars, belonging to the branch of the Franciscans known as the Récollets; and they were supposed to be free from the ambition for the aggrandizement of their Order which was imputed, and with reason, to the Jesuits. Whether the Récollets were free from it or not, no danger was to be feared from them; for Laval and the Jesuits were sure to oppose them, and they would need the support of the

[1] *Colbert à Duchesneau,* 1 *Mai,* 1677.
[2] *Ibid.,* 28 *Avril,* 1677.
[3] *Instruction pour M. Bouteroue,* 1668.
[4] *Mémoire succinct des principaux points des intentions du Roy sur le pays de Canada,* 18 *Mai,* 1669.

government too much to set themselves in opposition to it. "The more Récollets we have," says Talon, "the better will the too firmly rooted authority of the others be balanced."[1]

While Louis XIV. tried to confine the priests to their ecclesiastical functions, he was at the same time, whether from religion, policy, or both combined, very liberal to the Canadian Church, of which, indeed, he was the main-stay. In the yearly estimate of "ordinary charges" of the colony, the Church holds the most prominent place; and the appropriations for religious purposes often exceed all the rest together. Thus, in 1667, out of a total of 36,360 francs, 28,000 are assigned to Church uses.[2] The amount fluctuated, but was always relatively large. The Canadian curés were paid in great part by the King, who for many years gave eight thousand francs annually towards their support. Such was the poverty of the country that, though in 1685 there were only twenty-five curés,[3] each costing about five hundred francs a year, the tithes utterly failed to meet the expense. As late as 1700, the intendant declared that Canada without the King's help could

---

[1] *Talon au Ministre*, 10 Oct., 1670.

[2] Of this, 6,000 francs were given to the Jesuits, 6,000 to the Ursulines, 9,000 to the cathedral, 4,000 to the seminary, and 3,000 to the Hôtel-Dieu. (*État de dépense, etc.*, 1677.) The rest went to pay civil officers and garrisons. In 1682 the amount for Church uses was only 12,000 francs. In 1687 it was 13,500. In 1689 it rose to 34,000, including Acadia.

[3] Increased soon after to thirty-six by Saint-Vallier, Laval's successor.

not maintain more than eight or nine curés. Louis XIV. winced under these steady demands, and reminded the bishop that more than four thousand curés in France lived on less than two hundred francs a year.[1] "You say," he wrote to the intendant, "that it is impossible for a Canadian curé to live on five hundred francs. Then you must do the impossible to accomplish my intentions, which are always that the curés should live on the tithes alone."[2] Yet the head of the Church still begged for money, and the King still paid it. "We are in the midst of a costly war," wrote the minister to the bishop, "yet in consequence of your urgency the gifts to ecclesiastics will be continued as before."[3] And they did continue. More than half a century later, the King was still making them, and during the last years of the colony he gave twenty thousand francs annually to support Canadian curés.[4]

The maintenance of curés was but a part of his bounty. He endowed the bishopric with the revenues of two French abbeys, to which he afterwards added a third. The vast tracts of land which Laval had acquired were freed from feudal burdens, and emigrants were sent to them by the government in such numbers that, in 1667, the bishop's seigniory of Beaupré and Orleans contained more than a fourth

---

[1] *Mémoire à Duchesneau,* 15 *Mai,* 1678; *Le Roy à Duchesneau,* 11 *Juin,* 1680.

[2] *Le Roy à Duchesneau,* 30 *Avril,* 1681.

[3] *Le Ministre à l'Évêque,* 8 *Mai,* 1694.

[4] Bougainville, *Mémoire,* 1757.

of the entire population of Canada.[1] He had emerged from his condition of apostolic poverty to find himself the richest land-owner in the colony.

If by favors like these the King expected to lead the ecclesiastics into compliance with his wishes, he was doomed to disappointment. The system of movable curés, by which the bishop like a military chief could compel each member of his clerical army to come and go at his bidding, was from the first repugnant to Louis XIV. On the other hand, the bishop clung to it with his usual tenacity. Colbert denounced it as contrary to the laws of the kingdom.[2] "His Majesty has reason to believe," he writes, "that the chief source of the difficulty which the bishop makes on this point is his wish to preserve a greater authority over the curés."[3] The inflexible prelate, whose heart was bound up in the system he had established, opposed evasion and delay to each expression of the royal will; and even a royal edict failed to produce the desired effect. In the height of the dispute, Laval went to court, and, on the ground of failing health, asked for a successor in the bishopric. The King readily granted his prayer. The successor was appointed; but when Laval pre-

---

[1] Entire population, 4,312; Beaupré and Orleans, 1185. (*Recensement de* 1667.) Laval, it will be remembered, afterwards gave his lands to the seminary of Quebec. He previously exchanged the Island of Orleans with the Sieur Berthelot for the Island of Jesus. Berthelot gave him a large sum of money in addition.

[2] *Le Ministre à Duchesneau,* 15 *Mai,* 1678.

[3] *Instruction à M. de Meules,* 1682.

pared to embark again for Canada, he was given to understand that he was to remain in France. In vain he promised to make no trouble;[1] and it was not till after an absence of four years that he was permitted to return, no longer as its chief, to his beloved Canadian Church.[2]

Meanwhile Saint-Vallier, the new bishop, had raised a new tempest. He attacked that organization of the seminary of Quebec by which Laval had endeavored to unite the secular priests of Canada into an attached and obedient family, with the bishop as its head and the seminary as its home, — a plan of which the system of movable curés was an essential part. The Canadian priests, devoted to Laval, met the innovations of Saint-Vallier with an opposition which seemed only to confirm his purpose. Laval, old and worn with toil and asceticism, was driven almost to despair. The seminary of Quebec was the cherished work of his life, and, to his thinking, the citadel of the Canadian Church; and now he beheld it battered and breached before his eyes. His successor, in fact, was trying to place the Church of Canada on the footing of the Church of France. The conflict lasted for years, with the rancor that marks the quarrels of non-combatants of both sexes. "He"

---

[1] *Laval au Père la Chaise*, 1687. This forms part of a curious correspondence printed in the *Foyer Canadien* for 1866, from originals in the Archevêché of Quebec.

[2] From a *mémoire* of 18 Feb., 1685 (*Archives de Versailles*), it is plain that the court, in giving a successor to Laval, thought that it had ended the vexed question of movable curés.

[Saint-Vallier], says one of his opponents, "has made himself contemptible to almost everybody, and particularly odious to the priests born in Canada; for there is between them and him a mutual antipathy difficult to overcome."[1] He is described by the same writer as a person "without reflection and judgment, extreme in all things, secret and artful, passionate when opposed, and a flatterer when he wishes to gain his point." This amiable critic adds that Saint-Vallier believes a bishop to be inspired, in virtue of his office, with a wisdom that needs no human aid; and that whatever thought comes to him in prayer is a divine inspiration to be carried into effect at all costs and in spite of all opposition.

The new bishop, notwithstanding the tempest he had raised, did not fully accomplish that establishment of the curés in their respective parishes which the King and the minister so much desired. The Canadian curé was more a missionary than a parish priest; and Nature as well as Bishop Laval threw difficulties in the way of settling him quietly over his charge.

On the Lower St. Lawrence, where it widens to an estuary, six leagues across, a ship from France, the last of the season, holds her way for Quebec, laden with stores and clothing, household utensils, goods for Indian trade, the newest court fashions, wine, brandy, tobacco, and the King's orders from Ver-

---

[1] The above is from an anonymous paper, written apparently in 1695, and entitled *Mémoire pour le Canada*.

sailles. Swelling her patched and dingy sails, she glides through the wildness and the solitude where there is nothing but her to remind you of the great troubled world behind and the little troubled world before. On the far verge of the ocean-like river, clouds and mountains mingle in dim confusion; fresh gusts from the north dash waves against the ledges, sweep through the quivering spires of stiff and stunted fir-trees, and ruffle the feathers of the crow, perched on the dead bough after his feast of mussels among the sea-weed. You are not so solitary as you think. A small birch-canoe rounds the point of rocks, and it bears two men, — one in an old black cassock, and the other in a buckskin coat, — both working hard at the paddle to keep their slender craft off the shingle and the breakers. The man in the cassock is Father Morel, aged forty-eight, — the oldest country curé in Canada, most of his brethren being in the vigor of youth, as they had need to be. His parochial charge embraces a string of incipient parishes extending along the south shore from Rivière du Loup to Rivière du Sud, a distance reckoned at twenty-seven leagues, and his parishioners number in all three hundred and twenty-eight souls. He has administered spiritual consolation to the one inhabitant of Kamouraska; visited the eight families of La Bouteillerie and the five families of La Combe; and now he is on his way to the seigniory of St. Denis with its two houses and eleven souls.[1]

---

[1] These particulars are from the *Plan général de l'estat présent des missions du Canada, fait en l'année* 1683. It is a list and description

The father lands where a shattered eel-pot high and dry on the pebbles betrays the neighborhood of man. His servant shoulders his portable chapel, and follows him through the belt of firs and the taller woods beyond, till the sunlight of a desolate clearing shines upon them. Charred trunks and limbs encumber the ground; dead trees, branchless, barkless, pierced by the woodpeckers, in part black with fire, in part bleached by sun and frost, tower ghastly and weird above the labyrinth of forest ruins, through which the priest and his follower wind their way, the cat-bird mewing, and the blue-jay screaming as they pass. Now the golden-rod and the aster, harbingers of autumn, fringe with yellow and purple the edge of the older clearing, where wheat and maize, the settler's meagre harvest, are growing among the stumps.

Wild-looking women, with sunburnt faces and neglected hair, run from their work to meet the curé; a man or two follow with soberer steps and less exuberant zeal; while half-savage children, the *coureurs de bois* of the future, bareheaded, barefooted, and half-clad, come to wonder and stare. To set up his altar in a room of the rugged log-cabin; say mass, hear confessions, impose penance, grant absolution; repeat the office of the dead over a grave made weeks before; baptize, perhaps, the last infant;

of the parishes with the names and ages of the curés, and other details. (See *Abeille*, i.) This paper was drawn up by order of Laval.

marry, possibly, some pair who may or may not have waited for his coming; catechise as well as time and circumstance would allow the shy but turbulent brood of some former wedlock, — such was the work of the parish priest in the remoter districts. It was seldom that his charge was quite so scattered and so far extended as that of Father Morel; but there were fifteen or twenty others whose labors were like in kind, and in some cases no less arduous. All summer they paddled their canoes from settlement to settlement; and in winter they toiled on snow-shoes over the drifts, while the servant carried the portable chapel on his back, or dragged it on a sledge. Once, at least, in the year the curé paid his visit to Quebec, where, under the maternal roof of the seminary, he made his retreat of meditation and prayer, and then returned to his work. He rarely had a house of his own, but boarded in that of the seignior or one of the *habitants*. Many parishes or aggregations of parishes had no other church than a room fitted up for the purpose in the house of some pious settler. In the larger settlements there were churches and chapels of wood, thatched with straw, often ruinous, poor to the last degree, without ornaments, and sometimes without the sacred vessels necessary for the service.[1] In 1683 there were but seven stone churches in all the colony. The population was so thin and scattered that many of the settlers heard

---

[1] Saint-Vallier, *Estat présent de l'Église et de la Colonie Française*, 22 (ed. 1856).

mass only three or four times a year, and some of them not so often. The sick frequently died without absolution, and infants without baptism.

The splendid self-devotion of the early Jesuit missions has its record; so, too, have the unseemly bickerings of bishops and governors. But the patient toils of the missionary curé rest in the obscurity where the best of human virtues are buried from age to age. What we find set down concerning him is, that Louis XIV. was unable to see why he should not live on two hundred francs a year as well as a village curé by the banks of the Garonne. The King did not know that his cassock and all his clothing cost him twice as much and lasted half as long; that he must have a canoe and a man to paddle it; and that when on his annual visit the seminary paid him five or six hundred francs, partly in clothes, partly in stores, and partly in money, the end of the year found him as poor as before except only in his conscience.

The Canadian priests held the manners of the colony under a rule as rigid as that of the Puritan churches of New England, — but with the difference that in Canada a large part of the population was restive under their control, while some of the civil authorities, often with the governor at their head, supported the opposition. This was due partly to an excess of clerical severity, and partly to the continued friction between the secular and ecclesiastical powers. It sometimes happened, however, that a new governor arrived, who was so pious that the clerical party felt that they could rely on him. Of these rare instances the principal is that of Denonville, who, with a wife as pious as himself, and a young daughter, landed at Quebec in 1685. On this, Bishop Saint-Vallier, anxious to turn his good dispositions to the best account, addressed to him a series of suggestions or rather directions for the guidance of his conduct, with a view to the spiritual profit of those over whom he was appointed to rule. The document was put on file, and the following are some of the points in it. It is divided into five different heads, — "Touching feasts," "touching balls and dances," "touching comedies and other declamations," "touching dress," "touching irreverence in church." The governor and madame his wife are desired to accept no invitations to suppers, — that is to say, late dinners, — as tending to nocturnal hours and dangerous pastimes; and they are further enjoined to express dissatisfaction, and refuse to come again, should any entertainment offered them be too sumptuous. "Although," continues the bishop under the second head of his address, "balls and dances are not sinful in their nature, nevertheless they are so dangerous by reason of the circumstances that attend them and the evil results that almost inevitably follow, that, in the opinion of Saint Francis of Sales, it should be said of them as physicians say of mushrooms, that at best they are good for nothing;" and, after enlarging on their perils, he declares it to be of great importance to the glory of God and the sanctification of the colony, that the governor and his wife neither give such entertainments nor countenance them by their presence. "Nevertheless," adds the mentor, "since the youth and vivacity of mademoiselle their daughter requires some diversion, it is permitted to relent somewhat, and indulge her in a little moderate and proper dancing, provided that it be solely with persons of her own sex, and in the presence of madame her mother; but by no means in the presence of men or youths, since it is this mingling of sexes which causes the disorders that spring from balls and dances." Private theatricals in any form are next interdicted to the young lady. The bishop then passes to the subject of her dress, and exposes the abuses against which she is to be guarded. "The luxury of dress," he says, "appears in the rich and dazzling fabrics wherein the women and girls of Canada attire themselves, and which are far beyond their condition and their means; in the excess of ornaments which they put on; in the extraordinary head-dresses which they affect, their heads being uncovered and full of strange trinkets; and in the immodest curls so expressly forbidden in the epistles of Saint Peter and Saint Paul, as well as by all the fathers and doctors of the Church, and which God has often severely punished, — as may be seen by the example of the unhappy Pretextata, a lady of high quality, who, as we learn from Saint Jerome, who knew her, had her hands withered, and died suddenly five months after, and was precipitated into hell, as God had threatened her by an angel; because, by order of her husband, she had curled the hair of her niece, and attired her after a worldly fashion."[1]

Whether the Marquis and Marchioness Denonville profited by so apt and terrible a warning, or whether their patience and good-nature survived the episcopal onslaught, does not appear on record. The subject of feminine apparel received great attention, both from Saint-Vallier and his predecessor, each of whom issued a number of pastoral mandates concerning it. Their severest denunciations were aimed at low-necked dresses, which they regarded as favorite devices of the enemy for the snaring of souls; and they also used strong language against certain knots of ribbons called *fontanges*, with which the belles of Quebec adorned their heads. Laval launches strenuous invectives against "the luxury and vanity of women and girls, who, forgetting the promises of their baptism, decorate themselves with the pomp of

[1] "Témoin entr'autres l'exemple de la malheureuse Prétextate, dame de grande condition, laquelle au rapport de S. Jérôme, dont elle étoit connue, eut les mains desséchées et cinq mois après mourut subitement et fut précipitée en enfer, ainsi que Dieu l'en avoit menacée par un Ange pour avoir par le commandement de son mari frisé et habillé mondainement sa nièce." (*Divers points à représenter à Mr. le Gouverneur et à Madame la Gouvernante, signé Jean, évesque de Québec. Registre de l'Évêché de Québec.*) The bishop on another occasion holds up the sad fate of Pretextata as a warning to Canadian mothers; but in the present case he slightly changes the incidents to make the story more applicable to the governor and his wife.

Satan, whom they have so solemnly renounced; and, in their wish to please the eyes of men, make themselves the instruments and the captives of the fiend." [1]

In the journal of the superior of the Jesuits we find, under date of February 4, 1667, a record of the first ball in Canada, along with the pious wish, "God grant that nothing further come of it." Nevertheless more balls were not long in following; and, worse yet, sundry comedies were enacted under no less distinguished patronage than that of Frontenac, the governor. Laval denounced them vigorously, the Jesuit Dablon attacked them in a violent sermon; and such excitement followed that the affair was brought before the royal council, which declined to interfere.[2] This flurry, however, was nothing to the storm raised ten or twelve years later by other dramatic aggressions, an account of which will appear in the sequel of this volume.

The morals of families were watched with unrelenting vigilance. Frontenac writes in a mood unusually temperate, "They [the priests] are full of virtue and piety, and if their zeal were less vehement and more moderate, they would perhaps succeed better in their efforts for the conversion of souls; but

---

[1] *Mandement contre le luxe et la vanité des femmes et des filles*, 1682. (*Registres de l'Evêché de Québec.*) A still more vigorous denunciation is contained in *Ordonnance contre les vices de luxe et d'impureté*, 1690. This was followed in the next year by a stringent list of rules called *Réglement pour la conduite des fidèles de ce diocèse*.

[2] *Arrêts du 24 et 28 juin par lesquels cette affaire (des comédies) est renvoyée à Sa Majesté*, 1681. (?) *Registre du Conseil Souverain.*

they often use means so extraordinary, and in France so unusual, that they repel most people instead of persuading them. I sometimes tell them my views frankly and as gently as I can, as I know the murmurs that their conduct excites, and often receive complaints of the constraint under which they place consciences. This is above all the case with the ecclesiastics at Montreal, where there is a curé from Franche Comté who wants to establish a sort of inquisition worse than that of Spain, and all out of an excess of zeal." [1]

It was this curé, no doubt, of whom La Hontan complains. That unsanctified young officer was quartered at Montreal, in the house of one of the inhabitants. "During a part of the winter I was hunting with the Algonquins; the rest of it I spent here very disagreeably. One can neither go on a pleasure party, nor play a game of cards, nor visit the ladies, without the curé knowing it and preaching about it publicly from his pulpit. The priests excommunicate masqueraders, and even go in search of them to pull off their masks and overwhelm them with abuse. They watch more closely over the women and girls than their husbands and fathers. They prohibit and burn all books but books of devotion. I cannot think of this tyranny without cursing the indiscreet zeal of the curé of this town. He came to the house where I lived, and, finding some books on my table, presently pounced on the romance

[1] *Frontenac au Ministre*, 20 Oct., 1691.

of Petronius, which I valued more than my life because it was not mutilated. He tore out almost all the leaves, so that if my host had not restrained me when I came in and saw the miserable wreck, I should have run after this rampant shepherd and torn out every hair of his beard."[1]

La Mothe-Cadillac, the founder of Detroit, seems to have had equal difficulty in keeping his temper. "Neither men of honor nor men of parts are endured in Canada; nobody can live here but simpletons and slaves of the ecclesiastical domination. The count [Frontenac] would not have so many troublesome affairs on his hands if he had not abolished a Jericho in the shape of a house built by messieurs of the seminary of Montreal, to shut up, as they said, girls who caused scandal; if he had allowed them to take officers and soldiers to go into houses at midnight and carry off women from their husbands and whip them till the blood flowed because they had been at a ball or worn a mask; if he had said nothing against the curés who went the rounds with the soldiers, and compelled women and girls to shut themselves up in their houses at nine o'clock of summer evenings; if he had forbidden the wearing of lace, and made no objection to the refusal of the communion to women of quality because they wore a *fontange;* if he had not opposed excommunications flung about without sense or reason, — if I say, the count had been of this

---

[1] La Hontan, i. 60 (ed. 1709). Other editions contain the same story in different words.

way of thinking, he would have stood as a nonpareil, and have been put very soon on the list of saints, for saint-making is cheap in this country." [1]

While the Sulpitians were thus rigorous at Montreal, the bishop and his Jesuit allies were scarcely less so at Quebec. There was little good-will between them and the Sulpitians, and some of the sharpest charges against the followers of Loyola are brought by their brother priests at Montreal. The Sulpitian Allet writes: "The Jesuits hold such domination over the people of this country that they go into the houses and see everything that passes there. They then tell what they have learned to each other at their meetings, and on this information they govern their policy. The Jesuit, Father Ragueneau, used to go every day down to the Lower Town, where the merchants live, to find out all that was going on in their families; and he often made people get up from table to confess to him." Allet goes on to say that Father Châtelain also went continually to the Lower Town with the same object, and that some of the inhabitants complained of him to Courcelle, the governor. One day Courcelle saw the Jesuit, who was old and somewhat infirm, slowly walking by the château, cane in hand, on his usual errand, — on which he sent a sergeant after him to request that he would not go so often to the Lower Town, as the people were annoyed by the frequency of his visits. The father replied in wrath, "Go and tell Monsieur

[1] *La Mothe-Cadillac à ——, 28 Sept., 1694.*

de Courcelle that I have been there ever since he was governor, and that I shall go there after he has ceased to be governor;" and he kept on his way as before. Courcelle reported his answer to the superior, Le Mercier, and demanded to have him sent home as a punishment; but the superior effected a compromise. On the following Thursday, after mass in the cathedral, he invited Courcelle into the sacristy, where Father Châtelain was awaiting them; and here, at Le Mercier's order, the old priest begged pardon of the offended governor on his knees.[1]

The Jesuits derived great power from the confessional; and, if their accusers are to be believed, they employed unusual means to make it effective. Cavelier de la Salle says: "They will confess nobody till he tells his name, and no servant till he tells the name of his master. When a crime is confessed, they insist on knowing the name of the accomplice, as well as all the circumstances, with the greatest particularity. Father Châtelain especially never fails to do this. They enter as it were by force into the secrets of families, and thus make themselves formidable; for what cannot be done by a clever man devoted to his work, who knows all the secrets of every family; above all, when he permits himself to tell them when it is for his interest to do so?"[2]

[1] *Mémoire d'Allet.* The author was at one time secretary to Abbé Quélus. The paper is printed in the *Morale pratique des Jésuites.* The above is one of many curious statements which it contains.

[2] La Salle, *Mémoire,* 1678.

The association of women and girls known as the Congregation of the Holy Family, which was formed under Jesuit auspices, and which met every Thursday with closed doors in the cathedral, is said to have been very useful to the fathers in their social investigations.[1] The members are affirmed to have been under a vow to tell one another every good or evil deed they knew of every person of their acquaintance; so that this pious gossip became a copious source of information to those in a position to draw upon it. In Talon's time the Congregation of the Holy Family caused such commotion in Quebec that he asked the council to appoint a commission to inquire into its proceedings. He was touching dangerous ground. The affair was presently hushed, and the application cancelled on the register of the council.[2]

The Jesuits had long exercised solely the function of confessors in the colony, and a number of curious anecdotes are on record showing the reluctance with which they admitted the secular priests, and above all the Récollets, to share in it. The Récollets, of whom a considerable number had arrived from time to time, were on excellent terms with the civil powers, and were popular with the colonists; but with the bishop and the Jesuits they were not in

---

[1] See "La Salle, and the Discovery of the Great West," i. 111.

[2] *Représentation faite au conseil au sujet de certaines assemblées de femmes ou filles sous le nom de la Sainte Famille*, 1667. (*Registre du Conseil Souverain.*) The paper is cancelled by lines drawn over it; and the following minute, duly attested, is appended to it: "Rayé du consentement de M. Talon."

favor, and one or two sharp collisions took place. The bishop was naturally annoyed when, while he was trying to persuade the King that a curé needed at least six hundred francs a year, these mendicant friars came forward with an offer to serve the parishes for nothing; nor was he, it is likely, better pleased when, having asked the hospital nuns eight hundred francs annually for two masses a day in their chapel, the Récollets underbid him, and offered to say the masses for three hundred.[1] They, on their part, complain bitterly of the bishop, who, they say, would gladly have ordered them out of the colony, but, being unable to do this, tried to shut them up in their convent, and prevent them from officiating as priests among the people. "We have as little liberty," says the Récollet writer, "as if we were in a country of heretics." He adds that the inhabitants ask earnestly for the ministrations of the friars, but that the bishop replies with invectives and calumnies against the Order; and that when the Récollets absolve a penitent, he often annuls the absolution.[2]

In one respect this Canadian Church militant achieved a complete success. Heresy was scoured

---

[1] "Mon dit sieur l'evesque leur fait payer (*aux hospitalières* 800 *l.* par an pour deux messes qu'il leur fait dire par ses Séminaristes) que les Récollets leurs voisins leur offrent pour 300 *l.*" — *La Barre au Ministre*, 1682.

[2] *Mémoire instructif contenant la conduite des PP. Récollets de Paris en leurs missions de Canada*, 1684. This paper, of which only a fragment is preserved, was written in connection with a dispute of the Récollets with the bishop who opposed their attempt to establish a church in Quebec.

out of the colony. When Maintenon and her ghostly prompters overcame the better nature of the King, and wrought on his bigotry and his vanity to launch him into the dragonnades; when violence and lust bore the crucifix into thousands of Huguenot homes, and the land reeked with nameless infamies; when churches rang with *Te Deums*, and the heart of France withered in anguish, — when, in short, this hideous triumph of the faith was won, the royal tool of priestly ferocity sent orders that heresy should be treated in Canada as it had been treated in France.[1] The orders were needless. The pious Denonville replies, "Praised be God! there is not a heretic here." He adds that a few abjured last year, and that he should be very glad if the King would make them a present. The Jesuits, he further says, go every day on board the ships in the harbor to look after the new converts from France.[2] Now and then at a later day a real or suspected Jansenist found his way to Canada, and sometimes an *esprit fort*, like La Hontan, came over with the troops; but on the whole a community more free from positive heterodoxy perhaps never existed on earth. This exemption cost no bloodshed. What it did cost we may better judge hereafter.

If Canada escaped the dragonnades, so also she

[1] *Mémoire du Roy à Denonville*, 31 *Mai*, 1686. The King here orders the imprisonment of heretics who refuse to abjure, or the quartering of soldiers on them. What this meant, the history of the dragonnades will show.

[2] *Denonville au Ministre*, 10 *Nov*., 1686.

escaped another infliction from which a neighboring colony suffered deplorably. Her peace was never much troubled by witches. They were held to exist, it is true; but they wrought no panic. Mother Mary of the Incarnation reports on one occasion the discovery of a magician in the person of a converted Huguenot miller, who, being refused in marriage by a girl of Quebec, bewitched her, and filled the house where she lived with demons, which the bishop tried in vain to exorcise. The miller was thrown into prison, and the girl sent to the Hôtel-Dieu, where not a demon dared enter. The infernal crew took their revenge by creating a severe influenza among the citizens.[1]

If there are no Canadian names on the calendar of saints, it is not because in byways and obscure places Canada had not virtues worthy of canonization. Not alone her male martyrs and female devotees, whose merits have found a chronicle and a recognition; not the fantastic devotion of Madame d'Ailleboust, who, lest she should not suffer enough, took to herself a vicious and refractory servant girl, as an exercise of patience; and not certainly the mediæval pietism of Jeanne Le Ber, the venerated recluse of Montreal, — there are others quite as worthy of honor, whose names have died from memory. It is difficult to conceive a self-abnegation more complete than that of the hospital nuns of Quebec and Montreal. In the almost total absence

[1] Marie de l'Incarnation, *Lettre de — Septembre*, 1661.

of trained and skilled physicians, the burden of the sick and wounded fell upon them. Of the two communities, that of Montreal was the more wretchedly destitute, while that of Quebec was exposed, perhaps, to greater dangers. Nearly every ship from France brought some form of infection, and all infection found its way to the Hôtel-Dieu of Quebec. The nuns died, but they never complained. Removed from the arena of ecclesiastical strife, too busy for the morbidness of the cloister, too much absorbed in practical benevolence to become the prey of illusions, they and their sister community were models of that benign and tender charity of which the Roman Catholic Church is so rich in examples. Nor should the Ursulines and the nuns of the Congregation be forgotten among those who, in another field of labor, have toiled patiently according to their light.

Mademoiselle Jeanne Le Ber belonged to none of these sisterhoods. She was the favorite daughter of the chief merchant of Montreal, — the same who, with the help of his money, got himself ennobled. She seems to have been a girl of a fine and sensitive nature; ardent, affectionate, and extremely susceptible to religious impressions. Religion at last gained absolute sway over her. Nothing could appease her longings or content the demands of her excited conscience but an entire consecration of herself to Heaven. Constituted as she was, the resolution must have cost her an agony of mental conflict. Her story is a strange, and, as many will think, a very sad one. She renounced her suitors, and wished to renounce her inheritance; but her spiritual directors, too far-sighted to permit such a sacrifice, persuaded her to hold fast to her claims, and content herself with what they called "poverty of heart." Her mother died, and her father, left with a family of young children, greatly needed her help; but she refused to leave her chamber where she had immured herself. Here she remained ten years, seeing nobody but her confessor and the girl who brought her food. Once only she emerged, and this was when her brother lay dead in the adjacent room, killed in a fight with the English. She suddenly appeared before her astonished sisters, stood for a moment in silent prayer by the body, and then vanished without uttering a word. "Such," says her modern biographer, "was the sublimity of her virtue and the grandeur of her soul." Not content with this domestic seclusion, she caused a cell to be made behind the altar in the newly built church of the Congregation, and here we will permit ourselves to cast a stolen glance at her through the narrow opening through which food was passed in to her. Her bed, a pile of straw which she never moved, lest it should become too soft, was so placed that her head could touch the partition which alone separated it from the Host on the altar. Here she lay wrapped in a garment of coarse gray serge, worn, tattered, and unwashed. An old blanket, a stool, a spinning-wheel, a belt and shirt of haircloth, a scourge, and a pair of shoes made by herself of the husks of Indian-corn, appear to have formed the sum of her furniture and her wardrobe. Her employments were spinning and working embroidery for churches. She remained in this voluntary prison about twenty years; and the nun who brought her food testifies that she never omitted a mortification or a prayer, though commonly in a state of profound depression, and what her biographer calls "complete spiritual aridity." When her mother died, she had refused to see her; and, long after, no prayer of her dying father could draw her from her cell. "In the person of this modest virgin," writes her reverend eulogist, "we see, with astonishment, the love of God triumphant over earthly affection for parents, and a complete victory of faith over reason and of grace over nature."

In 1711, Canada was threatened with an attack by the English; and Mademoiselle Le Ber gave the nuns of the Congregation an image of the Virgin on which she had written a prayer to protect their granary from the invaders. Other persons, anxious for a similar protection, sent her images to write upon; but she declined the request. One of the disappointed applicants then stole the inscribed image from the granary of the Congregation, intending to place it on his own when the danger drew near. The English, however, did not come, their fleet having suffered a ruinous shipwreck ascribed to the prayers of Jeanne Le Ber. "It was," writes the Sulpitian Belmont, "the greatest miracle that ever happened since the days of Moses." Nor was this the only miracle of which she was the occasion. She herself declared that once when she had broken her spinning-wheel, an angel came and mended it for her. Angels also assisted in her embroidery, "no doubt," says Mother Juchereau, "taking great pleasure in the society of this angelic creature." In the church where she had secluded herself, an image of the Virgin continued after her death to heal the lame and cure the sick.[1]

Though Jeanne rarely permitted herself to speak, yet some oracular utterance of the sainted recluse would now and then escape to the outer world. One of these was to the effect that teaching poor girls to read, unless they wanted to be nuns, was robbing them of their time. Nor was she far wrong, for in Canada there was very little to read except formulas of devotion and lives of saints. The dangerous innovation of a printing-press had not invaded the colony,[2] and the first Canadian newspaper dates from the British conquest.

All education was controlled by priests or nuns. The ablest teachers in Canada were the Jesuits. Their college of Quebec was three years older than Harvard. We hear at an early date of public disputations by the pupils, after the pattern of those

---

[1] Faillon, *L'Héroine chrétienne du Canada, ou Vie de Mlle. Le Ber.* This is a most elaborate and eulogistic life of the recluse. A shorter account of her will be found in Juchereau, *Hôtel-Dieu.* She died in 1714, at the age of fifty-two.

[2] A printing-press was afterwards brought to Canada, but was soon sent back again.

tournaments of barren logic which preceded the reign of inductive reason in Europe, and of which the archetype is to be found in the scholastic duels of the Sorbonne. The boys were sometimes permitted to act certain approved dramatic pieces of a religious character, like the *Sage Visionnaire*. On one occasion they were allowed to play the *Cid* of Corneille, which, though remarkable as a literary work, contained nothing threatening to orthodoxy. They were taught a little Latin, a little rhetoric, and a little logic; but against all that might rouse the faculties to independent action, the Canadian schools prudently closed their doors. There was then no rival population, of a different origin and a different faith, to compel competition in the race of intelligence and knowledge. The Church stood sole mistress of the field. Under the old régime the real object of education in Canada was a religious and, in far less degree, a political one. The true purpose of the schools was: first, to make priests; and, secondly, to make obedient servants of the Church and the King. All the rest was extraneous and of slight account. In regard to this matter, the King and the bishop were of one mind. "As I have been informed," Louis XIV. writes to Laval, "of your continued care to hold the people in their duty towards God and towards me by the good education you give or cause to be given to the young, I write this letter to express my satisfaction with conduct so salutary, and to exhort you to persevere in it."[1]

[1] *Le Roy à Laval*, 9 *Avril*, 1667 (extract in Faillon).

The bishop did not fail to persevere. The school for boys attached to his seminary became the most important educational institution in Canada. It was regulated by thirty-four rules, "in honor of the thirty-four years which Jesus lived on earth." The qualities commended to the boys as those which they should labor diligently to acquire were "humility, obedience, purity, meekness, modesty, simplicity, chastity, charity, and an ardent love of Jesus and his Holy Mother."[1] Here is a goodly roll of Christian virtues. What is chiefly noticeable in it is, that truth is allowed no place. That manly but unaccommodating virtue was not, it seems, thought important in forming the mind of youth. Humility and obedience lead the list; for in unquestioning submission to the spiritual director lay the guaranty of all other merits.

We have seen already, that, besides this seminary for boys, Laval established another for educating the humbler colonists. It was a sort of farm-school; though besides farming, various mechanical trades were also taught in it. It was well adapted to the wants of a great majority of Canadians, whose tendencies were anything but bookish; but here, as elsewhere, the real object was religious. It enabled the Church to extend her influence over classes which the ordinary schools could not reach. Besides manual training, the pupils were taught to read and

[1] *Ancien réglement du Petit Séminaire de Québec*, see *Abeille*, viii. no. 32.

write; and for a time a certain number of them received some instruction in Latin. When, in 1686, Saint-Vallier visited the school, he found in all thirty-one boys under the charge of two priests; but the number was afterwards greatly reduced, and the place served, as it still serves, chiefly as a retreat during vacations for the priests and pupils of the seminary of Quebec. A spot better suited for such a purpose cannot be conceived.

From the vast meadows of the parish of St. Joachim, which here border the St. Lawrence, there rises like an island a low flat hill, hedged round with forests like the tonsured head of a monk. It was here that Laval planted his school. Across the meadows, a mile or more distant, towers the mountain promontory of Cape Tourmente. You may climb its woody steeps, and from the top, waist-deep in blueberry-bushes, survey, from Kamouraska to Quebec, the grand Canadian world outstretched below; or mount the neighboring heights of St. Anne, where, athwart the gaunt arms of ancient pines, the river lies shimmering in summer haze, the cottages of the *habitants* are strung like beads of a rosary along the meadows of Beaupré, the shores of Orleans bask in warm light, and far on the horizon the rock of Quebec rests like a faint gray cloud; or traverse the forest till the roar of the torrent guides you to the rocky solitude where it holds its savage revels. High on the cliffs above, young birch-trees stand smiling in the morning sun; while in the abyss beneath the snowy waters plunge from depth to depth, and, halfway down, the slender harebell hangs from its mossy nook, quivering in the steady thunder of the cataract. Game on the river; trout in lakes, brooks, and pools; wild fruits and flowers on meadows and mountains, — a thousand resources of honest and wholesome recreation here wait the student emancipated from books, but not parted for a moment from the pious influence which hangs about the old walls embosomed in the woods of St. Joachim. Around on plains and hills stand the dwellings of a peaceful peasantry, as different from the restless population of the neighboring States as the denizens of some Norman or Breton village.

Above all, do not fail to make your pilgrimage to the shrine of St. Anne. You may see her chapel four or five miles away, nestled under the heights of the Petit Cap. Here, when Ailleboust was governor, he began with his own hands the pious work, and a *habitant* of Beaupré, Louis Guimont, sorely afflicted with rheumatism, came grinning with pain to lay three stones in the foundation, in honor probably of Saint Anne, Saint Joachim, and their daughter the Virgin. Instantly he was cured. It was but the beginning of a long course of miracles continued more than two centuries, and continuing still. Their fame spread far and wide. The devotion to Saint Anne became a distinguishing feature of Canadian Catholicity, till at the present day at least thirteen parishes bear her name. But of all her shrines, none can match the fame of St. Anne du Petit Cap. Crowds flocked thither on the week of her festival, and marvellous cures were wrought unceasingly, as the sticks and crutches hanging on the walls and columns still attest. Sometimes the whole shore was covered with the wigwams of Indian converts who had paddled their birch canoes from the farthest wilds of Canada. The more fervent among them would crawl on their knees from the shore to the altar. And, in our own day, every summer a far greater concourse of pilgrims — not in paint and feathers, but in cloth and millinery, and not in canoes, but in steamboats — bring their offerings and their vows to the "Bonne Sainte Anne."[1]

To return to Laval's industrial school. Judging from repeated complaints of governors and intendants of the dearth of skilled workmen, the priests in charge of it were more successful in making good Catholics than in making good masons, carpenters, blacksmiths, and weavers; and the number of pupils, even if well trained, was at no time sufficient to meet the wants of the colony,[2] for, though the Canadians

---

[1] For an interesting account of the shrine at the Petit Cap, see Casgrain, *La Pèlerinage de la Bonne Sainte Anne*, a little manual of devotion printed at Quebec. I chanced to visit the old chapel in 1871, during a meeting of the parish to consider the question of reconstructing it, as it was in a ruinous state. Passing that way again two years later, I found the old chapel still standing, and a new one, much larger, half finished.

[2] Most of them were moreover retained, after leaving the school, by the seminary, as servants, farmers, or vassals. (La Tour, *Vie de Laval*, liv. vi.)

Sainte Anne du Petit Cap.

showed an aptitude for mechanical trades, they preferred above all things the savage liberty of the backwoods.

The education of girls was in the hands of the Ursulines and the nuns of the Congregation, of whom the former, besides careful instruction in religious duties, taught their pupils "all that a girl ought to know."[1] This meant exceedingly little besides the manual arts suited to their sex; and, in the case of the nuns of the Congregation, who taught girls of the poorer class, it meant still less. It was on nuns as well as on priests that the charge fell, not only of spiritual and mental, but also of industrial, training. Thus we find the King giving to a sisterhood of Montreal a thousand francs to buy wool, and a thousand more for teaching girls to knit.[2] The King also maintained a teacher of navigation and surveying at Quebec on the modest salary of four hundred francs.

During the eighteenth century, some improvement is perceptible in the mental state of the population. As it became more numerous and more stable, it also became less ignorant; and the Canadian *habitant*, towards the end of the French rule, was probably better taught, so far as concerned religion, than the mass of French peasants. Yet secular instruction was still extremely meagre, even in the *noblesse*.

---

[1] "À lire, à écrire, les prières, les mœurs chrétiennes, et tout ce qu'une fille doit savoir." — Marie de l'Incarnation, *Lettre du 9 Août*, 1668.

[2] *Denonville au Ministre*, 13 Nov., 1685.

"In spite of this defective education," says the famous navigator, Bougainville, who knew the colony well in its last years, "the Canadians are naturally intelligent. They do not know how to write, but they speak with ease, and with an accent as good as the Parisian."[1] He means, of course, the better class. "Even the children of officers and gentlemen," says another writer, "scarcely know how to read and write; they are ignorant of the first elements of geography and history."[2] And evidence like this might be extended.

When France was heaving with the throes that prepared the Revolution; when new hopes, new dreams, new thoughts — good and evil, false and true — tossed the troubled waters of French society, — Canada caught something of its social corruption, but not the faintest impulsion of its roused mental life. The torrent surged on its way; while, in the deep nook beside it, the sticks and dry leaves floated their usual round, and the unruffled pool slept in the placidity of intellectual torpor.[3]

---

[1] Bougainville, *Mémoire de* 1757 (see Margry, *Relations inédites*).

[2] *Mémoire de* 1736; *Détail de toute la Colonie* (published by the Hist. Soc. of Quebec).

[3] Several Frenchmen of a certain intellectual eminence made their abode in Canada from time to time. The chief among them are the Jesuit Lafitau, author of *Mœurs des Sauvages Américains;* the Jesuit Charlevoix, traveller and historian; the physician Sarrazin; and the Marquis de la Galisonnière, the most enlightened of the French governors of Canada. Sarrazin, a naturalist as well as a physician, has left his name to the botanical genus *Sarracenia*, of which the curious American species, *S. purpurea*, the "pitcher-

plant," was described by him. His position in the colony was singular and characteristic. He got little or no pay from his patients; and though at one time the only genuine physician in Canada (*Callières et Beauharnois au Ministre*, 3 *Nov.*, 1702), he was dependent on the King for support. In 1699 we find him thanking his Majesty for 300 francs a year, and asking at the same time for more, as he has nothing else to live on. (*Callières et Champigny au Ministre*, 20 *Oct.*, 1699.) Two years later the governor writes, that, as he serves almost everybody without fees, he ought to have another 300 francs. (*Ibid.*, 5 *Oct.*, 1701.) The additional 300 francs was given him; but, finding it insufficient, he wanted to leave the colony. "He is too useful," writes the governor again; "we cannot let him go." His yearly pittance of 600 francs, French money, was at one time reinforced by his salary as member of the Superior Council. He died at Quebec in 1734.

CHAPTER XXIII.

1640–1763.

MORALS AND MANNERS.

Social Influence of the Troops. — A Petty Tyrant. — Brawls. — Violence and Outlawry. — State of the Population. — Views of Denonville. — Brandy. — Beggary. — The Past and the Present. — Inns. — State of Quebec. — Fires. — The Country Parishes. — Slavery. — Views of La Hontan, — of Hocquart; of Bougainville; of Kalm; of Charlevoix.

The mission period of Canada, or the period anterior to the year 1663, when the King took the colony in charge, has a character of its own. The whole population did not exceed that of a large French village. Its extreme poverty, the constant danger that surrounded it, and, above all, the contagious zeal of the missionaries, saved it from many vices, and inspired it with an extraordinary religious fervor. Without doubt an ideal picture has been drawn of this early epoch. Trade as well as propagandism was the business of the colony, and the colonists were far from being all in a state of grace; yet it is certain that zeal was higher, devotion more constant, and popular morals more pure, than at any later period of the French rule.

The intervention of the King wrought a change. The annual shipments of emigrants made by him were, in the most favorable view, of a very mixed character, and the portion which Mother Mary calls *canaille* was but too conspicuous. Along with them came a regiment of soldiers fresh from the license of camps and the excitements of Turkish wars, accustomed to obey their officers and to obey nothing else, and more ready to wear the scapulary of the Virgin in campaigns against the Mohawks than to square their lives by the rules of Christian ethics. "Our good King," writes Sister Morin, of Montreal, "has sent troops to defend us from the Iroquois, and the soldiers and officers have ruined the Lord's vineyard, and planted wickedness and sin and crime in our soil of Canada."[1] Few, indeed, among the officers followed the example of one of their number, — Paul Dupuy, who, in his settlement of Isle aux Oies, below Quebec, lived, it is said, like a saint, and on Sundays and fête days exhorted his servants and *habitants* with such unction that their eyes filled with tears.[2] Nor, let us hope, were there many imitators of Major La Fredière, who, with a company of the regiment, was sent to garrison Montreal, where he ruled with absolute sway over settlers and soldiers alike. His countenance naturally repulsive was made more so by the loss of an eye; yet he was irrepressible in gallantry, and women and girls fled in

---

[1] *Annales de l'Hôtel-Dieu St. Joseph*, cited by Faillon.
[2] Juchereau, *Hôtel-Dieu de Québec*, 511.

terror from the military Polyphemus. The men, too, feared and hated him, not without reason. One morning a settler named Demers was hoeing his field, when he saw a sportsman gun in hand striding through his half-grown wheat. "Steady there, steady!" he shouted in a tone of remonstrance; but the sportsman gave no heed. "Why do you spoil a poor man's wheat?" cried the outraged cultivator. "If I knew who you were, I would go and complain of you." "Whom would you complain to?" demanded the sportsman, who then proceeded to walk back into the middle of the wheat, and called out to Demers, "You are a rascal, and I'll thrash you." "Look at home for rascals," retorted Demers, "and keep your thrashing for your dogs." The sportsman came towards him in a rage to execute his threat. Demers picked up his gun, which, after the custom of the time, he had brought to the field with him, and, advancing to meet his adversary, recognized La Frediére, the commandant. On this he ran off. La Frediére sent soldiers to arrest him, threw him into prison, put him in irons, and the next day mounted him on the wooden horse, with a weight of sixty pounds tied to each foot. He repeated the torture a day or two after, and then let his victim go, saying, "If I could have caught you when I was in your wheat, I would have beaten you well."

The commandant next turned his quarters into a dram-shop for Indians, to whom he sold brandy in large quantities, but so diluted that his customers, finding themselves partially defrauded of their right of intoxication, complained grievously. About this time the intendant Talon made one of his domiciliary visits to Montreal, and when, in his character of father of the people, he inquired if they had any complaints to make, every tongue was loud in accusation against La Fredière. Talon caused full depositions to be made out from the statements of Demers and other witnesses. Copies were deposited in the hands of the notary, and it is from these that the above story is drawn. The tyrant was removed, and ordered home to France.[1]

Many other officers embarked in the profitable trade of selling brandy to Indians, and several garrison posts became centres of disorder. Others of the regiment became notorious brawlers. A lieutenant of the garrison of Montreal named Carion, and an ensign named Morel, had for some reason conceived a violent grudge against another ensign named Lormeau. On Pentecost day, just after vespers, Lormeau was walking by the river with his wife. They had passed the common and the seminary wall, and were in front of the house of the younger Charles Le Moyne, when they saw Carion coming towards them. He stopped before Lormeau, looked him full in the face, and exclaimed, "Coward!" "Coward yourself," returned Lormeau; "take your-

---

[1] *Information contre La Fredière.* (See Faillon, *Colonie Française*, iii. 386.) The dialogue, as here given from the depositions, is translated as closely as possible.

self off!" Carion drew his sword, and Lormeau followed his example. They exchanged a few passes, then closed, and fell to the ground grappled together. Lormeau's wig fell off; and Carion, getting the uppermost, hammered his bare head with the hilt of his sword. Lormeau's wife, in a frenzy of terror, screamed *murder*. One of the neighbors, Monsieur Belêtre, was at table with Charles Le Moyne and a Rochelle merchant named Baston. He ran out with his two guests, and they tried to separate the combatants, who still lay on the ground foaming like a pair of enraged bull-dogs. All their efforts were useless. "Very well," said Le Moyne in disgust, "if you won't let go, then kill each other if you like." A former military servant of Carion now ran up, and began to brandish his sword in behalf of his late master. Carion's comrade, Morel, also arrived, and, regardless of the angry protest of Le Moyne, stabbed repeatedly at Lormeau as he lay. Lormeau had received two or three wounds in the hand and arm with which he parried the thrusts, and was besides severely mauled by the sword-hilt of Carion, when two Sulpitian priests, drawn by the noise, appeared on the scene. One was Frémont, the curé; the other was Dollier de Casson. That herculean father, whose past soldier life had made him at home in a fray, and who cared nothing for drawn swords, set himself at once to restore peace, — upon which, whether from the strength of his arm, or the mere effect of his presence, the two champions released

He made a Jump at the Guns and took them under his Arms like so many Feathers.

their gripe on each other's throats, rose, sheathed their weapons, and left the field.[1]

Montreal, a frontier town at the head of the colony, was the natural resort of desperadoes, offering, as we have seen, a singular contrast between the rigor of its clerical seigniors and the riotous license of the lawless crew which infested it. Dollier de Casson tells the story of an outlaw who broke prison ten or twelve times, and whom no walls, locks, or fetters could hold. "A few months ago," he says, "he was caught again, and put into the keeping of six or seven men, each with a good gun. They stacked their arms to play a game of cards, which their prisoner saw fit to interrupt to play a game of his own. He made a jump at the guns, took them under his arm like so many feathers, aimed at these fellows with one of them, swearing that he would kill the first who came near him, and so, falling back step by step, at last bade them good-by, and carried off all their guns. Since then he has not been caught, and is roaming the woods. Very likely he will become chief of our banditti, and make great trouble in the country when it pleases him to come back from the Dutch settlements, whither they say he is gone along with another rascal, and a French woman so depraved that she is said to have given or sold two of her children to the Indians."[2]

---

[1] *Requête de Lormeau à M. d'Aillebout. Dépositions de MM. de Longueuil [Le Moyne] de Baston, de Belêtre, et autres.* Cited by Faillon, *Colonie Française,* iii. 393.

[2] Dollier de Casson, *Histoire de Montréal,* 1671–72.

When the governor, La Barre, visited Montreal, he found there some two hundred reprobates gambling, drinking, and stealing. If hard pressed by justice, they had only to cross the river and place themselves beyond the seigniorial jurisdiction. The military settlements of the Richelieu were in a condition somewhat similar, and La Barre complains of a prevailing spirit of disobedience and lawlessness.[1] The most orderly and thrifty part of Canada appears to have been at this time the *côte* of Beaupré, belonging to the seminary of Quebec. Here the settlers had religious instruction from their curés, and industrial instruction also if they wanted it. Domestic spinning and weaving were practised at Beaupré sooner than in any other part of the colony.

When it is remembered that a population which in La Barre's time did not exceed ten thousand, and which forty years later did not much exceed twice that number, was scattered along both sides of a great river for three hundred miles or more; that a large part of this population was in isolated groups of two, three, five, ten, or twenty houses at the edge of a savage wilderness; that between them there was little communication except by canoes; that the settlers were disbanded soldiers, or others whose lives had been equally adverse to habits of reflection or self-control; that they rarely saw a priest, and that a government omnipotent in name had not arms long enough to reach them, — we may listen without

---

[1] *La Barre au Ministre*, 4 *Nov.*, 1683.

surprise to the lamentations of order-loving officials over the unruly condition of a great part of the colony. One accuses the seigniors, who, he says, being often of low extraction, cannot keep their vassals in order.[1] Another dwells sorrowfully on the "terrible dispersion" of the settlements where the inhabitants "live in a savage independence." But it is better that each should speak for himself, and among the rest let us hear the pious Denonville.

"This, Monseigneur," he says, "seems to me the place for rendering you an account of the disorders which prevail not only in the woods, but also in the settlements. They arise from the idleness of young persons, and the great liberty which fathers, mothers, and guardians have for a long time given them, or allowed them to assume, of going into the forest under pretence of hunting or trading. This has come to such a pass, that, from the moment a boy can carry a gun, the father cannot restrain him and dares not offend him. You can judge the mischief that follows. These disorders are always greatest in the families of those who are *gentilshommes,* or who through laziness or vanity pass themselves off as such. Having no resource but hunting, they must spend their lives in the woods, where they have no curés to trouble them, and no fathers or guardians to constrain them. I think, Monseigneur, that martial law would suit their case better than any judicial sentence. Monsieur de la Barre suppressed a certain

---

[1] Catalogne, *Mémoire addressé au Ministre,* 1712.

order of knighthood which had sprung up here, but he did not abolish the usages belonging to it. It was thought a fine thing and a good joke to go about naked and tricked out like Indians, not only on carnival days, but on all other days of feasting and debauchery. These practices tend to encourage the disposition of our young men to live like savages, frequent their company, and be forever unruly and lawless like them. I cannot tell you, Monseigneur, how attractive this Indian life is to all our youth. It consists in doing nothing, caring for nothing, following every inclination, and getting out of the way of all correction."

He goes on to say that the mission villages governed by the Jesuits and Sulpitians are models of good order, and that drunkards are never seen there except when they come from the neighboring French settlements; but that the other Indians, who roam at large about the colony, do prodigious mischief, because the children of the seigniors not only copy their way of life, but also run off with their women into the woods.[1] "Nothing," he continues, "can be finer or better conceived than the regulations framed for the government of this country; but nothing, I assure you, is so ill observed as regards both the fur-trade

---

[1] Raudot, who was intendant early in the eighteenth century, is a little less gloomy in his coloring, but says that Canadian children were without discipline or education, had no respect for parents or curés, and owned no superiors. This, he thinks, is owing to "la folle tendresse des parents qui les empêche de les corriger et de leur former le caractère qu'ils ont dur et féroce."

and the general discipline of the colony. One great evil is the infinite number of drinking-shops, which makes it almost impossible to remedy the disorders resulting from them. All the rascals and idlers of the country are attracted into this business of tavern-keeping. They never dream of tilling the soil; but, on the contrary, they deter the other inhabitants from it, and end with ruining them. I know seigniories where there are but twenty houses, and more than half of them dram-shops. At Three Rivers there are twenty-five houses, and liquor may be had at eighteen or twenty of them. Villemarie [Montreal] and Quebec are on the same footing."

The governor next dwells on the necessity of finding occupation for children and youths, — a matter which he regards as of the last importance. "It is sad to see the ignorance of the population at a distance from the abodes of the curés, who are put to the greatest trouble to remedy the evil by travelling from place to place through the parishes in their charge."[1]

La Barre, Champigny, and Duchesneau write in a similar strain. Bishop Saint-Vallier, in an epistolary journal which he printed of a tour through the colony made on his first arrival, gives a favorable account of the disposition of the people, especially as regards religion. He afterwards changed his views. An abstract made from his letters for the use of the King states that he "represents, like M. Denonville,

[1] *Denonville au Ministre*, 13 *Nov.*, 1685.

that the Canadian youth are for the most part wholly demoralized." [1]

"The bishop was very sorry," says a correspondent of the minister at Quebec, "to have so much exaggerated in the letter he printed at Paris the morality of the people here." [2] He preached a sermon on the sins of the inhabitants and issued a pastoral mandate, in which he says, "Before we knew our flock we thought that the English and the Iroquois were the only wolves we had to fear; but God having opened our eyes to the disorders of this diocese, and made us feel more than ever the weight of our charge, we are forced to confess that our most dangerous foes are drunkenness, luxury, impurity, and slander." [3]

Drunkenness was at this time the most destructive vice in the colony. One writer declares that most of the Canadians drink so much brandy in the morning that they are unfit for work all day.[4] Another says that a canoe-man when he is tired will lift a keg of brandy to his lips and drink the raw liquor from the bung-hole, after which, having spoiled his appetite, he goes to bed supperless; and that, what with drink and hardship, he is an old man at forty. Nevertheless the race did not deteriorate. The prevalence of early marriages, and the birth of numerous offspring before the vigor of the father had been

---

[1] *N. Y. Colonial Documents*, ix. 278.   [2] *Ibid.*, ix. 388.
[3] *Ordonnance contre les vices de Pivrognerie, luxe, et impureté*, 31 Oct., 1690.
[4] *N. Y. Colonial Documents*, ix. 398.

wasted, insured the strength and hardihood which characterized the Canadians. As Denonville describes them, so they long remained. "The Canadians are tall, well-made, and well set on their legs [*bien plantés sur leurs jambes*], robust, vigorous, and accustomed in time of need to live on little. They have intelligence and vivacity, but are wayward, light-minded, and inclined to debauchery."

As the population increased, as the rage for bush-ranging began to abate, and, above all, as the curés multiplied, a change took place for the better. More churches were built, the charge of each priest was reduced within reasonable bounds, and a greater proportion of the inhabitants remained on their farms. They were better watched, controlled, and taught by the Church. The ecclesiastical power, wherever it had a hold, was exercised, as we have seen, with an undue rigor, yet it was the chief guardian of good morals; and the colony grew more orderly and more temperate as the Church gathered more and more of its wild and wandering flock fairly within its fold. In this, however, its success was but relative. It is true that in 1715 a well-informed writer says that the people were "perfectly instructed in religion;"[1] but at that time the statement was only partially true.

During the seventeenth century, and some time after its close, Canada swarmed with beggars, — a singular feature in a new country where a good farm could be had for the asking. In countries intensely

[1] *Mémoire addressé au Régent.*

Roman Catholic begging is not regarded as an unmixed evil, being supposed to promote two cardinal virtues, — charity in the giver, and humility in the receiver. The Canadian officials nevertheless tried to restrain it. Vagabonds of both sexes were ordered to leave Quebec, and nobody was allowed to beg without a certificate of poverty from the curé or the local judge.[1] These orders were not always observed. Bishop Saint-Vallier writes that he is overwhelmed by beggars,[2] and the intendant echoes his complaint. Almshouses were established at Montreal, Three Rivers, and Quebec;[3] and when Saint-Vallier founded the General Hospital, its chief purpose was to serve, not as a hospital in the ordinary sense of the word, but as a house of refuge, after the plan of the General Hospital of Paris.[4] Appeal, as usual, was made to the King. Denonville asks his aid for two destitute families, and says that many others need it. Louis XIV. did not fail to respond, and from time to time he sent considerable sums for the relief of the Canadian poor.[5]

Denonville says, "The principal reason of the

---

[1] *Règlement de Police*, 1676.

[2] *N. Y. Colonial Documents*, ix. 279.

[3] *Édits et Ordonnances*, ii. 119.

[4] On the General Hospital of Quebec, see Juchereau, 355. In 1692, the minister writes to Frontenac and Champigny that they should consider well whether this house of refuge will not "augmenter la fainéantise parmi les habitans," by giving them a sure support in poverty.

[5] As late as 1701 six thousand livres were granted. *Callières au Ministre*, 4 *Nov.*, 1701.

poverty of this country is the idleness and bad conduct of most of the people. The greater part of the women, including all the *demoiselles*, are very lazy."[1] Meules proposes as a remedy that the King should establish a general workshop in the colony, and pay the workmen himself during the first five or six years.[2] "The persons here," he says, "who have wished to make a figure are nearly all so overwhelmed with debt that they may be considered as in the last necessity."[3] He adds that many of the people go half-naked even in winter. "The merchants of this country," says the intendant Duchesneau, "are all plunged in poverty, except five or six at the most; it is the same with the artisans, except a small number, because the vanity of the women and the debauchery of the men consume all their gains. As for such of the laboring class as apply themselves steadily to cultivating the soil, they not only live very well, but are incomparably better off than the better sort of peasants in France."[4]

All the writers lament the extravagant habits of the people; and even La Hontan joins hands with the priests in wishing that the supply of ribbons, laces, brocades, jewelry, and the like might be cut off by act of law. Mother Juchereau tells us, that, when the English invasion was impending, the belles of

---

[1] *Denonville et Champigny au Ministre, 6 Nov.*, 1687.
[2] *Meules au Ministre,* 12 *Nov.*, 1682.
[3] Meules, *Mémoire touchant le Canada et l'Acadie,* 1684.
[4] *Duchesneau au Ministre,* 10 *Nov.*, 1679.

Canada were scared for a while into modesty in order to gain the favor of Heaven; but, as may be imagined, the effect was short, and Father La Tour declares that in his time all the fashions except *rouge* came over regularly in the annual ships.

The manners of the mission period, on the other hand, were extremely simple. The old governor, Lauzon, lived on pease and bacon like a laborer, and kept no man-servant. He was regarded, it is true, as a miser, and held in slight account.[1] Magdeleine Bochart, sister of the governor of Three Rivers, brought her husband two hundred francs in money, four sheets, two table-cloths, six napkins of linen and hemp, a mattress, a blanket, two dishes, six spoons and six tin plates, a pot and a kettle, a table and two benches, a kneading-trough, a chest with lock and key, a cow, and a pair of hogs.[2] But the Bocharts were a family of distinction, and the bride's dowry answered to her station. By another marriage contract, at about the same time, the parents of the bride, being of humble degree, bind themselves to present the bridegroom with a barrel of bacon, deliverable on the arrival of the ships from France.[3]

Some curious traits of this early day appear in the license of Jean Boisdon as innkeeper. He is required to establish himself on the great square of Quebec, close to the church, so that the parishioners may con-

---

[1] *Mémoire d'Aubert de la Chesnaye*, 1676.

[2] *Contrat de mariage*, cited by Ferland, *Notes*, 73.

[3] *Contrat de mariage*, cited by Benjamin Sulte in *Revue Canadienne*, ix. 111.

veniently warm and refresh themselves between the services; but he is forbidden to entertain anybody during high mass, sermon, catechism, or vespers.[1] Matters soon changed; Jean Boisdon lost his monopoly, and inns sprang up on all hands. They did not want for patrons, and we find some of their proprietors mentioned as among the few thriving men in Canada. Talon tried to regulate them, and, among other rules, ordained that no innkeeper should furnish food or drink to any hired laborer whatever, or to any person residing in the place where his inn was situated. An innkeeper of Montreal was fined for allowing the syndic of the town to dine under his roof.[2]

One gets glimpses of the pristine state of Quebec through the early police regulations. Each inhabitant was required to make a gutter along the middle of the street before his house, and also to remove refuse and throw it into the river. All dogs, without exception, were ordered home at nine o'clock. On Tuesdays and Fridays there was a market in the public square, whither the neighboring *habitants*, male and female, brought their produce for sale, as they still continue to do. Smoking in the street was forbidden, as a precaution against fire; householders were required to provide themselves with ladders, and when the fire alarm was rung all able-bodied

---

[1] *Acte officielle*, 1648, cited by Ferland, *Cours d'Histoire du Canada*, i. 365.

[2] Faillon, *Colonie Française*, iii. 403.

persons were obliged to run to the scene of danger with buckets or kettles full of water.[1] This did not prevent the Lower Town from burning to the ground in 1682. It was soon rebuilt, but a repetition of the catastrophe seemed very likely. "This place," says Denonville, "is in a fearful state as regards fire; for the houses are crowded together out of all reason, and so surrounded with piles of cord-wood that it is pitiful to see."[2] Add to this the stores of hay for the cows kept by many of the inhabitants for the benefit of their swarming progeny. The houses were at this time low, compact buildings, with gables of masonry, as required by law; but many had wooden fronts, and all had roofs covered with cedar shingles. The anxious governor begs, that, as the town has not a *sou* of revenue, his Majesty will be pleased to make it the gift of two hundred crowns' worth of leather fire-buckets.[3] Six or seven years after, certain citizens were authorized by the council to import from France, at their own cost, "a pump after the Dutch fashion, for throwing water on houses in case of fire."[4]

How a fire was managed at Quebec appears from a letter of the engineer, Vasseur, describing the burning of Laval's seminary in 1701. Vasseur was then at Quebec, directing the new fortifications. On a Monday in November, all the pupils of the seminary

---

[1] *Règlement de Police*, 1672. *Ibid.*, 1676.
[2] *Denonville au Ministre*, 20 Août, 1685.
[3] *Ibid.*
[4] *Règlement de* 1691, extract in Ferland.

and most of the priests went, according to their weekly custom, to recreate themselves at a house and garden at St. Michel, a short distance from town. The few priests who remained went after dinner to say vespers at the church. Only one, Father Petit, was left in the seminary, and he presently repaired to the great hall to rekindle the fire in the stove and warm the place against the return of his brethren. His success surpassed his wishes. A firebrand snapped out in his absence and set the pine floor in a blaze. Father Boucher, curé of Point Levi, chanced to come in, and was half choked by the smoke. He cried *fire!* the servants ran for water; but the flames soon mastered them; they screamed the alarm, and the bells began to ring. Vasseur was dining with the intendant at his palace by the St. Charles, when he heard a frightened voice crying out, "Monsieur, you are wanted! you are wanted!" He sprang from table, saw the smoke rolling in volumes from the top of the rock, ran up the steep ascent, reached the seminary, and found an excited crowd making a prodigious outcry. He shouted for carpenters. Four men came to him, and he set them at work with such tools as they had to tear away planks and beams, and prevent the fire from spreading to the adjacent parts of the building; but when he went to find others to help them, they ran off. He sent new men in their place, and these too ran off the moment his back was turned. A cry was raised that the building was to be blown up, on which the crowd scattered for their lives. Vasseur now gave up the seminary for lost, and thought only of cutting off the fire from the rear of the church, which was not far distant. In this he succeeded, by tearing down an intervening wing or gallery. The walls of the burning building were of massive stone, and by seven o'clock the fire had spent itself. We hear nothing of the Dutch pump, nor does it appear that the soldiers of the garrison made any effort to keep order. Under cover of the confusion, property was stolen from the seminary to the amount of about two thousand livres, — which is remarkable, considering the religious character of the building, and the supposed piety of the people. "There were more than three hundred persons at the fire," says Vasseur: "but thirty picked men would have been worth more than the whole of them."[1]

August, September, and October were the busy months at Quebec. Then the ships from France discharged their lading, the shops and warehouses of the Lower Town were filled with goods, and the *habitants* came to town to make their purchases. When the frosts began, the vessels sailed away, the harbor was deserted, the streets were silent again, and like ants or squirrels the people set at work to lay in their winter stores. Fathers of families packed their cellars with beets, carrots, potatoes, and cabbages; and, at the end of autumn, with meat, fowls, game, fish, and eels, all frozen to stony hardness.

[1] *Vasseur au Ministre*, 24 *Nov.*, 1701. Like Denonville before him, he urges the need of fire-buckets.

Most of the shops closed, and the long season of leisure and amusement began. New Year's day brought visits and mutual gifts. Thence till Lent dinner-parties were frequent, sometimes familiar and sometimes ceremonious. The governor's little court at the château was a standing example to all the aspiring spirits of Quebec, and forms and orders of precedence were in some houses punctiliously observed. There were dinners to the military and civic dignitaries and their wives, and others, quite distinct, to prominent citizens. The wives and daughters of the burghers of Quebec are said to have been superior in manners to women of the corresponding class in France. "They have wit," says La Potherie, "delicacy, good voices, and a great fondness for dancing. They are discreet, and not much given to flirting; but when they undertake to catch a lover, it is not easy for him to escape the bands of Hymen."[1]

So much for the town. In the country parishes, there was the same autumnal stowing away of frozen vegetables, meat, fish, and eels, and unfortunately the same surfeit of leisure through five months of the year. During the seventeenth century, many of the people were so poor that women were forced to keep at home from sheer want of winter clothing. Nothing, however, could prevent their running from house to house to exchange gossip with the neighbors, who all knew one another, and, having nothing else to do, discussed each other's affairs with an industry

[1] La Potherie, i. 279.

which often bred bitter quarrels. At a later period, a more general introduction of family weaving and spinning served at once to furnish clothing and to promote domestic peace.

The most important persons in a parish were the curé, the seignior, and the militia captain. The seignior had his bench of honor in the church. Immediately behind it was the bench of the militia captain, whose duty it was to drill the able-bodied men of the neighborhood, direct roadmaking and other public works, and serve as deputy to the intendant, whose ordinances he was required to enforce. Next in honor came the local judge, if any there was, and the church-wardens.

The existence of slavery in Canada dates from the end of the seventeenth century. In 1688 the attorney-general made a visit to Paris, and urged upon the King the expediency of importing negroes from the West Indies as a remedy for the scarcity and dearness of labor. The King consented, but advised caution, on the ground that the rigor of the climate would make the venture a critical one.[1] A number of slaves were brought into the colony; but the system never flourished, the climate and other circumstances being hostile to it. Many of the colonists, especially at Detroit and other outlying posts, owned slaves of a remote Indian tribe, the Pawnees. The fact is

---

[1] *Instruction au Sr. de Frontenac*, 1689. On Canadian slavery, see a long paper, *L'Esclavage en Canada*, published by the Historical Society of Montreal.

remarkable, since it would be difficult to find another of the wild tribes of the continent capable of subjection to domestic servitude. The Pawnee slaves were captives taken in war and sold at low prices to the Canadians. Their market value was much impaired by their propensity to run off.

It is curious to observe the views of the Canadians taken at different times by different writers. La Hontan says: "They are vigorous, enterprising, and indefatigable, and need nothing but education. They are presumptuous and full of self-conceit, regard themselves as above all the nations of the earth, and, unfortunately, have not the veneration for their parents that they ought to have. The women are generally pretty; few of them are brunettes; many of them are discreet, and a good number are lazy. They are fond to the last degree of dress and show, and each tries to outdo the rest in the art of catching a husband."[1]

Fifty years later, the intendant Hocquart writes: "The Canadians are fond of distinctions and attentions, plume themselves on their courage, and are extremely sensitive to slights or the smallest corrections. They are self-interested, vindictive, prone to drunkenness, use a great deal of brandy, and pass for not being at all truthful. This portrait is true of many of them, particularly the country people: those of the towns are less vicious. They are all attached to religion, and criminals are rare. They are vola-

[1] La Hontan, ii. 81 (ed. 1709).

tile, and think too well of themselves, which prevents their succeeding as they might in farming and trade. They have not the rude and rustic air of our French peasants. If they are put on their honor and governed with justice, they are tractable enough; but their natural disposition is indocile."[1]

The navigator Bougainville, in the last years of the French rule, describes the Canadian *habitant* as essentially superior to the French peasant, and adds, "He is loud, boastful, mendacious, obliging, civil, and honest; indefatigable in hunting, travelling, and bush-ranging, but lazy in tilling the soil."[2]

The Swedish botanist, Kalm, an excellent observer, was in Canada a few years before Bougainville, and sketches from life the following traits of Canadian manners. The language is that of the old English translation: "The men here [at Montreal] are extremely civil, and take their hats off to every person indifferently whom they meet in the streets. The women in general are handsome; they are well bred and virtuous, with an innocent and becoming freedom. They dress out very fine on Sundays, and though on the other days they do not take much pains with the other parts of their dress, yet they are very fond of adorning their heads, the hair of which is always curled and powdered and ornamented with glittering bodkins and aigrettes. They are not averse to taking part in all the business of housekeeping;

---

[1] *Mémoire de* 1736.

[2] *Mémoire de* 1757, printed in Margry, *Relations Inédites*.

and I have with pleasure seen the daughters of the better sort of people, and of the governor [of Montreal] himself, not too finely dressed, and going into kitchens and cellars to look that everything be done as it ought. What I have mentioned above of their dressing their heads too assiduously is the case with all the ladies throughout Canada. Their hair is always curled, even when they are at home in a dirty jacket and short coarse petticoat that does not reach to the middle of their legs. On those days when they pay or receive visits, they dress so gayly that one is almost induced to think their parents possess the greatest honors in the state. They are no less attentive to have the newest fashions, and they laugh at one another when they are not dressed to one another's fancy. One of the first questions they propose to a stranger is, whether he is married; the next, how he likes the ladies of the country, and whether he thinks them handsomer than those of his own country; and the third, whether he will take one home with him. The behavior of the ladies seemed to me somewhat too free at Quebec, and of a more becoming modesty at Montreal. Those of Quebec are not very industrious. The young ladies, especially those of a higher rank, get up at seven and dress till nine, drinking their coffee at the same time. When they are dressed, they place themselves near a window that opens into the street, take up some needlework and sew a stitch now and then, but turn their eyes into the street most of the time. When a young fellow comes in, whether they are acquainted with him or not, they immediately lay aside their work, sit down by him, and begin to chat, laugh, joke, and invent *double-entendres;* and this is reckoned being very witty. In this manner they frequently pass the whole day, leaving their mothers to do the business of the house. They are likewise cheerful and content, and nobody can say that they want either wit or charms. Their fault is that they think too well of themselves. However, the daughters of people of all ranks without exception go to market and carry home what they have bought. The girls at Montreal are very much displeased that those at Quebec get husbands sooner than they. The reason of this is that many young gentlemen who come over from France with the ships are captivated by the ladies at Quebec and marry them; but as these gentlemen seldom go up to Montreal, the girls there are not often so happy as those of the former place." [1]

Long before Kalm's visit, the Jesuit Charlevoix, a traveller and a man of the world, wrote thus of Quebec in a letter to the Duchesse de Lesdiguières: "There is a select little society here which wants nothing to make it agreeable. In the *salons* of the wives of the governor and of the intendant, one finds circles as brilliant as in other countries." These circles were formed partly of the principal inhabitants, but chiefly of military officers and government

[1] Kalm, *Travels into North America*, translated into English by John Reinold Forster (London, 1771), 56, 282, etc.

officials, with their families. Charlevoix continues: "Everybody does his part to make the time pass pleasantly, with games and parties of pleasure, — drives and canoe excursions in summer, sleighing and skating in winter. There is a great deal of hunting and shooting, for many Canadian gentlemen are almost destitute of any other means of living at their ease. The news of the day amounts to very little indeed, as the country furnishes scarcely any, while that from Europe comes all at once. Science and the fine arts have their turn, and conversation does not fail. The Canadians breathe from their birth an air of liberty, which makes them very pleasant in the intercourse of life, and our language is nowhere more purely spoken. One finds here no rich persons whatever, and this is a great pity; for the Canadians like to get the credit of their money, and scarcely anybody amuses himself with hoarding it. They say it is very different with our neighbors the English; and one who knew the two colonies only by the way of living, acting, and speaking of the colonists would not hesitate to judge ours the more flourishing. In New England and the other British colonies there reigns an opulence by which the people seem not to know how to profit; while in New France poverty is hidden under an air of ease which appears entirely natural. The English colonist keeps as much and spends as little as possible; the French colonist enjoys what he has got, and often makes a display of what he has not got. The one labors for his heirs; the other leaves them to get on as they can, like himself. I could push the comparison further, but I must close here; the King's ship is about to sail, and the merchant vessels are getting ready to follow. In three days, perhaps, not one will be left in the harbor." [1]

And now we, too, will leave Canada. Winter draws near, and the first patch of snow lies gleaming on the distant mountain of Cape Tourmente. The sun has set in chill autumnal beauty, and the sharp spires of fir-trees on the heights of Sillery stand stiff and black against the pure cold amber of the fading west. The ship sails in the morning; and before the old towers of Rochelle rise in sight there will be time to smoke many a pipe, and ponder what we have seen on the banks of the St. Lawrence.

[1] Charlevoix, *Journal Historique*, 80 (ed. 1744).

CHAPTER XXIV.

1663-1763.

CANADIAN ABSOLUTISM.

FORMATION OF CANADIAN CHARACTER. — THE RIVAL COLONIES. — ENGLAND AND FRANCE. — NEW ENGLAND. — CHARACTERISTICS OF RACE. — MILITARY QUALITIES. — THE CHURCH. — THE ENGLISH CONQUEST.

NOT institutions alone, but geographical position, climate, and many other conditions unite to form the educational influences that, acting through successive generations, shape the character of nations and communities.

It is easy to see the nature of the education, past and present, which wrought on the Canadians and made them what they were. An ignorant population, sprung from a brave and active race, but trained to subjection and dependence through centuries of feudal and monarchical despotism, was planted in the wilderness by the hand of authority, and told to grow and flourish. Artificial stimulants were applied, but freedom was withheld. Perpetual intervention of government, — regulations, restrictions, encouragements sometimes more mischievous than restrictions, a constant uncertainty what the authorities would do next, the fate of each man resting less with himself than with another, volition enfeebled, self-reliance paralyzed, — the condition, in short, of a child held always under the rule of a father, in the main well-meaning and kind, sometimes generous, sometimes neglectful, often capricious, and rarely very wise, — such were the influences under which Canada grew up. If she had prospered, it would have been sheer miracle. A man, to be a man, must feel that he holds his fate, in some good measure, in his own hands.

But this was not all. Against absolute authority there was a counter influence, rudely and wildly antagonistic. Canada was at the very portal of the great interior wilderness. The St. Lawrence and the Lakes were the highway to that domain of savage freedom; and thither the disfranchised, half-starved seignior, and the discouraged *habitant* who could find no market for his produce naturally enough betook themselves. Their lesson of savagery was well learned, and for many a year a boundless license and a stiff-handed authority battled for the control of Canada. Nor, to the last, were Church and State fairly masters of the field. The French rule was drawing towards its close when the intendant complained that though twenty-eight companies of regular troops were quartered in the colony, there were not soldiers enough to keep the people in order.[1] One cannot but remember that in a neighboring colony,

---

[1] *Mémoire de* 1736 (printed by the Historical Society of Quebec).

far more populous, perfect order prevailed, with no other guardians than a few constables chosen by the people themselves.

Whence arose this difference, and other differences equally striking, between the rival colonies? It is easy to ascribe them to a difference of political and religious institutions; but the explanation does not cover the ground. The institutions of New England were utterly inapplicable to the population of New France, and the attempt to apply them would have wrought nothing but mischief. There are no political panaceas, except in the imagination of political quacks. To each degree and each variety of public development there are corresponding institutions, best answering the public needs; and what is meat to one is poison to another. Freedom is for those who are fit for it; the rest will lose it, or turn it to corruption. Church and State were right in exercising authority over a people which had not learned the first rudiments of self-government. Their fault was not that they exercised authority, but that they exercised too much of it, and, instead of weaning the child to go alone, kept him in perpetual leading-strings, making him, if possible, more and more dependent, and less and less fit for freedom.

In the building up of colonies, England succeeded and France failed. The cause lies chiefly in the vast advantage drawn by England from the historical training of her people in habits of reflection, forecast, industry, and self-reliance, — a training which enabled them to adopt and maintain an invigorating system of self-rule, totally inapplicable to their rivals.

The New England colonists were far less fugitives from oppression than voluntary exiles seeking the realization of an idea. They were neither peasants nor soldiers, but a substantial Puritan yeomanry, led by Puritan gentlemen and divines in thorough sympathy with them. They were neither sent out by the King, governed by him, nor helped by him. They grew up in utter neglect, and continued neglect was the only boon they asked. Till their increasing strength roused the jealousy of the Crown, they were virtually independent, — a republic, but by no means a democracy. They chose their governor and all their rulers from among themselves, made their own government and paid for it, supported their own clergy, defended themselves, and educated themselves. Under the hard and repellent surface of New England society lay the true foundations of a stable freedom, — conscience, reflection, faith, patience, and public spirit. The cement of common interests, hopes, and duties compacted the whole people like a rock of conglomerate; while the people of New France remained in a state of political segregation, like a basket of pebbles held together by the enclosure that surrounds them.

It may be that the difference of historical antecedents would alone explain the difference of character between the rival colonies; but there are deeper causes, the influence of which went far to determine the antecedents themselves. The Germanic race, and especially the Anglo-Saxon branch of it, is peculiarly masculine, and, therefore, peculiarly fitted for self-government. It submits its action habitually to the guidance of reason, and has the judicial faculty of seeing both sides of a question. The French Celt is cast in a different mould. He sees the end distinctly, and reasons about it with an admirable clearness; but his own impulses and passions continually turn him away from it. Opposition excites him; he is impatient of delay, is impelled always to extremes, and does not readily sacrifice a present inclination to an ultimate good. He delights in abstractions and generalizations, cuts loose from unpleasing facts, and roams through an ocean of desires and theories.

While New England prospered and Canada did not prosper, the French system had at least one great advantage. It favored military efficiency. The Canadian population sprang in great part from soldiers, and was to the last systematically reinforced by disbanded soldiers. Its chief occupation was a continual training for forest war; it had little or nothing to lose, and little to do but fight and range the woods. This was not all. The Canadian government was essentially military. At its head was a soldier nobleman, often an old and able commander; and those beneath him caught his spirit and emulated his example. In spite of its political nothingness, in spite of poverty and hardship, and in spite even of trade, the upper stratum of Canadian society was animated by the pride and fire of that gallant *noblesse* which held war as its only worthy calling, and prized honor more than life. As for the *habitant*, the forest, lake, and river were his true school; and here, at least, he was an apt scholar. A skilful woodsman, a bold and adroit canoe-man, a willing fighter in time of need, often serving without pay, and receiving from government only his provisions and his canoe, he was more than ready at any time for any hardy enterprise; and in the forest warfare of skirmish and surprise there were few to match him. An absolute government used him at will, and experienced leaders guided his rugged valor to the best account.

The New England man was precisely the same material with that of which Cromwell formed his invincible "Ironsides;" but he had very little forest experience. His geographical position cut him off completely from the great wilderness of the interior. The sea was his field of action. Without the aid of government, and in spite of its restrictions, he built up a prosperous commerce, and enriched himself by distant fisheries, neglected by the rivals before whose doors they lay. He knew every ocean from Greenland to Cape Horn, and the whales of the north and of the south had no more dangerous foe. But he was too busy to fight without good cause; and when he turned his hand to soldiering, it was only to meet some pressing need of the hour. The New England troops in the early wars were bands of raw fishermen and farmers, led by civilians, decorated with military titles, and subject to the slow and uncertain action of legislative bodies. The officers had not learned to command, nor the men to obey. The remarkable exploit of the capture of Louisburg, the strongest fortress in America, was the result of mere audacity and hardihood, backed by the rarest good luck.

One great fact stands out conspicuous in Canadian history, — the Church of Rome. More even than the royal power, she shaped the character and the destinies of the colony. She was its nurse and almost its mother; and, wayward and headstrong as it was, it never broke the ties of faith that held it to her. It was these ties which, in the absence of political franchises, formed under the old régime the only vital coherence in the population. The royal government was transient; the Church was permanent. The English conquest shattered the whole apparatus of civil administration at a blow, but it left her untouched. Governors, intendants, councils, and commandants, all were gone; the principal seigniors fled the colony; and a people who had never learned to control themselves or help themselves were suddenly left to their own devices. Confusion, if not anarchy, would have followed but for the parish priests, who, in a character of double paternity, half spiritual and half temporal, became more than ever the guardians of order throughout Canada.

This English conquest was the grand crisis of Canadian history. It was the beginning of a new life. With England came Protestantism, and the

Canadian Church grew purer and better in the presence of an adverse faith. Material growth; an increased mental activity; an education, real though fenced and guarded; a warm and genuine patriotism, — all date from the peace of 1763. England imposed by the sword on reluctant Canada the boon of rational and ordered liberty. Through centuries of striving she had advanced from stage to stage of progress, deliberate and calm, — never breaking with her past, but making each fresh gain the base of a new success, — enlarging popular liberties while bating nothing of that height and force of individual development which is the brain and heart of civilization; and now, through a hard-earned victory, she taught the conquered colony to share the blessings she had won. A happier calamity never befell a people than the conquest of Canada by the British arms.

APPENDIX.

SECTION FIRST.

A.

LA TOUR AND D'AUNAY.

Procès verbal d'André Certain.

[Literatim.]

Collection de M. Margry.

L'an mil six cent quarante quatre le vint cinq jour d'octobre deux mois après la signification faits de l'arrest du conseil en date du 5 mai de la mesme année au Sieur de la Tour et à tous ceux qui estoient avec luy dans le fort de la Rivière St. Jean par la Montjoie le 15 8bre 1644 Mr Charles de Menou chevalier Seigneur d'Aunay Charnisay, gouverneur et Lieutenant général pour le Roy dans toute l'Etendue descostes d'Acadie pais de la Nouvelle France, veu le refus du d. de la Tour et l'obstination dans laquelle estoient ses gens, equipa de rechef deux de ses chaloupes pour tenter par les voies de douceur de ramener ces esprits rebelles à l'obeissance qu'ils doivent à sa Majeste pour lequel effet mon dit Sieur deputa un lieutenant de son vaisseau pour commander une d'icelles et son sergent pour l'autre auec commandement de sa part d'aller à la riviere

St. Jean faire tout effort pour adroitement remonter quelqu'uns de ces esprits rebelles, les emboucher et leur donner lettres pour leur camarades signés de mon dit Sieur avec assurance d'abolition de leurs crimes et payements de leurs gages s'ils se rangeoient à leur devoir de veritables sujets, leur devant montrer comme les arrets du conseil obligeoient mon dit Sieur à pareils traitemens. Ce qu'ayant fidellement executé ils ne receurent pour toute reponse qu'injures et imprecations de ces malheureux et huit jours après la femme du dit Sieur de la Tour arrivant à la riviere de St. Jean conduite par un vaisseau anglois obligea son mary d'aller à Boston vers les Anglois se declarer de leur religion, comme elle venoit de faire et leur demander un ministre pour son habitation et par là obliger tout le corps des Anglois à les maintenir dans leurs biens avec offre qu'ils partageroient toute la coste d'Acadie après qu'ils s'en seroient rendus maistres: Et le 28 de Janvier 1645 la dite dame parla si insolemment aux réverends peres Recollects qui pour lors estoient dans son habitation que faisant la Démoniaque et mepris scandaleux de la religion Catholique, apostolique et Romaine son mary présent, qui adhéroit à toutes ses actions, ils furent contraints de sortir et chercher moyen de se retirer quoyque dans ces contrées l'Hiver soit très rigoureux, ce que le dit Sieur de la Tour et sa femme leur octroierent avec dérision et injures leur donnant pour cet effet une vieille pinasse qui couloid quasy bas d'eau avec deux bariques de bled d'Inde pour toutes vitailles, ce qui sera justifié par une attestation de ceux mesmes qui estoient dans le service du Sr de la Tour et sa femme et une lettre d'un des susdits pères Recollects superieur dans le d. lieu et huit ou neuf des gens du d. Sr de la Tour connoissant le deplorable estat de cette habitation ed la formelle rebellion du Sr de la Tour sa femme et du reste de leurs camarades contre le devoir qu'ils doivent à dieu et au Roy se retirérent

semblablement et accompagnerent les dits reverends pères
Recollects, lesquels avec beaucoup de perils se vinrent rendre
dans le Port Royal demeure ordinaire du Sr. d'Aunay,
lequel après avoir esté imbu de tout ce que dessus les receut
tous humainement envoiant les deux religieux Recollects
dans la maison des Reverends peres Capucins missionaires
qui les receurent avec tant d'affection et les firent tant de
charité et saints offices qu'ils en demeurent tous confus aussy
bien que les huid personnes qui les accompagnoient voyant
le favorable accueil que leur fit mon dit Sieur qui ne se con-
tenta pas de les loger et nourrir comme les siens propres mais
les paya leurs gages que le dit La Tour de tant d'années qu'ils
l'avoient servy leur avoid refusé. Ce qui est prouvé par une
reconnoissance de ces mesmes personnes pour les sommes qui
leur ont esté mises entre les mains, signée de leurs mains.
Ce régalement ayant esté donné comme dessus est dit, Mon
dit sieur s'informant plus particulierement de l'estat au quel
estoient ces miserables esprits, l'obstination du reste de ceux
qui estoient demeurez avec le dit la Tour, et qu'il estoit
party pour aller vers les Anglois dans Boston pour tascher
de renvoyer comme jà cy dessus est dit le traitté de paix fait
avec les dits Anglois et le sieur Marie confident de Mon
d. Sieur D'Aunay et engager par mesme moyen quelque
marchand pour amener quelques vitailles dans la riviere de
Saint Jean dans la quelle il n'avoit laissé que quarante cinq
personnes, ce que mon dit sieur considerant fit assemblées de
tous les officiers qui pour lors estoient auprès de sa personne,
où il fut conclud de prendre cette occasion aux cheveux. Et
quoyque ne le peut quasy permettre et qu'il falloit risquer
pour une affaire de telle consequence, ce qui obligea mon dit
sieur de monter le plus grand de ces navires du port de trois
cents tonneaux, equipé en guerre, pour se mettre en garde à
l'entrée de la Rivière St. Jean afin de surprendre le dit La
Tour avec une partie de son monde, qui pensoit à la faveur

de la rigueur de l'Hiver faire son voyage sans qu'il en fust aucune nouvelle, ce que mon dit sieur ayant executé et pris rade à une lieue du fort de la Rivière St. Jean assisté d'un religieux Capucin missionnaire et des deux susdits Recollects, envoya de rechef vers la dite femme La Tour et tous ceux qui pour lors estoient avec elle le Révérend Père André Recollect par une de ses chaloupes, le quel se promettoit d'attirer peutestre quelquuns à resipiscence, leur faisant connoitre le bon accueil que luy et leurs camarades avoient receu de mon dit Sieur, ce qui ne reussit non plus que les autres fois du passé. Deux mois s'ecoulèrent dans semblable attente, après quoy mon dit Sieur prid resolution de battre le fer pendant qu'il estoit chaud, voyant un de ses navires aussy equipé en guerre qui l'estoit venu trouver du Port Royal selon qu'il l'avoit ainsy ordonné accompagné d'une pinasse aussi chargée de monde et après avoir reallié de toutes ses Habitations les personnes capables de porter mousquets, il fit descendre une bonne partie de ses hommes à terre et mettre deux pièces de canon avec ordre de les mettre promptement en batterie le plus proche du fort de la Rivière de St. Jean qu'ils pourroient avec assurance qu'aussytost qu'ils avoient effectué son commandement ils approcheroient ce navire à la portée du pistolet, afin que sans donner jour aux assiegés de se reconnoistre on pust faire un tonnerre et par mer et par terre, donner à mesme temps qu'il y auroit breche faite, pendant l'exécution de ces ordres un petit navire Anglois se présenta pour entrer dans la dite rivière chargé de vitailles et munitions de guerre, dans lequel il y avoit un des domestiques du d. La Tour qui estoit chargé de Lettres de son maistre pour la ditte dame sa femme qui l'assuroit dans un mois ou deux venir la trouver en meilleur estat et posture qu'il pourroit. Le dit domestique avoit outre plus une lettre du gouverneur de la grande baye des anglois addressante à la dite dame par laquelle il l'exhortoit à faire son profit des instructions qu'elle avoit recues pendant sa residence. Le dit navire fut pris et arresté par mon dit Sieur et l'equipage renvoyé au lieu d'où il estoit party, avec une chaloupe que mon dit sieur leur donna pour cet effet, lequel estant une fois de retour fit rapport à Messieurs les magistrats du gouvernement des Anglois que leur navire avoid esté pris en negotiant avec les francois et que le traité de paix quils avoient fait avec le Sieur Marie nestoit gardé avec mil autres plaintes dont ils vouloient couvrir le sujet de leur voyage, ce qui obligea ces Messieurs de deputer un exprès vers mon dit Sieur pour luy demander raison du bien pris par luy sur un de leurs marchands contre les articles de paix que le Sieur Marie, confident, leur avoit laissé signer de sa part — À quoy mon dit Sieur leur fit response et déclara à leur député la fourbe de leur dit marchand, le quel par un désir de lucre abusoit de leur commission et au lieu d'aller négotiant dans les Habitations des véritables François, Il alloit rompant par luy mesmes ce traité de paix passé entre ses magistrats et le Sieur Marie, confident, portant ainsi frauduleusement des munitions de vivres et de guerre pour maintenir des rebelles dans leur desobeissance et contre le devoir qu'ils doivent à leur prince naturel. Toutes les quelles raisons payerent entièrement et le député et Messieurs les Magistrats de la Grande Baie le susdit député estant party et mon dit Sieur D'Aunay ayant recue nouvelle que la batterie estoit en estat et ses gens qui estoient à terre disposés à faire ce quil leur ordonneroit, se resolut de haster le pas et avant que le d. Sieur De la Tour en eust le vent faire tout son effort, ce qui luy arriva si Heureusement qu'après avoir encore une fois sommé ces malheureux, lesquels lui envoierent pour response une vollée de canon à balle, aborant le pavillon rouge sur leurs bastions avec mil injures et blasphemes et avoir fait battre le dit fort de la

Rivière de St Jean tant par terre que par son grand navire, qu'il avoit emmené à portée de pistolet d'iceluy ce qui rasa une partie de leur parapets il s'en rendit maistre par un assaut général qu'il fit donner sur le soir de la mesme Journée le Lendemain Pasques ce qui fut accompagné d'une si grande benediction de Dieu, que quoyque la perte des Hommes que mon dit sieur a fait soit grande elle eut esté encore plus sanglante. Une partie des assiegéz furent tuez dans la chaleur du combat et l'autre fait prisonniers entre autres la femme du dit La Tour, son fils et sa fille de Chambre et une autre femme qui est tout cequ'il y avoit dans le dit fort de sexe feminin toutes lesquelles ne recurent aucun tort ny à leur Honneur ny à leurs personnes. Une partie des prisonniers recut grace de mon dit Sieur et le reste des plus seditieux fut pendu et etranglé pour servir de memoire et d'exemple, à la postérité d'une si obstinée rébellion ce qui est prouvé par l'attestation qu'en ont rendue et signée une bonne partie de ceux qui ont recue la vie et pareille gratification. Le Lendemain 18 Avril 1645 mon dit sieur fit inhumer tous les morts tant de part que d'autre avec la distinction pour tant requise en telle rencontre du party faisant prier Dieu et faire un service solemnel à tous ceux que deux révérends pères Capucins missionnaires qui avoient esté presens à tout jugement estre deu, ce qui est prouvé aussi bien que tout ce que dessus par une attestation authentique des mesmes susd. révérends pères Capucins missionnaires après quoy mon dit Sieur fit travailler pour combler les travaux de dehors faits par les assiegeans et reparer ceux de la place mettre ordre aux deffauts d'icelle par luy reconnus et faire inventaire de tout ce qui se trouva de reste dans icelle après le pillage fait par les compagnons que mon dit sieur leur avoit donné et faire ensuite renvituailler le dit lieu de toutes choses necessaires pour la conservation d'iceluy et enfin poser une personne capable et fidele pour le service du Roi ce que dura l'espace de trois semaines ou un mois pendant le quel la femme du dit La Tour qui estoit dans le Commencement en Liberté fut resserrée par une Lettre qu'on trouva qu'elle ecrivoit à son mary et pratique qu'elle faisoit de lui faire tenir par le moyen des Sauvages afin de la pouvoir par la première occasion envoyer en France à nos Seigneurs du Conseil en bonne sauve garde, ce qui l'alarma de telle sorte que de depit et de rage elle tomba malade et nonobstant tous les bons traitemens et Charités que L'on exerça en son endroit mourut le 15 Juin après avoir abjuré publiquement dans le chapelle du mesme fort L'Heresie qu'elle avoit professée parmy les Anglois à la grande Baye. Ce qui est justifié par l'attestation désjà cy dessus alleguée des deux reverends pères Capucins Missionaires.

Le présent procés verbal a esté fait par nous, André Certain prevost et garde du Scel Royal de La Coste d'Acadie pays de la Nouvelle france à la requeste de Monsieur d'Aunay Charnisay Gouverneur et Lieutenant general pour le Roy en toute l'Etendue de la Coste d'Acadie pays de la Nouvelle France le 10ᵉ jour de may 1645 et rendu et dès le mesme jour et an que dessus pour lui servir et valoir aussi que de raison. Le tout en présence de tesmoins et principaux chefs des Francois qui sont dans la dite coste signé Longvilliers Poincy, Bernard Marot, Dubreuil Vismes, Javille, Jean Laurent, Henry Dansmartin, Barthelemy Aubert, Leclerc et Certain prevost et Garde du Sceau Royal.

[The following extracts are printed, letter for letter, from copies of the original documents.]

SECTION SECOND.

B.

THE HERMITAGE OF CAEN.

MÉMOIRE POUR FAIRE CONNOISTRE L'ESPRIT ET LA CONDUITE DE LA COMPAGNIE ESTABLIE EN LA VILLE DE CAEN, APPELÉE L'HERMITAGE.

(*Extrait.*)[1]   *Bibliothèque Nationale.*

C'EST en ce fameux Hermitage que le dit feu Sieur de Bernières a eslevé plusieurs jeunes gens auxquels il enseignoit une espèce d'oraison sublime et transcendante que l'on appelle l'oraison purement passive, parceque l'esprit n'y agit point, mais reçoit seulement la divine opération; c'est cette espèce d'oraison qui est la source de tant de visions et de révélations, dont l'Hermitage est si fécond; et après qu'il leur avoit subtilizé et presque fait évaporer l'esprit par cette oraison rafinée, il les rendoit capables de reconnoistre les Jansénistes les plus cachéz; en sorte que quelques uns de ces disciples ont dit qu'ils le connoissoient au flairer, comme les chiens font leur gibier, pour ensuite leur faire la chasse, néantmoins le dit Sieur de Bernières disoit qu'il n'avoit pas l'odorat si subtil, mais que la marque à laquelle il connoissoit les Jansénistes estoit quand

---

[1] This *mémoire* forms 116 pages in the copy in my possession.

on improuvoit sa conduite ou que l'on estoit opposé aux Jésuites. . . . Au commencement les personnes de cette compagnie ne se mesloient que de l'assistance des pauvres, mais depuis que le feu Sieur de Bernières qui estoit un simple laïque, qui n'avoit point d'estude, s'en estant rendu le maistre, il persuada a ceux qui en sont qu'elle n'estoit pas seulement establie pour prendre soin des pauvres, mais de toutes les autres bonnes œuvres, publiques ou particulières, qui regardent la Piété et la Religion et que Dieu les avoit suscitez, principalement pour suppléer aux défauts et négligences des Prélats, des Pasteurs, des Magistrats, des Juges et autres Supérieurs Ecclésiastiques et Politiques qui faute de s'appliquer assez aux devoirs de leurs charges, obmettent dans les occasions beaucoup de bien qu'ils pourroient procurer, et négligent de résister à beaucoup de maux, d'abus et d'erreurs qu'ils pourroient empêcher; et que pour remédier à ces manquements, il estoit expédient que Dieu suscitat plusieurs gens de bien de toutes sortes de conditions qui s'unissent ensemble pour travailler à l'avancement du bien qui se peut faire en chaque profession, et pour extirper les erreurs, les abus et les vices qui s'y glissent souvent, par la négligence ou connivence mesme de ceux qui sont le plus obligez par leur ministère d'y donner ordre.

Et c'est dans cette pensée que ces messieurs croyent avoir droit à se mesler de toutes choses, de s'ingérer de toutes les actions un peu éclantes qui regardent la Religion, de s'ingérer en censeurs publics, pour corriger et controller tout ce qui leur deplaist, d'entrer et de pénétrer dans les secrets des maisons et des familles particulières, comme aussi dans la conduite des communautez Religieuses pour y gouverner toutes choses à leur gré; et bien que ces messieurs soient fort ignorans, bien qu'ils n'ayent aucune experience des affaires et qu'ils passent dans le jugement de tous ceux qui les connoissent pour personnes qui n'ont qu'un Zèle impetueux et violent, sans lumières et sans discrétion, neantmoins ils présument avoir assez de capacité pour réformer la vie, les mœurs, les sentimens et la doctrine de tous les autres. Et ce qu'il y a de plus fascheux et de plus dangereux en cela, c'est que si on ne défère aveuglément à tous leurs sentimens, si on improuve leur conduite et si l'on oppose la moindre résistance à leurs entreprises, quoyqu'injustes et violentes, ils unissent toutes leur forces pour les faire réussir et pour cet effet ils réclament les secours de tous ceux qui leur sont unis, à Paris, à Rouen et ailleurs, pour décrier, pour diffamer et pour perdre ceux qui leur résistent et qui veulent s'opposer au cours de leurs violences et de leurs injustice, de sorte qu'on peut assurer avec vérité que cette compagnie a dégénéré en une cabale et en une faction dangereuse et pernicieuse, tant à l'Eglise qu'à la Patrie, estant certain que depuis peu d'années ils ont excité beaucoup de troubles et de divisions dans toute la ville de Caen, et notamment dans le clergé et mesme en plusieurs autres lieux de la Basse-Normandie ainsi qu'il paroistra par les articles suivants de ce mémoire.

Il est arrivé quelques fois qu'ayant eu de faux avis que des maris maltroitoient leurs femmes ou que des femmes n'estoient pas fidèles à leurs maris ou que des filles ne se gouvernoient pas bien, ils se sont ingérez sur le rapport qui en estoit fait en leur assemblée de chercher les moyens de remédier à ces maux, et ils en ont choisi de si impertinents et de si indiscrets que cela a esté capable de causer bien du désordre et de la division dans les familles et dans toute la ville; car souvent voulant empescher une légère faute, on en fait naistre de grands scandales, lorsque l'on agit par emportement plustost que par prudence.

Ce n'est pas seulement dans les familles particulières qu'ils s'introduisent pour en fureter les secrets, pour en connoitre les défauts et pour en usurper la direction et le gouvernement, mais encore dans les maisons Religieuses, dont les unes se sont soumises à leur domination, comme les Ursulines de Caen, les moynes de l'Abbaye d'Ardenne de l'ordre de Premontré, proche de cette ville et depuis peu les filles de Sainte-Marie ; et les autres leur ayant tesmoigné quelque résistance, ils ont employé toute leur industrie pour en venir à bout ; et où l'artifice a manqué, ils y ont adjouté les violences et les menaces. . . .

Mais il ne faut point chercher de marques plus visibles de la persévérance, pour mieux dire du progrès de ces faux ermites dans leurs emportemens que ce qu'ont fait cet hiver passé cinq jeunes hommes nourris en l'Hermitage et élevés sous la direction et discipline du feu Sieur de Bernières. On leur avoit si bien imprimé dans l'esprit que tout estoit rempli de Jansénistes dans la ville de Caen, et que les curez en estoient les fauteurs et protecteurs, qu'un d'entre eux s'imagina que Dieu l'inspiroit fortement advertir le peuple de Caen que les curez estoient des fauteurs d'Hérétiques et par conséquent des excomuniez ; et ayant persuadé à ses compagnons d'annoncer publiquement à toute la ville ce crime prétendu des Curez d'une manière qui touchast le peuple et qui fut capable de l'exciter contre ces Pasteurs, ils résolurent de faire cette publication le mercredi quatrième du mois de Febvrier dernier, et jugèrent que pour se disposer à exécuter dignement ce que Dieu leur avoit inspiré, il falloit faire ensemble une communion extraordinaire, immédiatement avant que de l'entreprendre. Ils assistèrent donc pour cet effet et dans la paroisse de Saint-Ouen à la messe d'un prestre qu'on dit estre de leur cabale, et communièrent tous cinq de sa main ; et après leur communion, le plus zélé mit bas son pourpoint et le laissa avec son chapeau dans l'Eglise ; et accompagné des quatre autres qui le suivoient sans chapeaux, sans colets et le pourpoint deboutonné, non-obstant la rigueur extrême du froid ; ils marchèrent en cet équipage par toute la ville, annonçant à haute voix que les curez de Caen à l'exception de deux qu'ils nommoient étoient fauteurs de Jansénistes et excommuniez, parce qu'ils avoient signé un acte devant l'official de Caen, où ils attestent qu'ils ne connoissent point de Jansenistes dans la dite ville et répétoient cet advertissement de dix pas en dix pas, ce qui emeut toute la ville et attira à leur suite une grande multitude de populace qui se persuadant que ces gens estoient envoyés de Dieu pour leur donner cet advertissement, témoignoient desja de l'emotion contre les curez. Mais les magistrats qui estoient alors au siège en ayant esté advertis, ils envoyèrent leurs huissiers pour les arrester et les emmener, et ayant esté interrogez par le juge sur le sujet d'une action si extraordinaire, ils respondirent hardiment qu'ils l'avoient entreprise pour le service de Dieu et qu'ils estoient prests de souffrir la mort pour soustenir la vérité de ce qu'ils annonçoient, qu'ils avoient connoissance certaine qu'il y avoit grand nombre de Jansénistes en la ville de Caen, et que les curez s'en estoient declarez les fauteurs, par la déclaration qu'ils avoient donnée qu'ils n'en connoissoient point; ensuitte de quoy quatre d'entre eux furent renvoyez en prison et le cinquième fut mis entre les mains de ses parents sur une attestation que donnèrent les médecins qu'il estoit hypocondriaque et peu de jours après le lieutenant criminel ayant instruit le procez, les quatre prisonniers furent condamnez à cent livres d'amende; il leur fut deffendu et à tous autres de s'assembler ni d'exciter aucun scandale, il fut ordonné qu'ils seroient mis entre les mains de leur parents pour s'en charger et en faire bonne et seure garde, avec deffense de les laisser entrer dans la ville et aux fauxbourgs, sur peines au cas appartenantes. . . .

Car de quelles entreprises ne sont pas capables des personnes d'esprit faible et d'humeur atrabilaire que d'ailleurs on a desséchées par des jeûnes, des veilles et d'autres austéritez continuelles et par des méditations de trois ou quatre heures par jour, lorsque l'on ne les entretient presque d'autre chose, si non que leur Religion et l'Eglise sont en un très grand danger de se perdre, par la faction et la conspiration des Jansénistes lesquels on leur représente dans les livres, dans les sermons et dans les conférences, comme des gens qui veulent renverser les fondements de la Religion et de la Piété Chrestienne, qui veulent détruire le mystère de l'Incarnation, qui ne croyent point à la Transubstantation ni l'Invocation des Saints, ni les Indulgences, qui veulent abolir le sacrifice de la messe et le sacrement de la Pénitence, qui combattent la dévotion et le culte de la Sainte-Vierge, qui nient le franc arbitre et qui substituent en sa place le destin et la fatalité des Turcs, et enfin qui machinent la ruine de l'authorité des Souverains Pontifes. Qu'y a-t-il de plus aisé que d'animer les esprits imbéciles d'eux mesmes et prévenus de ces fausses imaginations contre des Evesques, des Docteurs, des Curez, et contre d'autres personnes très vertueuses et très catholiques, lorsqu'on leur fait croire que toutes ces personnes conspirent à establir une hérésie abominable !

C.

LAVAL AND ARGENSON.

Lettre de l'Evesque de Petrée a M. d'Argenson, Frère du Gouverneur.

(*Extrait.*) *Papiers d'Argenson.*

J'ai reçeu dans mon entrée dans le pays de Monsieur votre frère toutes les marques d'une bienveillance extraordinaire; iay fait mon possible pour la recongnoistre et luy ay rendu tous les respects que je dois à une personne de sa vertu et de son mérite joint à la qualité qu'il porte; comme son plus véritable amy et fidelle serviteur iay cru estre obligé de luy donner un advis important pour le bien de l'Eglise et qui luy devoit estre utile s'il l'eust pris dans la mesme disposition que ie suis asseuré que vous l'auries receu; cestoit seul à seul à cœur ouvert avec marques assez évidentes que ce que ie luy disois estoit vray veu qu'il estoit fondé sur des sentimens que i'avois veu moy mesme paroistre en diverses assemblées publiques; cependant il ne fist que trop congnoistre qu'il ne trouvoit auqunnement bon que ie luy donnaisses cet advertissement et me voullut faire embrasser le party de ceux qui avaient tout subject de se plaindre de son procédé envers eux, mais que je ne pretendois auqunnement justifier n'en ayant auqunne plainte de leur part pour luy faire et d'ailleurs estans asses desintéressés; vous pouvez bien iuger quels sont ceux dont ie veux parler sans vous les nommer puisque vous mesme qui avez une affection sincère et bien réglée pour ces dignes ouvriers évangéliques m'avez avoué que vous aviez doulleur de le voir partir dans les sentiments où il estoit à leur esgard sans beaucoup de fondement du moins suffisamment recongneu pour lors; ce que ie luy dis avoir sceu de vous pour ne rien omettre de ce que je me persuadois qui estoit capable de lui faire avouer une vérité qui nestoit que trop apparente, ce qui devoit un peu le calmer son esprit sembla l'aigrir et se fascha de ce que vous m'aviez faict cette ouverture, ie ne scais depuis ce qu'il a pensé de moy, mais il semble que je luy sois suspect et qu'il aye crû que i'embrasse la cause de ces bons serviteurs de Dieu à son preiudice, mais ie puis bien asseurer qu'ils n'ont pour luy que des sentimens de respect et que la plus forte passion que iaye est de le voir dans une parfaite union et intelligence avec eux.

QUEBEC, ce 20 Octobre 1659.

APPENDIX. 219

Lettre de M. d'Argenson, 1660.

(*Extrait.*) *Papiers d'Argenson.*

Monsieur de Petrée a une telle adherence à ses sentiments et un zèle qui le porte souvent hors du droict de sa charge qu'il ne faict aucune difficulté d'empieter sur le pouvoir des aultres et avec tant de chaleur qu'il n'écoute personne. Il enleva ces jours derniers une fille servente d'un habitant d'icy, et la mit de son autorité dans les Hursulines sur le seul prétexte qu'il vouloit la faire instruire, et par là il priva cet habitant du service qu'il prétendoit de sa servente qui luy avoit faict beaucoup de dépense a amener de France. Cet habitant est Mr Denis lequel ne cognoissant pas qui l'avoit soubstret me présenta requeste pour l'avoir. Je gardé [*sic*] la requeste sans la répondre trois jours pour empescher l'éclat de cette affaire. Le R. P. Lalement avec lequel j'en communiqué et lequel blasma fort le procedé de Mr de Petrée s'employa de tout son pouvoir pour la faire rendre sans bruit et n'y gaigna rien, si bien que je fus obligé de repondre la requeste et de permettre à cet habitant de reprendre sa servente où il la trouveroit, et si je n'eusse insinué soubs main d'accommoder cette affaire et que l'habitant a qui on refusa de la rendre l'eut poursuivi en justice j'eusse esté obligé de la luy rendre et de pousser tout avec beaucoup de scandal et cela (*à cause de*) la volonté de Mr de Petrée qui dict *qu'un evesque peult se qu'il veult, et ne menace que dexcommunication.*

Lettre de M. d'Argenson.

(*Extraits.*) *Papiers d'Argenson.*

Kebec le 7 Juillet, 1660.

Mr de Petrée a faist naistre cette contestation et ie puis dire auec verité que son zèle en plusieurs rencontres approche fort d'une grande atache à son sentiment et d'empietement sur la charge des aultres comme vous le verrez par un billet icy joint. . . . De toutes ces contestations que i'ay eu auec Mr de Petrée i'ay tousjours faist le R. P. Lalemand médiateur; c'est une personne d'un si grand merite et d'un sens si achevé que ie pense qu'on ne peult rien y adjouter; il seroit bien à souhaiter que touts ceux de sa maison suivissent ses sentiments; ils ne se mesleroient pas de censurer plusieurs choses comme ils font et laisseroient le gouvernement des affaires a ceux que Dieu a ordonné pour cela.

D.

PÉRONNE DUMESNIL.

LE SIEUR GAUDAIS DU PONT À MONSEIGNEUR DE COLBERT. 1664.

(Extrait.) Archives de la Marine.

QUELQUE 7 ou 8 jours après l'etablissement du Conseil Souverain, en consequence des lettres patentes de Sa majesté, le Procureur Général du dit Conseil jugeant qu'il était de sa charge de reprendre les (*papiers*) de cette plainte pour ne pas laisser un tel attentat impuni, fit sa requête verbale au dit Conseil tendante à ce qu'il lui fut donné commission pour informer contre le dit Sieur Du Mesnil; et que si le dit Sieur Du Mesnil, avait avis de la dite commission qu'il ne manquerait pas de détourner ces dits papiers demandant qu'il lui fut permis de saisir et de sequestrer ici et apposer le sceau au coffre ou armoire en laquelle se trouveraient les dits papiers, et pour ce faire qu'il plut au dit Conseil nommer tel Commissaire qu'il jugerait à propos.

Le dit Conseil entérinant la requête du dit Procureur Général, nomma le Sieur de Villeray, pour, en la présence du dit Procureur Général et assistance de son Greffier vaquer à la dite information, &c.

Et d'autant que le dit Sieur Du Mesnil était estimé homme violent et qu'il pourrait faire quelque boutade, pour donner main forte à la justice, Mr. le Gouverneur fut prié par les dits Conseillers de faire escorter le dit Sieur Commissaire par quelque nombre de soldats.

Le dit Sieur de Villeray assisté, comme dit est pour l'execution de sa commission, se transporta au logis du dit Sieur Du Mesnil, laissant à quartier l'escorte de soldats pour s'en servir en cas de besoin.

Le dit Sieur Du Mesnil ne trompa pas l'opinion que l'on avait eue de sa violence, fit grand bruit, cria aux voleurs, voulant emouvoir son voisinage, outrageant d'injures les dits Sieurs de Villeray et Procureur Général au grand mépris de l'autorité du Conseil, refusant même de le reconnaître. Ce qui n'empêcha pas le dit Sieur de Villeray d'exécuter sa commission de saisir les papiers du dit Sieur Du Mesnil, qui en donna la clef, y fit apposer le sceau et icelui sequestrer es mains d'un voisin du dit Sieur Du Mesnil et de son consentement.

Le lendemain le dit Sieur de Villeray rapporta son procès verbal au dit conseil, attesté du dit Procureur Général, et signé du Greffier du dit Conseil et sur les injures, violences et irrévérences y contenues tant contre le dit Sieur Commissaire que l'autorité du Conseil, fit decerner un décret de prise de corps contre le dit Sieur Du Mesnil, dont j'empêchai l'exécution.

Memoire de Dumesnil concernant les affaires du Canada.

(*Extrait.*)   Archives de la Marine.

10 Septembre, 1671.

Les dits Sieurs de Mésy, Gouverneur, de l'étrée, Evêque, et Dupont Gaudais, arrivés au dit Quebec le 16ᵉ jour de Septembre 1663, furent le lendemain salués et visités par le dit Du Mesnil précédent juge, lequel par devoir et civilité leur dit par forme d'avis que par des arrêts du conseil du Roi, qu'il leur représenta en date du 27 Mars 1647 et 13 Mai 1659 tous les commis et receveurs des dits deniers publics étaient exclus de toutes charges publiques, jusqu'à ce qu'ils eussent rendu et assuré leurs comptes, et le nommé Villeray chassé du conseil de la traite pour y avoir entré par voies et moyens illicites; et ordonné qu'il viendrait en France pour le purger de ses crimes; ce qu'il n'a pas fait, et pour nommer les autres commis, receveurs, auxquels il aurait commencé à faire le procès pendant qu'il était juge.

Nonobstant lesquels dires, actes et arrêts représentés, les dits Sieurs de Mésy, Evêque de l'étrée, et Dupont Gaudais, n'ont délaissé de prendre et admettre avec eux au dit Conseil Souverain les dits comptables; lesquels par ce moyen se prétendent à couvert et exempts de rendre les dits comptes. Le dit établissement de conseil fait et arrêté par les dits Commissaires le 18 du mois de Septembre, deux jours après leur arrivée; et pour Procureur Général prennent un nommé Jean Bourdon, boulanger et cannonier au fort et aussi comptable de 8 à 900,000 livres, comme il sera montré et qu'il a prêté son nom.

Le 20 du mois de Septembre, deux jours après l'établissement du dit conseil, les dits Villeray soi-disant conseiller et commissaire et Bourdon, Procureur Général accompagnés de deux sergents, d'un serrurier et de dix soldats du fort, bien armés vont en la maison du dit Du Mesnil, Intendant et Contrôleur Général, et peu auparavant leur juge souverain, sur les 7 a 8 heures du soir pour piller sa maison ; ce qu'ils firent ; ayant fait rompre la porte de son cabinet, ses armoires et un coffret ; pris et emporté ce qu'ils ont trouvé dedans et notamment tous ses papiers dans lesquels étaient leurs procès presque faits, et les preuves de leurs péculats, concussions et malversations, sans aucun inventaire ni forme de justice, étant le dit Du Mesnil, lors des dites violences, tenu et arrêté sur un siége et rudement traité par les soldats jusques à l'empêcher d'appeler du secours et des témoins pour voir ce qui se passait en sa maison et comme il était lié et arrêté.

Cette action violente ainsi faite et le dit Du Mesnil se voyant délivré du massacre de sa personne dont il était menacé, et d'être assassiné comme son fils s'en va trouver le dit Sieur Dupont Gaudais prenant qualité d'Intendant pour lui en faire plainte, qu'il ne voulut entendre, disant que c'était de son ordonnance et du dit Conseil que la dite action et prise de papiers avait été faite ; à quoi le dit Du Mesnil repartit qu'il s'en plaindrait au Roi, et lui en demanderait justice, ce qui obligea le dit Dupont Gaudais de dire au dit Du Mesnil qu'il donnât sa requête ; ce qui fut fait, et sur laquelle fut par le dit Conseil ordonné le 22 du dit mois de Septembre, deux jours après cette violence que le dit Dupont Gaudais serait commissaire pour vérifier les faits d'icelle requête ; ce que poursuivant le dit Du Mesnil, il eut ordre verbal du dit Sr. Gaudais de mettre au Greffe ses causes et moyens de récusation, de nullité de prise à partie et de demandes ; ce que le dit Du Mesnil fit comme appert par l'acte signé du Greffier du dit Conseil du 28 du dit mois de Septembre sur lesquelles récusations, prises à partie et demandes, le dit Conseil n'a rien voulu ordonner, comme appert par autre acte du dit Greffier du 21 Octobre ensuivant, jour ordonné pour l'embarquement et départ des vaisseaux du dit Quebec pour retourner en France.

Mais au lieu de statuer et ordonner sur les faits, moyens et conclusions du dit Du Mesnil, le dit Conseil sans plainte, sans partie et sans information a dressé emprisonnement du dit Du Mesnil et caché le décret sans le mettre au Greffe dans l'intention de le faire paraître et executer du même temps que le dit Du Mesnil se voudrait embarquer pour revenir en France, afin qu'il n'eût pas le temps de donner avis des violences qu'on lui faisait: de quoi averti il s'embarqua quelques jours auparavant les autres et fut reçu par le Capitaine Gardeur dans son navire, nonobstant les défenses qui lui en avaient été faites par le dit nouveau Conseil et que six pièces de canon de la plate forme d'en bas fussent pointées contre son navire pour le faire obéir à leurs ordonnances.

Tous ces massacres, assassins et pillages n'ont été faits au dit Du Mesnil, Intendant, par les dits comptables, ordonnateurs et preneurs de bien public et leurs parents et alliés que pour tâcher à couvrir et s'exempter de compter, payer et rendre ce qu'ils ont pillé, savoir. . . .

E.

LAVAL AND MÉSY.

Ordre de Mr de Mésy de faire sommation a l'Evêque de Pétrée.

(*Extrait.*) *Registre du Conseil Supérieur.*

13 Fevrier, 1664.

Le Sieur d'Angoville, Major de la Garnison entretenue par le Roi dans le Fort de St Louis à Québec pays de la Nouvelle France, est commandé par nous Sieur de Mésy,

Lieutenant Général et Gouverneur pour Sa Majesté dans toute l'étendue du dit pays, aller dire et avertir Monsieur l'Evêque de Pétrée étant présentement dans la chambre qui servait ci-devant aux Assemblées du Conseil au dit pays, que les Sieurs nommés pour Conseillers et le Sieur Bourdon pour Procureur du Roi au dit conseil à la persuasion du dit Sieur de Pétrée qui les connaissait entièrement ses créatures s'étant voulu rendre les maîtres declarés et portés en diverses manières dans le dit Conseil contre les Intérêts du Roi et du public pour appuyer et autoriser les intérêts d'autrui en particulier, il leur a été commandé par notre ordre pour la conservation des intérêts du Roi en ce pays, de s'absenter du dit Conseil jusqu'à ce que à notre diligence par le retour des premiers vaisseaux qui viendront. Sa Majesté ait été informée de leur conduite, et qu'ils se soient justifiés des cabales qu'ils ont formées, fomentées et entretenues contre leur devoir et le serment de fidélité qu'ils étaient obligés de garder à Sa dite Majesté.

Priant le dit Sieur Evêque acquiescer à la dite interdiction pour le bien du service du Roi, et vouloir procéder par l'avis d'une Assemblée publique à nouvelle nomination des Conseillers en la place des dits Sieurs Interdits pour pouvoir rendre la justice aux peuples et habitants de ce pays, Déclarant que nous Sieur de Mésy ne pouvons en nommer aucun de notre part en la façon en laquelle nous avons été surpris par notre facilité lors de la première nomination manque d'une parfaite connaissance, et que s'il est fait quelque chose au préjudice de cet avertissement par aucun des dits Conseillers interdits, ils seront traités comme désobéissants, fomenteurs de rebellions et contraires au repos public.

(Signé) Mésy.

Réponse de l'Evêque de Pétrée.

Registre du Conseil Supérieur.

16 Fev. 1664.

Laissant à part les paroles offensives et accusations injurieuses qui me regardent dans l'affiche mise au son du tambour le treizième de ce mois de Fevrier, au poteau public, dont je prétends me justifier devant Sa Majesté je réponds à la prière que Monsieur le Gouverneur m'y fait d'agréer l'interdiction des personnes qui y sont comprises, et de vouloir procéder à la nomination d'autres Conseillers ou Officiers et ce par l'avis d'une assemblée publique, que ni ma conscience ni mon honneur, ni le respect et obéissance que je dois aux volontés et commandements du Roi, ni la fidélité et l'affection que je dois à son service ne me le permettent aucunement jusques à ce que dans un jugement légitime les desnommés dans la susdite affiche soient convaincus des crimes dont on les y accuse.

A Quebec ce seizième Février mil-six-cent-soixante-quatre.

(Signé)   Francois, Evêque de Quebec.

Enrégistré à la requête de Mgr. l'Evêque de Pétrée ce 16 Fevrier 1664 par moi Secrétaire au Conseil Souverain soussigné.

(Signé)   Peuvret, Secret^{re}
avec paraphe.

Lettre de Mésy aux Jésuites.

(*Extrait.*)   Collection de l'Abbé Ferland.

Comme ainsi soit que la gloire de Dieu, le service du Roi et le service du public nous aient engagés de venir en ce pays pour y rencontrer notre salut par la sollicitation de

M. l'Evêque de Pétrée qui nous a fait agréer au Roi pour avoir l'honneur d'être son Lieutenant Général et Gouverneur de toute la Nouvelle France, représenter sa personne dans le Conseil Souverain qu'il a établi dans ce dit pays pour exercer la justice, police et finance, ce qui nous tient lieu d'obligation vers mon dit Sieur l'Evêque pour lui donner des marques de reconnaissance en toutes rencontres. A quoi nous sommes aussi obligés par son mérite particulier et par le respect qui est dû à son caractère, mais qui ne doit entrer en nulle consideration pour le regard du service et de la fidélité que nous sommes obligé de rendre à S. M.; n'étant pas ni de notre conscience ni de notre honneur d'avoir accepté la commission dont il nous a honoré, pour n'en pas faire le deub de notre charge et de trahir les intérêts de Sa dite Majesté; lui en ayant fait le serment de fidélité entre ses mains et d'en avoir reçu le commandement par sa bouche. Pourquoi ayant rencontré plusieurs pratiques que nous avons cru en conscience par devoir être obligé d'en empêcher la suite, nous aurions fait publier notre déclaration du 13ᵉ jour de Février dernier, et ne l'ayant pu faire faire sans y intéresser le Sʳ Evêque, notre dite déclaration nous fait passer dans son esprit et de tous Messieurs les Ecclésiastiques qui considèrent ce point d'une prétendue offense sans avoir égard aucunement aux intérêts du Roy pour un calomniateur, mauvais juge, un ingrat et conscience erronée et plusieurs autres termes injurieux qui se publient journellement contre l'autorité du Roy, en faisant un point de réprobation de la dite prétendue offense, un des principaux nous étant venu avertir que l'on nous pourrait faire fermer la porte des Eglises et nous empêcher de recevoir les Sᵗˢ Sacrements, si nous ne réparions la dite prétendue offense, ce qui nous donne un scrupule en l'âme; et de plus ne pouvant nous adresser pour nous en éclaircir qu'à des personnes qui se déclarent nos parties et qui jugent du fait sans en savoir la cause; mais n'y ayant rien de si important au monde que le salut et la fidélité que nous devons garder pour les intérêts du Roi que nous tenons inséparables l'un de l'autre, et reconnaissant qu'il n'y a rien de si certain que la mort et rien de si inconnu que l'heure, et que le temps est long pour informer Sa Majesté de ce qui se passe, pour en recevoir ses ordres, et qu'en attendant, une âme est toujours dans la crainte quoiqu'elle se connaisse dans l'innocence, nous sommes obligé avoir néanmoins recours aux Révérends Pères Casuistes de la maison de Jesus pour nous dire en leur conscience ce que nous pouvons pour la décharge de la nôtre et pour garder la fidélité que nous devons avoir pour le service du Roi, les priant qu'ils aient agréable signer ce qu'ils jugeront au bas de cet écrit, afin de nous servir de garantie vers sa Majesté.

Fait au Château de Quebec, ce dernier jour de Fevrier, 1664.

Mésy.

SECTION THIRD.

F.

MARRIAGE AND POPULATION.

Lettre de Colbert a Talon.

(*Extrait.*) *Archives de la Marine.*

Paris, 20 Fevrier, 1668.

Sa Majesté a fait une gratification de 1500 livres à Mr de Lamotte, 1er Capitaine au Régiment de Carignan-Salières, tant en considération du service qu'il rend en Canada, de la construction des forts et de ses expéditions qui ont été faites contre les Iroquois, que du mariage qu'il a contracté dans le pays, et de la résolution qu'il a prise de s'y habituer. Elle a ordonné de plus la somme de 6000 livres pour être distribuées aux officiers des mêmes troupes, ou qui s'y sont déjà mariés ou qui s'y marieront afin de leur donner des moyens de s'établir et de mieux s'affermir dans la pensée ou ils sont de ne pas revenir en France. Elle fait un autre fond de 12,000 livres pour être distribué aux soldats qui resteront aux pays et qui s'y marieront, autres que ceux des quatre compagnies qu'elle y laisse, ces derniers étant entretenus par le paiement de leur solde. . . . 1200 livres pour celui des meilleurs habitants qui a 15 enfants, et 800 livres pour l'autre qui en a dix. Elle a aussi gratifié M. l'Evêque de Pétrée d'une somme de 6000 livres pour continuer à l'assister pour soutenir sa dignité, fournir aux besoins de son Eglise et de son séminaire, et enfin 40,000 livres pour être employées à la levée de 150 hommes et de 50 filles depuis 16 jusqu'a 30 ans et non au dela ; outre 235 que la Compagnie y fait passer cette année, et qui devaient y être passées l'année dernière ; 12 Cavales, 2 étalons, 2 gros ânes de Mirbelais et 50 brebis ; à quoi l'on travaille dans les provinces du royaume, et l'on n'oublie rien pour l'embarquement partant de la Rochelle vers la fin du mois prochain.

. . . Je vous prie de bien faire considérér à tout le pays que leur bien, leur subsistance, et tout ce qui peut les regarder de plus près dépend d'une résolution publique à laquelle il ne soit jamais contrevenu de marier les garçons à 18 ou 19 ans, et les filles à 14 ou 15 ans ; que les oppositions de n'avoir pas suffisamment pour vivre doivent être rejetées, parceque dans ces pays et le Canada premièrement où tout le monde travaille, il se produit pour tous la subsistance et que l'abondance ne peut jamais leur venir que par l'abondance des hommes. . . . Il serait bon de rendre les charges et servitudes doubles à l'égard des garçons qui ne se marieraient point à cet age . . . et à l'egard de ceux qui sembleraient avoir absolument renoncé au mariage, il serait à propos de leur augmenter les charges, de les priver de tous honneurs, même d'y ajouter quelque marque d'infamie.

. . . Bien que le Royaume de France soit autant peuplé qu'aucun pays du monde, il est certain qu'il serait difficile d'entretenir de grandes armées et de faire passer en même temps de grandes Colonies dans les pays éloignés. . . . Il faut donc se réduire à tirer seulement chaque année avec précaution un nombre d'habitants de l'un et de l'autre sexe, pour les envoyer au Canada, et fonder principalement l'augmentation de la colonie sur l'augmentation des mariages, à mesure que le nombre des colons augmentera.

LETTRE DE TALON A COLBERT.

(*Extrait.*) *Archives de la Marine.*

10 Novembre, 1670.

... De toutes les filles venues cette année au nombre de 165, il n'en reste pas 30 à marier. Après que les soldats venus cette année auront travaillé à faire une habitation, il se porteront au mariage; pour quoi il serait bon qu'il plût à Sa Majesté d'envoyer encore 150 à 200 filles.

... Il serait bon de recommander que les filles destinées à ce pays ne soient nullement disgrâciées de la nature, qu'elles n'aient rien de rebuttant à l'extérieur; qu'elles soient saines et fortes pour le travail de campagne, ou du-moins qu'elles aient quelqu'industrie pour les ouvrages de main.

... Trois ou quatre filles de naissance et distinguées par la qualité serviraient peut-être utilement à lier par le mariage des officiers qui ne tiennent au pays que par les appointements et l'emolument de leurs terres, et qui par la disproportion des conditions ne s'engagent pas davantage. Si le Roi fait passer d'autres filles ou femmes veuves de l'Ancienne à la Nouvelle-France, il est bon de les faire accompagner d'un certificat de leur Curé ou du juge du lieu qui fasse connaître qu'elles sont libres et en état d'être mariées, sans quoi les Ecclésiastiques d'ici font difficulté de leur conférer ce sacrement; à la vérité ce n'est pas sans raison, 2 ou 3 doubles mariages s'étant reconnus ici; on pourrait prendre la même précaution pour les hommes veufs.

LETTRE DE TALON A COLBERT.

(*Extrait.*) *Archives de la Marine.*

2 Novembre, 1671.

... Le nombre des enfants nés cette année est de 6 à 700. ... J'estime qu'il n'est plus nécessaire de faire passer des demoiselles, en ayant reçu cette année quinze ainsi qualifiées au lieu de quatre que je demandais pour faire des alliances avec les officiers ou les principaux habitants d'ici. ...

G.

CHÂTEAU ST. LOUIS.

THIS structure, destined to be famous in Canadian history, was originally built by Samuel de Champlain. The cellar still remains, under the wooden platform of the present Durham Terrace. Behind the château was the area of the fort, now an open square. In the most famous epoch of its history, the time of Frontenac, the château was old and dilapidated, and the fort was in a sad condition. "The walls are all down," writes Frontenac in 1681; "there are neither gates nor guard-house; the whole place is open." On this the new intendant, Meules, was ordered to report what repairs were needed. Meanwhile La Barre had come to replace Frontenac, whose complaints he repeats. He says that the wall is in ruin for a distance of a hundred and eighty *toises*. "The workmen ask 6,000 francs to repair it. I could get it done in France for 2,000. The cost frightens me. I have done nothing." (*La Barre au Ministre,* 1682.) Meules, however, received orders to do what was necessary; and, two years later, he reports that he has rebuilt the wall, repaired the fort, and erected a building, intended at first for the council, within the area. This building stood near the entrance of the present St. Louis Street, and was enclosed by an extension of the fort wall.

Denonville next appears on the scene, with his usual disposition to fault-finding. The so-called château, he says (1685), is built of wood, "and is dry as a match. There is a place where with a bundle of straw it could be set on fire at any time; . . . some of the gates will not close; there is no watch-tower, and no place to shoot from." (*Denonville au Ministre*, 20 *Août*, 1685.)

When Frontenac resumed the government, he was much disturbed at the condition of the château, and begged for slate to cover the roof, as the rain was coming in everywhere. At the same time the intendant, Champigny, reports it to be rotten and ruinous. This was in the year made famous by the English attack and the dramatic scene in the hall of the old building, when Frontenac defied the envoy of Admiral Phipps, whose fleet lay in the river below. In the next summer, 1691, Frontenac again asks for slate to cover the roof, and for 15,000 or 20,000 francs to repair his mansion. In the next year the King promises to send him 12,000 francs, in instalments. Frontenac acknowledges the favor; and says that he will erect a new building, and try in the mean time not to be buried under the old one, as he expects to be every time the wind blows hard. (*Frontenac au Ministre*, 15 *Sept.*, 1692.) A misunderstanding with the intendant, who had control of the money, interrupted the work. Frontenac writes the next year that he had been obliged to send for carpenters, during the night, to prop up the château, lest he should be crushed under the ruins. The wall of the fort was however strengthened, and partly rebuilt to the height of sixteen feet, at a cost of 13,629 francs. It was a time of war, and a fresh attack was expected from the English. (*Frontenac et Champigny au Ministre,* 4 *Nov.*, 1693.) In the year 1854, the workmen employed in demolishing a part of this wall, adjoining the garden of the château, found a copper plate bearing an inscription in Latin as follows: " In the year of Redemption 1693, under the reign of the most august, most invincible, and most Christian King of France, Louis the Great, fourteenth of that name, the most excellent Louis de Buade, Count of Frontenac, governor for the second time of all New France, seeing that the rebellious inhabitants of New England, who three years ago were repulsed, routed, and completely vanquished by him when they besieged this town of Quebec, are threatening to renew the siege this very year, has caused to be built, at the expense of the king, this citadel, with the fortifications adjoining thereto, for the defence of the country, for the security of the people, and for confounding yet again that nation perfidious alike towards its God and its lawful king. And he [Frontenac] has placed here this first stone."

A year later, the rebuilding of the château was begun in earnest. Frontenac says that nothing but a miracle has saved him from being buried under its ruins; that he has pulled everything down, and begun again from the foundation, but that the money has given out. (*Frontenac au Ministre,* 4 *Nov.*, 1694.) Accordingly, he and the intendant sold six licenses for the fur trade; but at a rate unusually low, for they brought only 4,400 francs. The King, hearing of this, sent 6,000 more. Frontenac is profuse in thanks; and at the same time begs for another 6,000 francs, " to complete a work which is the ornament and beauty of the city " (1696). The minister sent 8,000 more, which was soon gone; and Frontenac drew on the royal treasurer for 5,047 in addition. The intendant complains of his extravagance, and says that he will have nothing but perfection; and that, besides the château, he has insisted on building two guard-houses, with Mansard roofs, at the two sides of the gate. "I must do as he says," adds the intendant, "or there will be a quarrel." (*Champigny au Ministre*, 13 *Oct.*, 1697.) In a letter written two days after, Frontenac speaks with great complacency of his château, and asks for another 6,000 francs to finish it. As the case was urgent, he sold six more licenses, at 1,000 francs each; but he died too soon to see the completion of his favorite work (1698). The new château was not finished before 1700, and even then it had no cistern. In a pen-sketch of Quebec on a manuscript map of 1699, preserved in the Dépôt des Cartes de la Marine, the new château is distinctly represented. In front is a gallery or balcony, resting on a wall and buttresses at the edge of the cliff. Above the gallery is a range of high windows along the face of the building, and over these a range of small windows and a Mansard roof. In the middle is a porch opening on the gallery; and on the left extends a battery, on the ground now occupied by a garden along the brink of the cliff. A water-color sketch of the château taken in 1804, from the land-side, by William Morrison, Jr., is in my possession. The building appears to have been completely remodelled in the interval. It is two stories in height; the Mansard roof is gone, and a row of attic windows surmounts the second story. In 1809 it was again remodelled, at a cost of ten thousand pounds sterling. A third story was added; and the building, resting on the buttresses which still remain under the balustrade of Durham Terrace, had an imposing effect when seen from the river. It was destroyed by fire in 1834.

H.

TRADE AND INDUSTRY.

(Extrait.) *Archives de la Marine.*

LETTRE DE DENONVILLE AU MINISTRE.

A QUEBEC LE 13 NOVEMBRE, 1685.

... J'ai remarqué, Monseigneur que les femmes et filles, y sont assez paresseuses par le manque de menus ouvrages à se donner, il y a un peu trop de luxe dans la pauvreté générale des demoiselles ou soi disantes; les menus ouvrages de capots et de chemises de traite les occupent un peu, pendant l'hiver, et leur font gagner quelque chose, mais cela ne dure pas, l'endroit de pauvreté de ce pays, est le manque de toiles et de serges ou draps, cependant c'est ici le pays du monde le plus propre à faire des chanvres, et du fil, et par consequent de la toille, si on s'en voulait donner la peine. Mr. Talon s'y est donné du soin pour cela, aussi y a-t-il une côte qui est celle de Beaupré, ou on en fait, mais ce n'est que chez quelques habitans. J'ai fort exorté la dessus tous les peuples d'y travailler, pour y réussir, il faut y apporter de la sévérité et de l'utilité si il y a moyen, ce dernier avec le temps et l'industrie arrivera, et le premier de ma part ne manquera pas, je n'ai pu avoir d'autre raison, pourquoi on ne faisait point de chanvres, si ce n'est que l'on n'avait pas assez de temps, à cause que les saisons de labourer, semer et recueillir sont trop courtes, car en ce pays le bled ne se sème qu'en Avril et May. Si le Roy voulait acheter les chanvres un peu plus cher jusques à ce que l'on fut en train, cela pourait les animer, avec un ordre à chacun d'en fournir une certaine quantité on pourra les faire agir, si outre cela on avait quelques ouvriers tisserands à distribuer par paroisses, et qui ne fussent à la charge du peuple que pour leurs nouritures, ce serait un moyen pour faire apprendre aux enfants. Les Curés nous rendraient compte du nombre de ceux qui apprendraient à préparer la chanvre et fillasse, et à faire de la toille ; avant que d'en venir là il faudrait montrer à filer aux filles et aux femmes, car il y en a très peu, qui sachent tenir le fuseau, c'est en cela que les filles de la congrégation de Montréal feront merveilles. Il nous est venu de la part de Mr. Arnoul deux bariques de graine de chanvre que je ferai distribuer et dont je me ferai rendre compte.

Je croyais, Monseigneur, une ordonnance necessaire encore à faire pour engager chaque habitant à avoir deux ou trois brebis, n'y en ayant pas suffisament dans le pays.

. . . Il n'est pas possible qu'on ne puisse faire une verrerie en ce pays, la plus grande affaire sont les ouvriers qui enchérissent tout car l'on donne ordinairement et communément à chaque ouvrier par jour quarente sols nouris, cinquante sols et un écu, et tous ces maraux n'en sont pas plus riches car ils mettent tout à boire.

(Signé)   LE M^{qris} DE DENONVILLE.

MÉMOIRE A MONSEIGNEUR LE MARQUIS DE SEIGNELAY, SUR L'ÉTABLISSEMENT DU COMMERCE EN CANADA, PRÉSENTÉ PAR LES SIEURS CHALONS ET RIVERIN.

(*Extrait.*)   *Archives de la Marine.*

(JOINT A LA LETTRE DU SIEUR DE RIVERIN, DU 7 FEVRIER, 1686.)

. . . En effet si cette colonie n'a pas avancé depuis le temps de son établissement, c'est que les habitants qui la composent ou par leur négligence ou par leur peu d'expérience dans les affaires, ou enfin par leur impuissance ne se sont pas mis en estat de se servir des avantages qu'elle renferme en elle-mesme et des moyens qu'elle leur fournit pour un commerce solide et considerable.

Car il ne faut pas regarder la traitte des pelleteries à laquelle seule on s'est attaché jusqu'à présent et qui finira avec le temps par la destruction des bestes, comme un moyen propre à son avancement, au contraire l'expérience a fait connoistre qu'elle rend les habitans fainéans et vagabonds, qu'elle les détourne de la culture des terres, de la pesche, de la navigation et des autres entreprises.

MÉMOIRE DU SIEUR DE CATALOGNE, INGÉNIEUR, SUR LES PLANS DES HABITATIONS ET SEIGNEURIES DES GOUVERNEMENS DE QUEBEC, DE MONTRÉAL ET DES TROIS-RIVIÈRES.

(*Extrait.*)[1] *Archives de la Marine.*

7 NOVEMBRE, 1712.

. . . .

Observations sur l'établissement. — Que par rapport à la grande étendue qu'on a donnée à l'établissement, il n'y a pas le quart des ouvriers qu'il faudroit pour bien étendre et cultiver les terres.

Que les laboureurs ne se donnent pas assez de soin pour cultiver les terres, étant certain que la semence d'un minot de blé, semé sur de la terre cultivée comme en France, produira plus que deux autres comme on sème en Canada.

Que comme les saisons sont trop courtes et souvent très mauvaises, il serait à souhaiter que l'Eglise permit les travaux indispensables, que les fêtes d'été obligent de chômer, étant très vrai que depuis le mois de Mai que les semences commencent jusques à la fin de Septembre, il n'y

---

[1] This *mémoire* is 70 pages in length.

a pas 90 journées de travail, par rapport aux fêtes et au mauvais temps. C'est pourtant dans cette espace que roule la solidité de cet établissement. Il faudrait assujetir les habitans négligens à travailler à la culture des terres, en les privant des voyages qui les dispensent de travailler, et cela parce qu'un voyage de deux ou trois mois leur produit 30 ou 40 escus en perdant la saison du travail à la terre, qui les fait demeurer en friche.

Les obliger de semer quantité de chanvre et lin qui vient en ce pays plus gros qu'en Europe. Ils s'en relâchent parceque, disent-ils, il y a trop de peine et de soins à le mettre en œuvre. Il est vrai qu'il y a peu de gens qui s'entendent et qui le font payer bien cher.

Assujetir les habitans à nourrir et à élever des bêtes à cornes, au lieu du grand nombre de chevaux qui ruinent le l'acage et qui entraînent les habitans à des grosses dépenses, tant que pour leurs équipages qui sont fort chers que par la grande quantité de fourages et de grains qu'il faut pendant 7 ou 8 mois de l'année, étant très vrai que l'entretien d'un cheval coûte autant que deux bœufs.

Obliger les Seigneurs pour faciliter l'établissement de leurs Seigneuries de donner suffisamment des terres pour commencer à un prix modique et à construire des moulins et les commodités publiques; plusieurs consomment le tiers de leur temps à aller faires leur farines à 15 ou 20 lieues, et que les Seigneurs, dès que les Seigneuries sont établies, concèdent des terres sans que les tenanciers soient obligés de payer des rentes qu'après 6 ans que les terres soient en valeur.

Ordonner au grand voyer de donner son application à faire établir les chemins et ponts nécessaires au public, qui est une nécessité fort essentielle.

Obliger les habitans ou ceux qui sont en état, de faire des greniers pourque chacun fût en état de conserver du grain pour deux années; cela fait une fois, l'abondance se trouvera toujours au Canada au lieu que la plupart, faute de cette commodité, en manquent très souvent, étant obligé de le vendre à vil prix.

Châtier sévérement tous ceux qui sont convaincus de fraude, mauvaise foi et imposture, qui est un mal qui commence à être bien en racine et qui indubitablement le privera de tout commerce, les marchands des îles et de Plaisance s'en étant déjà plaints.

Que comme il n'y a pas de notaires dans tous les lieux, que les conventions et les marchés faits en présence de deux témoins vaudront pendant un temps fixé.

Il serait à souhaiter que S. M. voulût établir dans chaque ville des conseils à juger sans frais sur le fait du commerce et des affaires qui n'entrent pas dans la coutume. Ces sortes de procédures aussi bien que les autres, ne prennent aucune fin que lorsque les parties n'ont plus d'argent pour plaider, qui est la ruine des familles.

Engager un certain nombre de gens du pays à étudier le pilotage, même les officiers des troupes, particulièrement du fleuve St. Laurent qui est très dangereux, la plupart du temps ne se trouvant pas un seul pilote en Canada, et cependant on commence à donner dans la construction; le capitaine du Port et M. Duplessis ayant mis un vaisseau de 3 à 400 tonneaux sur les chantiers.

Congédier de temps en temps des soldats en leur permettant de se marier, après qu'ils auront un établissement.

Il s'est établi une coutume dans ce pays autorisée par le magistrat, qui même ne me parait pas naturelle, de laisser des bestiaux à l'abandon qui la plupart gâtent les grains et les prairies, n'y ayant presque point de terres closes qui causent des contestes et de la mesintelligence entre les voisins; pour obvier à cela il faudrait qu'il y eut des gardiens pour chaque nature d'animaux pour les mener dans les communes, car tel qui n'a pas un pouce de terre, envoie ses animaux paître sur les terres de ses voisins, en disant que l'abandon est donné; si S. M. voulait couper la racine à une pépinière de procès et de mésintelligence entre les Seigneurs et habitans, il serait à souhaiter qu'elle voulut donner une ordonnance tendante à ce que les Seigneuries et autres concessions demeureraient dans les limites qu'elles se trouvent à présent, sans avoir égard aux titres portés dans les contrats, pour la quantité et les rumbs de vent qui y sont annoncés, étant à remarquer que les anciens Seigneurs et habitans se sont établis de bonne foi, que les terres ont été limitées par des arpenteurs peu intelligens, et aujourd'hui que la chicane est en vogue, chacun veut suivre les termes de son contrat qui tendent la plupart à l'impossible. Mr. Raudot a donné une ordonnance à ce sujet pour l'île de Montréal seulement.

Comme la plupart des rues de Quebec et de Montréal sont souvent impraticables, tant par les rochers que par les bourbiers, s'il plaisait à S. M. d'ordonner que les deniers qui proviennent des amendes et certaines confiscations seraient employés à les mettre en état.

Que la subordination du vassal à son Seigneur n'est point objet à   . Cette erreur vient qu'il a été accordé des Seigneuries à des roturiers qui non pas su maintenir le droit que la raison leur donne à l'égard de leur co-sujets, même les officiers de milice qui leur sont dépendants, n'ont la plupart aucun égard pour leur superiorité et veulent dans les occasions passer pour indépendants.

Il serait à souhaiter que S. M. voulût envoyer dans ce pays toute sorte d'artisans, particulièrement des ouvriers en cordages et filages, des potiers et un verrier, et ils trouveraient à s'occuper. Si S. M. voulait faire envoyer en marchandises une partie des appointemens de Messrs. les officiers, cela leur adoucirait la dureté qu'eux seuls trouvent dans le pays, par la grande cherté des marchandises causée par le mauvais retour de la monnaie de cartes qui fait acheter 3 et 4 pour 100.

  Veu : Vaudreuil.

  Veu : Bégon.   Catalogne.

I.

LETTER OF FATHER CARHEIL.

Lettre du Père Etienne de Carheil, de la Compagnie de Jésus, a l'Intendant de Champigny.

(*Extrait.*)[1] *Archives Nationales.*

A Michilimakina, le 30 d'Aoust, 1702.

... Nos Missions sont réduites à une telle extrémité, que nous ne pouvons plus les soutenir contre une multitude infinie de désordres, de brutalitez, de violences, d'injustices, d'impietez, d'impudicitez, d'insolences, de mépris, d'insultes que l'infâme et funeste traitte d'eau-de-vie y cause universellement dans toutes les nations d'icy haut, où l'on vient la faire, allant de villages en villages et courant les lacs avec une quantité prodigieuse de barils, sans garder aucune mesure. Si Sa Majesté avoit veu une seule fois ce qui se passe et icy et à Montréal, dans tous les temps qu'on y fait cette malheureuse traitte, je suis sur qu'elle ne balanceroit pas un moment, dès la première vue, à la déffendre pour jamais sous les plus rigoureuses peines.

Dans le désespoir où nous sommes, il ne nous reste point d'autre party à prendre que celui de quitter nos Missions et de les abandonner aux traittants d'eau-de-vie, pour y établir

[1] This letter is 15 pages long.

le domaine de leur traitte, de l'ivrognerie et de l'impureté. C'est ce que nous allons proposer à nos supérieurs en Canada et en France, y étant contraints par l'état d'inutilité et d'impuissance de faire aucun fruit où l'on nous a réduits par la permission de cette déplorable traitte, permission que l'on n'a obtenue de Sa Majesté que sous un pretexte aparent de raisons que l'on scait être fausses, permission qu'elle n'accorderoit point, si ceux auxquels elle se raporte de la vérité la lui fesoient connoistre comme ils la connoissent eux-mêmes et tout le Canada avec eux, permission enfin qui est le plus grand mal et le principe de tous les maux qui arrivent présentement au pays, et surtout des naufrages dont on n'entendoit point encore parler ici et que nous apprenons arriver maintenant presque touttes les années ou dans la venue ou dans le retour de nos vaisseaux en France, par une juste punition de Dieu qui fait périr par l'eau ce que l'on avoit mal acquis par l'eau-de-vie, ou qui entend empêcher le transport pour prévenir le mauvais usage qu'on en feroit. Si cette permission n'est révoquée par une déffense contraire, nous n'aurons plus que faire de demeurer dans aucune de nos Missions d'icy haut, pour y perdre le reste de notre vie, et touttes nos peines dans une pure inutilité sous l'empire d'une continuelle ivrognerie et d'une impureté universelle qu'on ne permet pas moins aux traitteurs d'eau-de-vie que la traitte même dont elle est l'accompagnement et la suite. Si Sa Majesté veut sauver nos missions et soutenir l'établissement de la Religion, comme nous ne doutons point qu'elle le veuille, nous la suplions très-humblement de croire, ce qui est très véritable, qu'il n'y a point d'autre moyen de le pouvoir faire que d'abolir les deux infâmes commerces qui les ont réduites à la nécessité prochaine de périr et qui ne tarderont pas à achever de les perdre, s'ils ne sont au plus tost abolis par ses ordres et mis hors d'état d'être rétablis. Le premier est le commerce de l'eau-de-vie; le second est le commerce des femmes sauvages avec les François, qui sont tous deux aussy publics l'un que l'autre, sans que nous puissions y remédier, pour n'estre pas appuyez des commandans qui, bien loin de les vouloir empêcher par les remontrances que nous leur faisons, les exercent eux-mêmes avec plus de liberté que leurs inférieurs, et les autorisent tellement par leur exemple qu'en le regardant on s'en fait une permission générale et une assurance d'impunité qui les rend communs à tout ce qui vient icy de François en traitte, de sorte que tous les villages de nos Sauvages ne sont plus que des cabarets pour l'ivrognerie et des Sodomes pour l'impureté, d'où il faut que nous nous retirions, les abandonnant à la juste colère de Dieu et à ses vengeances.

Vous voyez par là que, de quelque manière qu'on établisse le commerce François avec les Sauvages, si l'on veut nous retenir parmi eux, nous y conserver et nous y soutenir en qualité de missionnaires dans le libre exercice de nos fonctions avec espérance d'y faire du fruit, il faut nous délivrer des commandans et de leur garnisons qui, bien loin d'estre nécessaires, sont au contraire si pernicieuses que nous pouvons dire avec vérité qu'elles sont le plus grand mal de nos missions, ne servant qu'à nuire à la traitte ordinaire des voyageurs et à l'avancement de la Foy. Depuis qu'elles sont venues icy haut, nous n'y avons plus veu que corruption universelle qu'elles ont répandues par leur vie scandaleuse dans tous les esprits de ces nations qui en sont présentement infectées. Tout le service prétendu qu'on veut faire croire au Roy qu'elles rendent se réduit à quatre principales occupations dont nous vous prions instamment de vouloir bien informer le Roy.

La première est de tenir un cabaret public d'eau-de-vie où ils la traittent continuellement aux Sauvages qui ne cessent point de s'enyvrer, quelques opositions que nous y puissions faire. C'est en vain que nous leur parlons pour les arrêter; nous n'y gagnons rien que d'être accusez de nous oposer nous-mêmes au Service du Roy en voulant empêcher une traitte qui leur est permise.

La seconde occupation des soldats est d'estre envoyez d'un poste à l'autre par les Commandans, pour y porter leurs marchandises et leur eau-de-vie, après s'être accommodés ensemble, sans que les uns et les autres ayent d'autre soin que celuy de s'entr'ayder mutuellement dans leur commerce, et afin que cela s'exécute plus facilement des deux costez comme ils le souhaitent, ils faut que les commandans se ferment les yeux pour user de connivence et ne voir aucun des désordres de leur soldats, quelques visibles, publics et scandaleux qu'ils soient, et il faut réciproquement que les soldats, outre qu'ils traittent leurs propres marchandises, se fassent encore les traitteurs de celles de leurs Commandans qui souvent même les obligent d'en acheter d'eux pour leur permettre d'aller où ils veulent.

Leur troisième occupation est de faire de leur fort un lieu que j'ay honte d'apeler par son nom, où les femmes ont apris que leurs corps pouvoient tenir lieu de marchandises et qu'elles seroient mieux reçues que le castor, de sorte que c'est présentement le commerce le plus ordinaire, le plus continuel et le plus en vogue. Quelques efforts que puissent faire tous les missionnaires pour décrier et pour l'abolir, au lieu de diminuer, il augmente et se multiplie tous les jours de plus en plus; tous les soldats tiennent table ouverte à touttes les femmes de leur connaissance dans leur maison; depuis le matin jusqu'au soir, elles y passent les journées entières, les unes après les autres, assises à leur feu et souvent sur leur lit dans des entretiens et des actions propre de leur commerce qui ne s'achève ordinairement que la nuit, la foule étant trop grande pendant la journée pour qu'ils puissent l'achever, quoyque souvent aussy ils s'entrelaissent une maison vide de monde pour n'en pas différer l'achêvement jusqu'à la nuit.

La quatrième occupation des soldats est celle du jeu qui a lieu dans les tems où les traitteurs se rassemblent; il y va quelquefois à un tel point que n'étans pas contens d'y passer le jour, ils y passent encore la nuit entière, et il n'arrive même que trop souvent dans l'ardeur de l'aplication qu'ils ne se souviennent pas, ou s'ils s'en souviennent, qu'ils méprisent de garder les postes. Mais ce qui augmente en cela leur désordre, c'est qu'un attachement si opiniâtre au jeu n'est presque jamais sans une ivrognerie commune à tous les joueurs, et que l'ivrognerie est presque toujours suivie de querelles qui s'excitent entre eux lesquelles venant à paroître publiquement aux yeux des Sauvages, causent parmi eux trois grands scandales: le premier de les voir ivres, le second de les voir s'entrebatre avec fureur les uns contre les autres jusqu'à prendre des fusils en main pour s'entretuer, le troisième de voir que les Missionnaires n'y peuvent apporter aucun remède.

Voila, Monseigneur, les quatre seules ocupations des garnisons que l'on a tenues ici pendant tant d'années. Si ces sortes d'ocupations peuvent s'apeler le service du Roy, j'avoue qu'elles luy ont actuellement et toujours rendu quelqu'un de ces quatre services, mais je n'en ai point veu d'autres que ces quatre-là; et par conséquent, si on ne juge pas que ce soit là des services nécessaires au Roy, il n'y a point eu jusqu'à présent de nécessité de les tenir icy, et après leur rapel, il n'y en aura point de les y rétablir.

Cependant comme cette nécessité prétendue des Garnisons est l'unique pretexte que l'on prend pour y envoyer des Commandans, nous vous prions, Monseigneur, d'être bien persuadé de la fausseté de ce prétexte, afin que, sous ces spécieuses aparences du service du Roy, on ne se fasse pas une obligation d'en envoyer, puisque les Commandans ne viennent icy que pour y faire la traitte de concert avec leurs soldats sans se mettre en peine de tout le reste. Ils n'ont de liaison avec les Missionnaires que par les endroits où ils les croient utiles pour leur temporel, et hors de là ils leur sont contraires dès qu'ils veulent s'opposer au désordre qui, ne s'accordant ny avec le service de Dieu ny avec le service du Roy, ne laisse pas d'être avantageux à leur commerce, au quel il n'est rien qu'ils ne sacrifient. C'est là l'unique cause qui a mis le déréglement dans nos Missions, et qui les a tellement désolées par l'ascendant que les Commandans ont pris sur les Missionnaires en s'attirant toute l'autorité soit à l'égard des François, soit à l'égard des Sauvages, que nous n'avons pas d'autre pouvoir que celui d'y travailler inutilement sous leur domination qui s'est élevée jusqu'à nous pour nous faire des crimes civils et des accusations prétendues juridiques des propres fonctions de notre état et de notre devoir, comme l'a toujours fait Monsieur de la Motte qui ne voulait pas même que nous nous servissions du mot de désordre et qui intente en effet procez au père Pinet pour s'en être servi.

. . . Vous voyez, Monseigneur, que je me suis beaucoup étendu sur les articles des Commandans et des garnisons pour vous faire comprendre que c'est là qu'est venu tout le malheur de nos Missions. Ce sont les Commandans, ce sont les garnisons, qui, se joignant avec les traitteurs d'eau-de-vie les ont entièrement désolées par l'ivrognerie et par une impudicité presque universelle que l'on y a établie par une continuelle impunité de l'une et de l'autre, que les puissances civiles ne tolèrent pas seulement, mais qu'elles permettent, puisque les pouvant empêcher, elles ne les empêchent pas. Je ne crains donc point de vous déclarer que si l'on remet icy haut dans nos missions des Commandans traitteurs et des garnisons de soldats traitteurs, nous ne doutons point que nous ne soyons contraints de les quitter, n'y pouvant rien faire pour le salut des âmes. C'est à vous d'informer Sa Majesté de l'extrémité où l'on nous réduit et de luy demander pour nous notre délivrance, afin que nous puissions travailler à l'établissement de la Religion sans ces empêchemens qui l'ont arrêté jusqu'à présent.

J.

THE GOVERNMENT AND THE CLERGY.

Mémoire de Talon sur l'Etat présent du Canada, 1667.

(Extrait.) *Archives de la Marine.*

. . . L'ECCLÉSIASTIQUE est composé d'un Evesque, ayant le tiltre de Pétrée, In partibus infidelium, et se servant du caractère et de l'autorité de Vicaire Apostolique.

Il a soubs [*sous*] luy neuf Prestres, et plusieurs clercs qui vivent en communauté quand ils sont près de lui dans son Séminaire, et séparément à la campagne quand ils y sont envoyez par voye de mission pour desservir les cures qui ne sont pas encore fondées. Il y a pareillement les Pères de la Compagnie de Jésus, au nombre de trente-cinq, la pluspart desquels sont employez aux Missions étrangères: ouvrage digne de leur zèle et de leur piété s'il est exempt du meslange de l'intérest dont on les dit susceptibles, par la traitte des pelleteries qu'on assure qu'ils font aux Sta8aks [*Outaouaks*], et au Cap de la Magdelaine; ce que je ne sçay pas de science certaine.

La vie de ces Ecclésiastiques, par tout ce qui paroist au dehors, est fort réglée, et peut servir de bon exemple et d'un bon modèle aux séculiers qui la peuvent imiter; mais comme ceux qui composent cette Colonie ne sont pas tous d'esgale force, ny de vertu pareille, ou n'ont pas tous les mesmes dispositions au bien, quelques-uns tombent aysément dans leur disgrâce pour ne pas se conformer à leur manière de vivre, ne pas suivre tous leurs sentimens, et ne s'abandonner pas à leur conduite qu'ils estendent jusques sur le temporel, empiétant mesme sur la police extérieure qui regarde le seul magistrat.

On a lieu de soupçonner que la pratique dans laquelle ils sont, qui n'est pas bien conforme à celle des Ecclésiastiques de l'Ancienne France, a pour but de partager l'autorité temporelle qui, jusques au temps de l'arrivée des troupes du Roy en Canada, résidoit principalement en leur personnes.

À ce mal qui va jusques à géhenner [*gêner*] et contraindre les consciences, et par là desgoûter les colons les plus attachez au pays, on peut donner pour remède l'ordre de balancer avec adresse et modération cette autorité par celle qui réside ez [*dans les*] personnes envoyées par Sa Majesté pour le Gouvernement: ce qui a desjà été pratiqué; de permettre de renvoyer un ou deux Ecclésiastiques de ceux qui reconnoissent moins cette autorité temporelle, et qui troublent le plus par leur conduite le repos de la Colonie, et introduire quatre Ecclésiastiques entre les séculiers ou les réguliers, les faisant bien autoriser pour l'administration des Sacremens, sans qu'ils puissent estre inquiétez: autrement ils deviendroient inutiles au pays, parce que s'ils ne se conformoient pas à la pratique de ceux qui y sont aujourd'huy M. l'Evesque leur deffendroit d'administrer les Sacremens.

Pour estre mieux informé de cette conduite des consciences, on peut entendre Monsieur Dubois, Aumosnier au régiment de Carignan, qui a ouy plusieurs Confessions en secret, et a la desrobée, et Monsieur de Bretonvilliers sur ce qu'il a appris par les Ecclésiastiques de son Séminaire establi à Mont-Réal.

Lettre du Ministre a Mr. Talon, 20 Fevrier, 1668.

(*Extrait.*)   *Archives de la Marine.*

. . . Il faut que l'application d'un Gouverneur et d'un Intendant aide a adoucir le mal, et non à l'effet que le Gouverneur ne se porte à aucune extrémité, contre les Sieurs Evêque et les P. P. Jésuites, quand bien même ils auraient abusé du pouvoir que leur habit et le respect qu'on a naturellement pour la religion leur donne. En se contentant par des conférences particulières de resserrer ce pouvoir, autant que se pourra, dans les bornes d'une légitime autorité et espérant que, quand le pays sera plus peuplé, qui est la seule et unique chose que doit convier le dit Sr. Gouverneur et Intendant à y donner leurs soins quand à présent, l'autorité Royale qui sera la plus reconnue des peuples prévaudra sur l'autre et la contiendra dans de justes limites.

. . . Je ne m'explique point avec vous sur ce sujet, parceque je sais qu'à part ses bonnes qualités il [*M. de Courcelle*] a usé d'emportement dont il est bon qu'il se corrige. Insinuez lui aussi honnêtement les sentiments qu'il doit avoir et ce que je viens de vous dire au sujet du Sieur de Ressan, et qu'il ne doit jamais blâmer la conduite de l'Evêque de Pétrée ni des Jésuites en public, étant assez d'en user avec eux avec grande circonspection, se contentant seulement lorsqu'ils entreprendront trop de leur faire connaître et d'en envoyer des mémoires, afin que je confère avec leurs Supérieurs de ces entreprises et en cas qu'ils en fassent qu'on puisse les interdire.

INSTRUCTION POUR M. DE BOUTEROUE, 1668.

(Extrait.)   Archives de la Marine.

Il faut empescher autant qu'il se pourra la trop grande quantité des prestres, religieux, et religieuses . . . s'entremettre quelquefois et dans les occasions pour les porter à adoucir cette trop grande sévérité, estant très-important que lesdits evesque et Jésuites ne s'aperçoivent jamais qu'il veuille blasmer leur conduite.

(Signé)   COLBERT.

For the instructions on this subject, more precise and emphatic than the above, given by the King to Talon in 1665, see N. Y. Colonial Docs., ix. 24.

LETTRE DE COLBERT A DUCHESNEAU, 15 AVRIL, 1676.

(Extrait.)   Archives de la Marine.

Eviter les contestations . . . sans toutefois préjudicier aux précautions qui sont à prendre et aux mesures à garder pour empescher que la puissance ecclésiastique n'entreprenne rien sur la temporelle, à quoy les ecclésiastiques sont assez portés.

LETTRE DU MINISTRE A DUCHESNEAU, LE 28 AVRIL, 1677.

(Extrait.)   Archives de la Marine.

. . . Je vous dirai premièrement que Sa Majesté est bien persuadée de la piété de tous les Ecclésiastiques et de leurs bonnes intentions pour le succez du sujet de leurs missions, mais Sa Majesté veut que vous preniez garde qu'ils n'entreprennent rien tant sur son authorité Royalle que sur la justice et police du pays et que vous les resserriez précisement dans les bornes de l'authorité que les Ecclésiastiques ont dans le Royaume, sans souffrir qu'ils les passent en quelque sorte et manière que ce soit, et cette maxime généralle vous doit servir pour toutes les difficultez de cette nature qui pourront survenir; mais pour parvenir à ce point il seroit nécessaire que vous-mesme vous travailliassiez à vous rendre habil sur ces matières en lisant les autheurs qui en ont traitté, observer tout ce qui se passe et à envoyer tous les ans des mémoires sur les difficultez que vous aurez et auxquelles vous n'aurez pas pu remédier; considerez cette matière comme très importante et à laquelle vous ne sçauriez donner trop d'application.

Lettre du Ministre a Duchesneau, le premier May, 1677.

(*Extrait.*) *Archives de la Marine.*

... Je suis encore obligé de vous dire que l'on voit clairement qu'encore que le dit Sieur Evesque soit un homme de bien et qu'il fasse fort bien son devoir, il ne laisse pas d'affecter une domination qui passe de beaucoup au delà des bornes que les Evesques ont dans tout le monde chrestien et particulièrement dans le Royaume et ainsy vous devez vous appliquer à bien connoistre et à sçavoir le plus parfaitement que vous pourrez l'estendue du pouvoir des Evesques et les remèdes que l'authorité Royalle a apporté pour en empescher l'abus et leur trop grande domination, afin que vous puissiez de concert avec Monsieur le Comte de Frontenac dans les occasions importantes y apporter les mesmes remèdes, en quoy vous devez toujours agir avec beaucoup de modération et de retenue. . . . Comme je vois que Monsieur l'Evesque de Quebec, ainsi que je viens de vous dire affecte une authorité un peu trop indépendante de l'authorité Royalle et que par cette raison il seroit peut-estre bon qu'il n'eust pas de seance dans le conseil, vous devez bien examiner toutes les occasions et tous les moyens que l'on pourrait pratiquer, pour luy donner à luy-mesme l'envie de n'y plus venir; mais vous devez en cela vous conduire avec beaucoup de retenue, et bien prendre garde que qui ce soit ne descouvre ce que je vous escris sur ce point.

Mémoire du Roi aux Sieurs de Frontenac et de Champigny, Année 1692.

(*Extrait.*) *Archives de la Marine.*

. . . Sa Majesté veut aussy qu'ils [*Frontenac et Champigny*] assistent de leur authorité les Jesuites et les Récolets et tous autres Ecclésiastiques sans néantmoins souffrir qu'ils portent l'autorité ecclésiastique plus loin qu'elle ne doit s'estendre. Elle ne veut pas qu'ils se dispensent de faire doucement et avec toute la discrétion possible des remonstrances au dit Sieur Evesque dans les occasions où ils reconnoistront que les Ecclésiastiques agissent par un zèle immodéré ou par d'autres passions, afin de l'engager à y remédier et à faire tout ce qui dépend avec lui pour procurer le repos des consciences. Les dits Sieurs de Frontenac et de Champigny doivent se tenir en cela dans les voyes de la seule excitation et informer sa Majesté de tout ce qui se passera à cet égard.

Lettre de Monsieur de la Mothe Cadillac.

(*Extrait.*) *Archives de la Marine.*

28 Septembre, 1694.

... La chose ne se passa pas ainsi qu'il l'a raconté dans cet article et le suivant; ceux qui savent l'histoire de ce temps là en parlent autrement et voicy le fait: Monsieur de Laval fit diverses tentatives à peu près comme celles qu'on void aujourd'huy dont le but a toujours été de prévaloir sur l'autorité du gouvernement; Monsieur de Tracy pour lors Vice-roy de ce pays, voyait tranquillement le désir de cette élévation, et comme c'estoit un homme dévot, il ne jugea pas à propos de prêter le colet à cette cohorte Ecclésiastique, dont la puissance étoit redoutable. Monsieur Talon dans cette conjoncture fit paroître une plus forte résolution et risqua pour l'intérest du Roy de perdre son crédit et sa fortune; il vid qu'il falloit étouffer cet orage dans son berceau et enfin par ses remontrances et par ses soins, il fit donner un arrêt favorable et tel qu'il se l'étoit proposé. Monsieur de Laval voyant alors qu'on l'avoit rengainé et qu'on l'avoit coupé à demi-vent, il creut suivant la politique de l'Eglise qu'il falloit attendre un temps plus favorable; ayant donc mis armes bas, on tacha de rajuster les affaires par l'entremise même de Monsieur de Tracy qui obtint de Monsieur Talon au jour de sa réconciliation que l'arrêt en question seroit rayé et batonné, non pas pour le désaprouver ou pour l'avoir trouvé contraire à toute bonne justice, comme le veut persuader le procureur général; mais afin que Monsieur de Laval ne fut pas reprochable de ses écarts et de ses injustes pretentions; ce fut une foiblesse à Monsieur Talon de s'être laissé vaincre par de telles soumissions.

... Il faut être ici pour voir les menées qui se font tous

les jours pour renverser le plan et les projets d'un Gouverneur. Il faut une tête aussi ferme et aussi plombée que celle de Monsieur le Comte pour se soutenir contres les ambusches que partout on lui dresse; s'il veut la paix cela suffit pour qu'on s'y oppose et qu'on crie que tout est perdu; s'il veut faire la guerre, on lui expose la ruine de la collonie. Il n'auroit pas tant d'affaires sur les bras, s'il n'avoit pas aboli un Hiericho qui etait une maison que Messieurs du Séminaire de Montreal avoient fait bâtir pour renfermer, disoient-ils, les filles de mauvaise vie. S'il avoit voulu leur permettre de prendre des soldats et leur donner des officiers pour aller dans les maisons arracher des femmes à minuit et couchées avec leurs maris, pour avoir été au bal ou en masque et les faire fesser jusques au sang dans ce Hiericho; s'il n'avait rien dit encore contre des Curés qui faisoient la ronde avec des soldats et qui obligeoient en esté les filles et les femmes à se renfermer à neuf heures chez elles, s'il avoit voulu déffendre de porter de la dentelle, s'il n'avoit rien dit sur ce qu'on refusoit la communion à des femmes de qualité pour avoir une fontange, s'il ne s'opposoit point encore aux excommunications qu'on jette à tort et à travers, aux scandales qui s'en suivent, s'il ne faisoit les officiers que par la voye des communautés, s'il vouloit déffendre le vin et l'eau de vie aux sauvages, s'il ne disoit mot sur le sujet des cures fixes et droits de patronage, si Monsieur le Comte estoit de ces avis-là, ce seroit assurément un homme sans pareil et il seroit bientôt sur la liste des plus grands saints, car on les canonise dans ce pais à bon marché.

K.

CANADIAN CURÉS. EDUCATION. DISCIPLINE.

LETTRE DU MARQUIS DE DENONVILLE AU MINISTRE.

(*Extrait.*)   *Archives de la Marine.*

A QUEBEC 15 NOVEMBRE, 1685.

... Vous me permettrez, Monseigneur, de vous demander la grâce de faire quelques réflexions sur les moyens d'occuper la jeunesse du pays, dans son bas âge, et dans l'âge le plus avancé, que je vous rende compte de mes pensées la dessus, puisque c'est une des choses la plus essentielle de la colonie.

Pour y parvenir, Monseigneur, le premier moyen à mon gré, est de multiplier le nombre des Curés, et de les rendre plus fixes et résidentaires, Mr. notre Evêque en est si convaincu par la connaissance qu'il a prise de son diocèse dans ses visites, et dans le voyage que nous avons fait ensemble, qu'il n'a point de plus grand empressement que de pouvoir contribuer à cet établissement qui serait un moyen sur, pour faire des écoles, auxquelles les curés s'occuperaient et ainsi accoutumeraient les enfans de bonne heure à s'assugétir et à s'occuper: Mais, Monseigneur, pour faire cet établissement utilement, il faudrait multiplier le nombre des curés jusques au nombre de cinquante et un. Le mémoire que je vous en envoye, vous fera assez bien voir, que si on les étend davantage et qu'il faille que les curés passent et repassent la rivière, comme ils font à présent pour faire leurs fonctions, ils employent avec bien du travail tout le temps qu'ils pourraient donner à instruire la jeunesse, si leurs cures étaient moins étendues. Outre cela, Monseigneur, à l'entrée et à la sortie de l'hiver, il y a près de deux mois que l'on ne saurait passer la rivière, qui en bien des endroits a une lieue de largeur, et beaucoup plus en d'autres. Si bien que dans ces temps il faut que les malades demeurent sans aucun secours spirituel.

C'est une pitié, Monseigneur, que de voir l'ignorance dans laquelle les peuples éloignés du séjour des Curés vivent en ce pays, et les peines que les missionnaires et Curés se donnent pour y remédier en parcourant leurs cures, sur le pied qu'elles sont selon le mémoire que je vous en envoye. Vous y verrez, Monseigneur, le chemin qu'il leur faut faire pour visiter leurs paroisses dans les rigueurs de l'hiver.

Puisque j'ai entamé l'affaire des Curés vous me permettrez d'achever de vous dire que pour la subsistance d'un curé selon les connaissances que j'ai pu prendre du pays, depuis que j'y suis, selon le prix des denrées, on ne saurait donner moins à un curé pour sa subsistance que quatre cents livres, monoye de France, attendu qu'il ne faut pas compter sur aucun revenant bon du dedans de l'Eglise. Il est bien vrai qu'il y a quelques cures qui sont mieux peuplées dont les dismes sont assez raisonables pour pouvoir suffir à leur entretien, mais il y en a très peu sur ce pied là.

J'ai trouvé ici dans le Séminaire de l'Evêché, le commencement de deux établissements qui seraient admirables pour la Colonie, si on les pouvait augmenter, ce sont, Monseigneur, deux maisons où l'on retire des enfans pour les instruire, dans l'une on y met ceux auxquels on trouve de la disposition pour les lettres, auxquelles on s'attache de les former pour l'Eglise, qui dans la suite peuvent rendre plus de service que les prêtres Français étants plus faits que les autres aux fatigues et aux manieres du pays.

Dans l'autre maison on y met ceux qui ne sont propres que pour être artisans, et à ceux là on apprends des métiers.

Je croirais que ce serait là un moyen admirable pour commencer un établissement de manufactures, qui sont absolument nécessaires pour le secours de ce pays.

Mr. notre Evêque est charmé de ces établissements, et voudrait bien être en état de les soutenir et augmenter. Mais comme tout cela ne se peut faire sans dépense tant pour l'augmentation du nombre des Curés que pour cette espèce de manufacture, et qu'il conviendrait d'en faire de grandes, pour y réussir, je ne vois qu'un moyen assuré pour cela, qui serait que le Roy voulut bien donner une grosse abbaye à Mr. notre Evêque sans l'attacher à l'Evêché, comme il n'a l'esprit et le cœur occupés que des soins de faire du bien aux pauvres et augmenter la foi et le salut des âmes, il est certain que Sa Majesté, aurait le plaisir de voir employer le revenu de ce bénéfice en bonnes et saintes œuvres, qui feraient merveille pour le bien de la colonie son soutien et son augmentation.

J'ai trouvé à Villemarie en l'isle de Montreal, un établissement de sœurs de la congrégation, sous la conduite de la sœur Bourgeois, qui fait de grands biens à toute la colonie, elles furent brulées l'an passé où elles perdirent tout; il seroit fort nécessaire qu'elles se rétablissent, elles n'ont pas le premier sol, j'y ai trouvé un autre établissement de filles de la providence qui travaillent ensemble, elles pourront commencer quelque manfacture de ce côté là, si vous avez la bonté de continuer la gratification de mil livres pour les laines, et mil livres pour apprendre à tricoter. Il y a encore un troisième établissement pour faire des maîtres d'écoles.

Il faut revenir s'il vous plait, Monseigneur, à voir ce qui se peut faire pour dissipliner les grands garçons, et pour donner de l'occupation aux enfans des gentilshommes et autres soi-disans et vivans comme tels.

Avant tout, Monseigneur, vous me permettrez de vous

dire que la noblesse de ce pays nouveau, est tout ce qu'il y a de plus gueux et que d'en augmenter le nombre est augmenter le nombre des fainéants. Un pays neuf demande des gens laborieux et industrieux, et qui mettent la main à la hache et à la pioche. Les enfans de nos conseillers ne sont pas plus laborieux, et n'ont de ressource que les bois, où ils font quelque traite, et la plupart font tous les désordres dont j'ai eu l'honneur de vous entretenir, je ne m'oublierai en rien de ce qu'il y aurait à faire pour les engager à entrer dans le commerce, mais comme nos nobles et conseillers sont tous fort pauvres et accablés de debtes, ils ne sauraient trouver de crédit pour un écu.

Le seul moyen qui me parait le plus assuré pour discipliner cette jeunesse serait que le Roy voulut bien entretenir en ce pays, quelques compagnies, dont on donnerait le commandement à gens d'authorité et de bonnes mœurs et appliqués, comme à Mr. le Chevalier de Caillière, a Mr. de Varénes, Gouverneur des trois Rivières, ou au Sr. Prévot, Major de Quebec, avec des Lieutenants du pays que l'on choisirait, lesquels ne devraient point avoir peine d'obeir, a ceux auxquels naturellement ils doivent obéir.

INDEX.

INDEX.

ABENAKI Indians, the, at Port Royal, i. 13; ii. 118.

Absolutism, in Canada, ii. 78, 197-204.

Acadia, quarrel between England and France over, i. 3; the French keep a feeble hold on, i. 5; Charles de la Tour applies for a commission to command in, i. 5; French settlements transferred by conquest to England, i. 8; restored to France by the treaty of St. Germain, i. 8; France and the company of New France in sole possession of, i. 8; D'Aunay succeeds Razilly in command in, i. 9; inexact assertion of Charlevoix concerning division of, i. 14; invaded by the Plymouth traders, i. 15; i. 50; Le Borgne gets a lion's share of, i. 52; conquered for England by Major Robert Sedgwick, i. 52; restored to France by the treaty of Breda, i. 52; recaptured by Sir William Phips, i. 52; again restored to France by the treaty of Ryswick, i. 52; finally seized for England by General Nicholson, i. 52; Talon tries to open a road to, ii. 9; ii. 59, 119.

Adirondacks, the, i. 248.

Africa, i. 234, 235.

Agariata, Chief, i. 252.

Ailleboust, the family of, ii. 55.

Ailleboust, D', succeeds Charny as governor of Quebec, i. 88; his dealings with the Iroquois, i. 88; insanely pious, i. 165, 166, 167; Argenson complains of, i. 176; ii. 129, 165.

Ailleboust, Madame d', i. 106, 144; fantastic devotion of, ii. 157.

Aix, i. 156.

Albanel, Father Charles, the Jesuit, at the Fort of St. Louis, i. 250; penetrates to Hudson's Bay, ii. 9; ii. 130.

Albany, i. 113, 188, 249.

Alexander, Sir William, grant made by James I. to, i. 4; attacks Charles de la Tour at Fort Loméron, i. 5; makes Claude de la Tour a baronet of Nova Scotia, i. 6; sends Claude de la Tour to Cape Sable, i. 6; makes the La Tours baronets of Nova Scotia, i. 7; grants Charles de la Tour land near Cape Sable, i. 7; jealous of the company of New France, i. 7; fits out a private expedition under the brothers Kirke, i. 7; succeeds in transferring by conquest the French settlements in Acadia and Canada to England, i. 7; gives up Port Royal to Razilly, i. 8; i. 9.

264 INDEX.

Algonquins, French, i. 124.
Algonquin Indians, the, i. 68, 88, 126, 134.
Algonquin missions, the, ii. 119.
Allen's River, i. 12.
Allet, Father, the Sulpitian, i. 95, 141, 156; on the Jesuits at Quebec, ii. 152.
Almshouses, established in Canada, ii. 182.
Amazon River, the, i. 234.
American Revolution, the, i. 164.
Amours, D', Matthieu, the councillor, i. 195, 213; ii. 57.
Amours, D' (son), ii. 73.
Andaraqué, largest and strongest of the Mohawk forts, i. 257; taken by the French, i. 257; description of, i. 258.
André, Père, tries to seduce La Tour's men, i. 38; ii. 208.
Angoville, Major d', i. 208, 217; ii. 224.
Annahotaha, Etienne, i. 130; offers to reinforce Daulac, i. 131; at the Long Saut, i. 131-133; deserts Daulac, i. 134, 138.
Annapolis River, the, i. 11, 12, 48.
Anne of Austria, i. 144, 220, 230.
Anne, St., shrine of, ii. 165; Canadian devotion to, ii. 165.
Anticosti, the island of, ii. 93.
Antilles, the, i. 234, 235.
Antinomianism, the ghastly spectre of, i. 25.
Aoutarisati, the Iroquois Chief, i. 58.
Arabia, i. 166.
Argall, lawless inroads of, i. 4.
Argenson, Vicomte d', i. 105; becomes governor of the colony, i. 120; his efforts to save the colony, i. 121; on the desertion of Daulac by the Hurons, i. 138; i. 144, 155, 157, 158; characteristics of, i. 166; Laval quarrels with, i. 166, 167; his memorial to the council of State, i. 169; his reception by the Jesuits, i. 173; difficulties of, i. 174; the company of New France refuses aid to, i. 175; annoyed by the virtual independence of Montreal, i. 175; complains of Ailleboust, i. 176; his troubles, i. 177; resigns his position in disgust, i. 177; Laval urges the removal of, i. 178; his opinion of Villeray, i. 196; i. 203.
Argenson, D' (brother of the governor), i. 170, 178; correspondence between Laval and, ii. 217-220.
Argentau, town of, i. 150.
Arnoul, M., ii. 237.
Arts of ornament, the, in Canada, ii. 98.
Associates of Montreal, the, see *Montreal, the Association of*.
Aubert, Barthelemy, ii. 211.
Aubert, Felix, i. 217.
Austrian War, the, i. 242.
Auteuil, Ruette d', appointed councillor at Quebec, i. 195; removed from the council by Mézy, i. 208; i. 213.
Auteuil, D' (son), ii. 73.
Avangour, Baron Dubois d' takes Argenson's place, i. 178; description of, i. 178; his reception, i. 179; wished to be on good terms with the Jesuits, i. 179; the brandy quarrel, i. 180; Laval urges the removal of, i. 182; summoned home, i. 187; his memorial to Colbert, i. 187; death of, i. 188; i. 193.

Bagot, the Jesuit, i. 145, 147.
Balls, in Canada, ii. 149.

INDEX.

Bardy, Father, ii. 134.
Baronies, ii. 50.
Basques, the, ii. 92.
Baston, the merchant, ii. 174, 175.
Bayeux, the Bishop of, i. 148.
Beaufort, i. 230.
Beauharnois, Marquis de, ii. 49, 97, 169.
Beauport, Monsieur de, ii. 44.
Beauport, settlement of, census of, ii. 35, 43.
Beaupré, Laval's seigniory of, i. 224; ii. 34; census of, ii. 35; ii. 138; population of, ii. 139; ii. 164, 165, 176, 236.
Beaver-skins, serve as currency, ii. 98; effect produced by, ii. 119.
Beaver-trade, the, Canada dependent upon, i. 58; largeness of, i. 58; Oudiette granted monopoly in, ii. 102; ii. 107; a surfeit in, ii. 108; the West Indian Company given a monopoly in, ii. 109.
Becancour, the seigniory of, ii. 38.
Béchefer, the Jesuit, i. 251.
Bégon, the intendant, ii. 97, 242.
Belêtre, M., ii. 174, 175.
Belmont, the Sulpitian, on the desertion of Daulac by the Hurons, i. 138; on the struggle for the bishopric of Canada, i. 156; ii. 160.
Bernières, Sieur de, see *Louvigni, Bernières de.*
Bernon, ii. 90.
Berthelot, François, ii. 43, 60, 139.
Berthier, Captain, i. 243; ii. 37.
Biencourt, keeps a feeble hold on Acadia, i. 4, 5; takes the name of Poutrincourt, i. 5; at Fort Loméron, i. 5; La Tour becomes attached to the service of, i. 5; bequeaths his property to La Tour, i. 5.
Bienville, ii. 59.
Bigot, the intendant, ii. 78.
"Blue Coats" of Montreal, the, i. 247, 254.
Blue Hill in Milton, the, i. 23.
Bochart, Du Plessis, defeated and killed by the Mohawk Iroquois, i. 55.
Bochart, Magdeleine, ii. 184.
Bochart, Marie, ii. 24.
Boisdon, Jacques, ii. 36.
Boisdon, Jean, ii. 184.
Bologna, the Concordat of, i. 153; Canada excluded from, i. 154.
Bouchard, the surgeon of Montreal, i. 99.
Bousecours, the seigniory of, ii. 44.
Bossuet, i. 232.
Boston, site of, i. 4; La Tour sails for, i. 20; La Tour arrives in, i. 21; description of, i. 23; undesirable neighbors of, i. 23; antagonisms of the Pequot Indians, i. 23; dangers of the theological quarrels to, i. 24; training-day in, i. 26; Governor Winthrop allows La Tour to hire allies in, i. 28; Madame La Tour in, i. 36; D'Aunay sends envoys to, i. 41; ii. 94, 206.
Boucher, Father Pierre, curé of Point Levi, i. 189; ii. 18, 99, 187.
Boucherville, the seigniory of, ii. 38.
Boudrot, Michel, Lieutenant-General in Acadia, i. 13.
Bougainville, the famous navigator, ii. 138, 168; his view of the Canadians, ii. 192.
Boullé, ii. 43.
Bourbon, i. 229.

Bourbons, the, ii. 52.
Bourdon, Jean, appointed attorney-general at Quebec, i. 195, 196; early life of, i. 197; removed from the council by Mézy, i. 208; i. 213; banished to France, i. 214; ii. 222, 225.
Bourdon, Madame Jean, ii. 20.
Bourdon, Jean François, i. 173.
Bourgeoys, Marguerite, returns to Canada, i. 96; her labors at Montreal, i. 98; returns to France, i. 99; gains recruits in Troyes, i. 102; on the miracles at Montreal, i. 112; ii. 20.
Bourget, Bishop of Montreal, fiftieth anniversary of, i. 226.
Bourg la Reine, village of, ii. 33.
Bourg Royal, village of, ii. 33.
Bourg Talon, village of, ii. 33.
Bourse, the, established at Quebec, ii. 101.
Bouteroue, the intendant, ii. 26, 73, 136; Colbert's instructions regarding the government and the clergy in Canada, ii. 251.
Bradstreet, signs the "Ipswich Letter," i. 30; Governor Winthrop's reply to, i. 31; letter to Governor Winthrop, i. 31.
Brandy, love of the Indians for, i. 180; ii. 123; quarrel between Laval and Avaugour concerning, i. 180; a fiend with all crimes and miseries in his train, ii. 124; its sale necessary to the interests of the fur-trade, ii. 124; penalties for selling, ii. 125; question of its sale submitted to the fathers of the Sorbonne, ii. 126; the King's views concerning, ii. 127.
Brandy quarrel, the, i. 180; ii. 122–129.
Braun, Father, i. 226.

Brébeuf, Jean de, the Jesuit, i. 73, 226, 240.
Breda, the treaty of, restores Acadia to France, i. 52, 160.
Brésoles, Sister Judith de, i. 101; early life of, i. 106; made Superior at Montreal, i. 106, 109.
Bretonvilliers, M. de, ii. 249.
Brigeac, Claude de, i. 112; tortured to death by the Iroquois, i. 113.
British colonies, the, i. 4.
British conquest, the, ii. 161.
Brittany, ii. 13.
Bruyas, the Jesuit, ordered to the Oneidas, i. 266; takes the Mission of the Martyrs, ii. 116.
Bullion, Madame de, visited by Mlle. Mance, i. 100; designated as "the unknown benefactress," i. 100.

Cabots, the, discovery of North America by, i. 3.
Caen, i. 145; the zealots at, i. 147, 148, 149; i. 204; the Jacobin convent at, i. 205; i. 207; ii. 215, 216.
Cæsar, i. 153.
Caillière, Chevalier de, ii. 259.
Callières, ii. 169, 182.
Calvin, John, the extreme dogmas of, i. 24.
Canada, charter of the country and lordship of, i. 4; French settlements transferred by conquest to England, i. 8; restored to France by the treaty of St. Germain, i. 8; turned to fasting and penance, i. 54; the beaver her only sustenance, i. 58; the Iroquois wish for peace with, i. 66; writhes under the scourge of the Iroquois War, i. 118; still a mission, i. 120; domestic

quarrels in, i. 140; struggle for the bishopric of, i. 141-160; excluded from the Concordat of Bologna, i. 154; entering into a state of transition, i. 165; the chief sufferer from the monopoly of the Company of the West, i. 235; Louis XIV. has at heart the prosperity of, i. 236; an object of very considerable attention at court, i. 237; not to be wholly abandoned to a trading company, i. 239; little capital and little enterprise in, ii. 5; Talon sets himself to galvanize, ii. 5; concern of Colbert for the prosperity of, ii. 5; Talon's attempt to establish trade between the West Indies and, ii. 7; the peopling of, ii. 11; emigration to, ii. 13; young women sent to, ii. 15; premium placed on marriage, ii. 17; celibacy punished, ii. 23; bounties offered for children, ii. 23; satisfactory results, ii. 25; persists in attenuating herself, ii. 34; the settler of, ii. 31; the river settlements, ii. 37; feudalism of, ii. 40; Richelieu first plants feudalism in, ii. 41; not governed to the profit of a class, ii. 51; its condition in 1712, ii. 51; becomes infatuated with *noblesse*, ii. 53; the King the dispenser of charity for all, ii. 57; its government, ii. 62; the intendant, ii. 62; the Governor-General, ii. 63; the council, ii. 65; the King alone supreme in, ii. 65; inferior courts, ii. 67; the judge, ii. 68; the spirit of absolutism everywhere apparent in, ii. 78, 197-204; justice in, ii. 80-82; abuses, ii. 83; neglected, ii. 87; its organs of nutrition, ii. 88; its trade in fetters, ii. 89; appeals for help, ii. 95; manufactures of, ii. 97; ship-building in, ii. 98; condition of ornamental arts in, ii. 98; finances of, ii. 98; a coinage ordered for, ii. 99; a card currency issued, ii. 99; importance of the fur-trade to, ii. 102; the forest-trade, ii. 104; filled with distress and consternation, ii. 107; the *coureurs de bois*, ii. 109; the first ball in, ii. 149; clerical severity in, ii. 149; heresy scoured out of, ii. 155; never troubled by witches, ii. 157; threatened with an attack by the English, ii. 160; miracles in, ii. 161; education in, ii. 161; catches some of the French corruption, ii. 168; extreme poverty of, ii. 170; influence of the troops on, ii. 171; lawlessness in, ii. 171-177; drunkenness the most destructive vice in, ii. 180; swarms with beggars, ii. 181; slavery in, ii. 190; formation of character in, ii. 197; the very portal of the great interior wilderness, ii. 198; compared with New England, ii. 199-203; the Church of Rome stands out conspicuous in the history of, ii. 203; the English Conquest a happy calamity to, ii. 204; memorial of Dumesnil concerning the affairs of, ii. 222-224; marriage and population in, ii. 229-232; trade and industry in, ii. 236-242; the government and the clergy in, ii. 248-255.

"Canada, the River and Gulf of," i. 4.

Canadian Church, the, i. 103; its influence paramount and pervading, i. 120; i. 159; Laval the father of, i. 224; liberality of the King to, ii. 137; grows purer in the presence of Protestantism, ii. 204.

Canadian fisheries, the, see *Fisheries.*

Canadian government, the, ii. 62-82; essentially military, ii. 201.

Canadian *noblesse*, ii. 51.

Canadian settler, the, ii. 31.

Canadians, the, strength of, ii. 181; views of different writers on, ii. 191.

Capet, Hugh, i. 229; ii. 40.

Cap Rouge, i. 56, 59; ii. 37.

Capuchin Friars, the, at Port Royal, i. 13; supported by Richelieu, i. 13; the missions of, ii. 119.

Capucins, the, ii. 207, 208, 210, 211.

Card currency, in Canada, ii. 99; loses its value, ii. 100; converted into bills of exchange, ii. 100.

Carheil, Father Etienne, his letter to Champigny, ii. 115, 242-248; takes the mission of Saint Joseph, ii. 116; in despair over the Jesuit missions, ii. 119; his severe condemnation of the *coureurs de bois*, ii. 121; his suggestions concerning the government of Canada, ii. 122.

Carignan, the Prince of, i. 242.

Carignan-Salières, the regiment of, i. 237, 240, 241; history of, i. 242; ordered back to France. ii. 14; ii. 28, 29, 53, 229, 249.

Carillon, i. 131.

Carion, Lieutenant, attacks on Lormeau, ii. 173, 174.

Carleton, supposed site of Fort La Tour at, i. 39.

Casgrain, Abbé, ii. 36, 93; on the shrine at the Petit Cap, ii. 166.

Casson, Dollier de, i. 94, 104; on the miracles at Montreal, i. 111, 112; on the death of Major Closse, i. 114; on the year of disaster at Montreal, i. 115; on the principal fault of Frenchmen, i. 130; on the desertion of Daulac by the Hurons, i. 138; on Courcelle's "Blue Coats," i. 247; great strength of, i. 254; sent to St. Anne, i. 261; description of, i. 263; at Fort St. Anne, i. 264; on the policy of Talon, ii. 9; on the frenzy for marriage in Canada, ii. 23; on the advantages of the Canadian climate for women, ii. 25; at Montreal, ii. 174; on the outlaw of Montreal, ii. 175.

Castine, i. 15.

"Castle," the, i. 45.

Catalogne, the engineer, ii. 95, 96, 98, 177; his memorial, ii. 238-242.

Catholics, the, of France, divided by two great parties, i. 153; Laval an object of veneration to, i. 163.

Caughnawaga, Jesuit mission at, ii. 118.

Cayenne, i. 234.

Cayuga Indians, the, i. 57, 66; at Onondaga, i. 82; the Jesuits among, i. 84; send an embassy to Quebec, i. 245; sue for peace, i. 266; Carheil among, ii. 116.

Celibacy, punishment of, ii. 23.

Censitaire, the, ii. 46, 77, 79.

Certain, André, his official report on La Tour and D'Aunay, ii. 205-211.

INDEX.

Chalons, Sieur, ii. 92; memorial presented by, on the establishment of commerce in Canada, ii. 94, 237, 238.

Chambly, the chief proprietor on the Richelieu, ii. 30.

Chambly, Fort of, i. 250, 262.

Chambly, Rapids of, i. 244, 245, 247.

Chambly, town of, ii. 28, 30.

Champagne, Philippe de, i. 230.

Champigny, the intendant, on the Canadian nobility, ii. 55, 56; ii. 93, 95, 96; letter from Father Carheil to, ii. 115, 242–248; ii. 122, 169, 179, 182, 183; on Château St. Louis, ii. 233–235; his memorial to the King, ii. 253.

Champlain, Lake, i. 244, 248, 253, 260, 262.

Champlain, Samuel de, on the political influence of women among the Indians, i. 85; his earnestness in converting the Indians, i. 165; builds Château St. Louis, ii. 232.

Charbonnier, Marie Magdeleine, ii. 23.

Charlemagne, the Capitularies of, ii. 49.

Charles I., ii. 80.

Charlestown, i. 45, 52.

Charlevoix, Father, inexact assertion concerning division of Acadia, i. 14; on the Medicine Feast, i. 94; on the brandy quarrel, i. 182; on the earthquake at Quebec, i. 184; on the copper-mines of Lake Superior, ii. 7; on the early colonists of Canada, ii. 13; in Canada, ii. 168; his letter to the Duchesse de Lesdiguières, ii. 194.

Charnisay, Charles de Menou d'Aunay, in Razilly's company, i. 8; succeeds Razilly in command in Acadia, i. 9; dissensions with La Tour, i. 9; his position and qualities compared with La Tour, i. 9; his reign at Port Royal, i. 11; returns to France, i. 11; marries Jeanne Molin, i. 11; his life at Port Royal, i. 11–13; on good terms with the Indians, i. 12; reduced financial condition of, i. 13; bitter enmity for La Tour, i. 14; his feud with La Tour, i. 14, 15; attacks the Plymouth trading station at Penobscot, i. 15; La Tour plots against, i. 16; battle with La Tour, i. 17; takes La Tour prisoner, i. 17; releases La Tour, i. 17; ordered to seize La Tour's forts, i. 18; returns to France, i. 18; endeavors to seize La Tour, i. 19, 20; La Tour asks Governor Winthrop for aid against, i. 22, 27, 28; La Tour hires allies against, i. 28, 30; flees from La Tour and his allies, i. 32; letter from the Massachusetts magistrates to, i. 33; ordered by the King to keep peace with the Puritans, i. 33; makes overtures of friendship to the Puritans, i. 33; joined by the Récollet friars, i. 38; attacks and captures Fort St. Jean, i. 39; captures Madame La Tour, i. 40; his treatment of his prisoners, i. 40; sends envoys to the Puritans, i. 41; their reception in Boston, i. 41; makes a treaty with D'Aunay, i. 43, 44; royal favors to, i. 46; his hopes, i. 47; his death, i. 48; tribute to his character, i. 48, 49; his children, i. 52; no trace of his blood left in the land, i. 53; official report of André Certain on La Tour and, ii. 205-211.

Charnisay, Madame Charles de Menou d'Aunay, see *Molin, Jeanne*.

Charnisay, Joseph de Menou d'Aunay, i. 47.

Charny, son and successor of Lauson, i. 86; weakness of his character, i. 86; resigns the government and becomes a priest, i. 88.

Charron, chosen alderman of Quebec, i. 212.

Chartier, Sieur de, appointed attorney-general by Mézy, i. 212.

Chasy, nephew of Tracy, i. 251; murder of, i. 252.

Châtelain, Father, at Quebec, ii. 152; his episode with Courcelle, ii. 152, 153.

Châtel, Sister, i. 102.

Chaulmer, on the French colony among the Onondagas, i. 75.

Chaumonot, sent among the Onondagas, i. 69; arrival at Onondaga, i. 70; harangues the Indians, i. 71, 82; at Onondaga, i. 79, 80; sets out for the Cayugas, i. 84; on the Seneca mission, i. 94; on the Jesuits' belief in torture, i. 127; on the desertion of Daulac by the Hurons, i. 137.

Chaumont, Chevalier de, i. 238, 254.

Cheruel, on Colbert, i. 233; ii. 65, 87.

Children, bounties offered on, ii. 24.

Choisy, Abbé de, i. 230.

Chomedey, Paul de, see *Maisonneuve, Chomedey de*.

Clément, on Colbert, i. 233, 236;

on the paupers of Paris, ii. 19; on the premium on marriage in Canada, ii. 22.

Closse, Major, killed by the Iroquois, i. 114.

Colbert, Jean Baptiste, the true antagonist of Laval, i. 165; his opinion of Avaugour, i. 179; Avaugour's memorial to, i. 187; i. 197; Dumesnil reports his grievances to, i. 200; on the mutual accusations of Laval, Mézy, and the Jesuits, i. 217; the intendant of Mazarin's household, i. 232; reforms of, i. 233; defects in his policy, i. 233; Talon a true disciple of, ii. 4; his concern for the prosperity of Canada, ii. 5; reluctantly recalls Talon, ii. 10; peoples Canada, ii. 11, 18, places a premium on marriage in Canada, ii. 22; offers a bounty on children in Canada, ii. 25; satisfactory results, ii. 25; his letters to Duchesneau, ii. 75; report on the brandy question to, ii. 125, 126; orders Courcelle to be kept within bounds, ii. 133; his letter to Courcelle, ii. 133; on the relations of Laval and the King, ii. 135; plans against the Jesuits, ii. 136; letter from Du Pont concerning Dumesnil to, ii. 220; his correspondence with Talon regarding marriage and population, ii. 229-232; letter from Denonville concerning trade and industry in Canada, ii. 236, 237; his letter to Talon on the government and the clergy in Canada, ii. 250; his instructions to Bouterone regarding the government and the clergy in Canada, ii. 251; his letters to Du

INDEX.

chesneau, ii. 251, 252; letter from Denonville on Canadian curés, education, and discipline in Canada, ii. 256, 259.
Colden, i. 252.
Colombière, the vicar-general, pronounces the funeral eulogy of Laval, i. 225.
Comet, the, appears above Quebec, i. 119.
Commerce, in Canada, ii. 94, 237.
Commune, the, i. 178.
Company of New France, the, North America given by Louis XIII. to, i. 7; Richelieu at the head of, i. 7; Sir William Alexander jealous of, i. 7; in sole possession of Acadia, i. 8; Charles de la Tour made commander at Cape Sable for, i. 9; grants land to La Tour on the St. John, i. 14; i. 27; refuses aid to Argenson, i. 175; Argenson replaced by Avaugour, i. 178; shows signs of returning life, i. 190; called upon to resign its claims, i. 193; grants made by, ii. 46.
Company of the Hundred Associates, the, ii. 41.
Company of the West, the, i. 234; monopoly of trade granted to, i. 235; fails to prosper, i. 236.
Comtés, ii. 50.
Condé, i. 230, 231, 242.
Congregation of the Holy Family, the, ii. 154, 158, 160, 167.
Contrecœur, town of, ii. 30, 38.
Copper-mines of Lake Superior, the, ii. 7.
Corlaer (Schenectady), Dutch hamlet of, i. 249.
Côte, a, ii. 31, 77.
Cotton, Rev. John, i. 28.
Couillard, i. 239.

Couillard, Madame, i. 223.
Council of Canada, the, powers of, ii. 65.
Courcelle, Sieur de, see *Rémy, Daniel de*.
Courcelles, Seigneur de, i. 11.
Coureurs de bois, ii. 57, 104; an object of horror to the King, ii. 109; edicts directed against, ii. 109; their return to Montreal, ii. 112; build palisades, ii. 112; spoiled for civilization, ii. 113; had their uses, ii. 113; their riotous invasions of Michilimackinac, ii. 119; Father Carheil's severe condemnation of, ii. 121.
Coutume de Paris, the, ii. 49, 66.
Créquy, Duc de, ambassador of France at Rome, i. 220.
Croatia, i. 188.
Crolo, Sister, i. 102.
Cromwell, Captain, i. 44.
Cromwell, Oliver, i. 52, 202.
Crown, William, obtains a grant of Acadia from Cromwell, i. 53.
Cuillérier, René, i. 113.
Curés, Canadian, ii. 256.

Dablon, the Jesuit, sent among the Onondagas, i. 69; arrival at Onondaga, i. 70; harangues the Indians, i. 70; his journey home, i. 73; at Quebec, i. 73; joins the colony among the Onondagas, i. 74; denounces balls in Canada, ii. 149.
D'Amours, see *Amours, D'*.
Daniel, 123.
Dansmartin, Henry, ii. 211.
Daulac, Adam, early life of, i. 128; his expedition against the Iroquois, i. 129; Chief Anna-

hotaha offers to reinforce, i. 130; his encounter with the Iroquois at the Long Saut, i. 131-139; deserted by Annahotaha, i. 134; death of, i. 137; saved Canada from a disastrous invasion, i. 138.

D'Aulnay, D'Aulney, see *D'Aunay*.

D'Aunay, see *Charnisay, Charles de Menou d'Aunay*.

Dauphiny, ii. 56.

Danversière, see *La Danversière, Le Royer de*.

Demers, ii. 172.

De Monts, grant made by Henry IV. to, i. 3.

Denis, Charles, i. 173, 213.

Denis, M., i. 171; ii. 219.

Denonville, Marquis, the governor, on the Canadian nobility, ii. 54, 56, 57, 90, 91, 93, 96, 105; on the *coureurs de bois*, ii. 111; his arrival in Canada, ii. 146; the directions of Bishop Saint-Vallier to, ii. 146; ii. 156; on the education of girls in Canada, ii. 167; on the lawlessness in Canada, ii. 177-179; on the strength of the Canadians, ii. 181; asks aid from the King for the Canadian poor, ii. 182; ii. 186; on Château St. Louis, ii. 233; his letter to Colbert concerning trade and industry in Canada, ii. 236, 237; his letter to Colbert on Canadian curés, education and discipline in Canada, ii. 256-259.

Denonville, Marchioness, ii. 146.

Denonville, Mademoiselle, ii. 146.

Denys, Nicolas, the trader, i. 6; at Fort Loméron, i. 11; his title in Acadia, i. 14; on the capture of Fort St. Jean by D'Aunay, i. 40; keeps a feeble hold on his possessions, i. 52.

De Quen, see *Quen, De*.

Des Islets, ii. 10, 43, 50.

Desjardins, La Tour's agent, i. 16; taken prisoner by D'Aunay, i. 17; released by D'Aunay, i. 17; sends a ship to La Tour, i. 19.

Des Touches, Péronne, i. 192; his murder, i. 192.

Detroit, ii. 59; post of the *coureurs de bois* at, ii. 112; La Mothe-Cadillac the founder of, ii. 151; slavery at, ii. 190.

Diamond, Cape, i. 75, 238; ii. 82.

Dieppe, ii. 12.

Dollard, see *Daulac, Adam*.

Dollier, see *Casson, Dollier de*.

Dontre, ii. 67, 82, 101.

Dream Feast, the, i. 72.

Dreams, the oracles of the Iroquois, i. 91.

Drunkenness, the most destructive vice in the colony, ii. 180.

Du Bois, Jean Baptiste, i. 258.

Dubois, M., ii. 249.

Du Buisson, ii. 44.

Duchesneau, the intendant, on the Canadian nobility, ii. 54, 55, 73; letters from Colbert to, ii. 75, 136; letters from the King to, ii. 75, 130; attempts to apply a stimulus to Canadian trade, ii. 94; appeals for help, ii. 95; on the *coureurs de bois*, ii. 110; his report on the brandy question, ii. 125; ii. 138, 139, 179; on the poverty of Canada, ii. 183; letters from Colbert to, ii. 251, 252.

Dufresne, Jacques, i. 113.

Du Lhut, ii. 59, 110; the leader of the *coureurs du bois*, ii. 112.

INDEX. 273

Dumesnil, Jean Péronne, i. 190; his power not recognized, i. 191; his life threatened, i. 192, 193; his statements rejected by the council, i. 195; his papers seized by the council, i. 198; designs of the council against, i. 199; his escape, i. 200; returns to France, i. 200; reports his grievances to Colbert, i. 200; memorials of, i. 202; ii. 125; on the brandy quarrel, ii. 126; on the trade of the Jesuits, ii. 130; letter of Du Pont to Colbert concerning, ii. 220, 221; his memorial concerning affairs in Canada, ii. 222-224.

Dumont, i. 189; journal of, i. 190.

Dunkin, Mr., ii. 51.

Duplessis, ii. 98, 240.

Du Pont, Gaudais, letter to Colbert concerning Dumesnil from, ii. 220; ii. 222, 223.

Dupuy, Paul, ii. 80, 171.

Du Puys, Major Zachary, i. 74; at Onondaga, i. 79, 89; admirable coolness of, i. 90.

Du Quet, Pierre, i. 173.

Durham Terrace, ii. 232, 235.

Dutch, the, i. 63, 71, 75, 84; ii. 117, 124.

Dutch War, the, outbreak of, ii. 27.

Eboulemens, the, i. 185; ii. 34.

Education, in Canada, ii. 256.

Endicott, Governor John, warns Governor Winthrop against La Tour, i. 30; La Tour asks aid from, i. 32; refuses to grant La Tour's petition, i. 33; D'Aunay proposes terms of peace to, i. 34, 35.

England, claims the North American continent, i. 3; Sir William Alexander transfers the French settlements in Acadia and Canada by conquest to, i. 8; restored by treaty of St. Germain, i. 8; war breaks out between France and, i. 52; i. 121; jealousy of colonial manufactures shown by, ii. 97; succeeded in the building up of colonies, ii. 199.

English, the, attack Fort Loméron, i. 6; ii. 117, 124; threaten to attack Canada, ii. 160.

English colonist, the, compared with the French colonist, ii. 195.

English conquest, the, the grand crisis of Canadian history, ii. 203.

English gentry, the, ii. 52.

English revolution, the, i. 164.

Erie Indians, the, at war with the Iroquois, i. 57; the best hope of peace for the French lay in the Iroquois' war with, i. 67.

Estrades, the Maréchal d', viceroy for America, i. 237.

Evreux, in Normandy, i. 10.

Faillon, Abbé, on Dauversière and the Sisterhood of St. Joseph, i. 98; on the miraculous cure of Mlle. Mance, i. 100; on the reticence and dissimulation practised by the Jesuits and the Montrealists, i. 104; on the privations of the nuns at Montreal, i. 106; tribute to, i. 117; on the heroism of Daulac, i. 138; on the struggle for the bishopric of Canada, i. 155; on Laval's letter to the Pope, i. 159; on Laval's desire for the title of Bishop of Quebec, i. 219; on Dollier de Casson at

St. Anne, i. 264; on Tracy's expedition against the Iroquois, i. 267; on the peopling of Canada, ii. 12, 20; on the premium placed on marriage in Canada, ii. 22, 25; on the right of Montreal to trade with France, ii. 88; on the ornamental arts in Canada, ii. 98; on Mlle. Le Ber, ii. 161; on education in Canada, ii. 162; on the influence of the troops on Canada, ii. 171; on the brawls at Montreal, ii. 175; on the laws controlling innkeepers, ii. 185.

Félicité, Saint, i. 241.

Ferland, Abbé, his admiration of Laval, i. 172; ii. 44; on the trade of the Jesuits, ii. 131; ii. 184, 185, 186; on the letter from Mézy to the Jesuits, ii. 226.

"Festins à manger tout," i. 90, 94.

Fête Dieu, the, i. 168.

Feudalism, in Europe, ii. 40; in Canada, ii. 40; in France, ii. 40; first planted in Canada by Richelieu, ii. 41.

Fillion, Sieur, i. 203.

Finances of Canada, the, not prosperous, ii. 98.

Fisheries of Canada, the, ii. 93, 94.

Flavian, Saint, i. 241.

Flemish Bastard, the, i. 64, 252, 266.

Florida, i. 4, 7, 234.

Follin, Sieur, ii. 7.

Fontainebleau, the forest of, i. 229.

Fontanges, i. 231.

Forestier, at Fort St. Anne, i. 264.

Forest-trade, the, ii. 104.

Forster, John Reinold, ii. 194.

Fouquet, the arrest of, i. 231.

Fowle, Mr., i. 34.

France, claims the North American continent, i. 3; the French settlements in Acadia and Canada restored by the treaty of St. Germain to, i. 8; in sole possession of Acadia, i. 8; war breaks out between England and, i. 52; drifting toward the triumph of the *parti dévot*, i. 227; feudalism loses its vitality in, ii. 40; past and present stand side by side throughout, ii. 62; failed in the building up of colonies, ii. 199.

France, the Church of, i. 153.

Franche Comté, ii. 150.

Franchetot, Mathurin, captured by the Iroquois, i. 56; burned by the Iroquois, i. 61.

Francis, Saint, i. 13.

Francis Borgia, Saint, i. 225.

Francis I., of France, i. 153, 155, 156.

Francis of Assisi, Saint, i. 225.

Francis of Sales, Saint, i. 225; ii. 146.

Franciscans, the, ii. 136.

Frémin, Father, joins the colony among the Onondagas, i. 74; at Three Rivers, i. 250; ordered to the Mohawks, i. 266; ii. 130.

Frémont, the curé, ii. 174.

French, the, keep a feeble hold on Acadia, i. 4; make a lodgment on the rock of Quebec, i. 7; peace concluded with the Indians at Quebec, i. 61; their best hope of peace lay in the Iroquois' war with the Eries, i. 67; Mohawk attacks on, i. 68; the Mohawks make insolent de-

INDEX.   275

mands of, i. 86; abandon the Hurons to their fate, i. 86; the principal fault of, i. 130.
French Celt, the, ii. 201.
French colonist, the, compared with the English colonist, ii. 195.
French fisheries of Newfoundland, the, ii. 94.
French *noblesse*, the, ii. 52.
Fronde, i. 242.
Frontenac, Count, i. 197; ii. 16; on the life of Chambly on the Richelieu, ii. 30; on the younger Charles Le Moyne, ii. 60; reports on the *coureurs de bois* to, ii. 110; on the brandy quarrel, ii. 128, 129; his patronage of balls in Canada, ii. 149; on the clerical severity in Canada, ii. 149, 150; ii. 182; on Château St. Louis, ii. 232, 233–235; his memorial to the King, ii. 253.
Fundy, Bay of, i. 14, 38.
Fur-trade, the, not held inconsistent with *noblesse*, i. 10; disputes concerning, i. 52; again restored to Canada after the Iroquois War, i. 58; rendered worthless by the Iroquois War, i. 175; the Montrealists want to monopolize, i. 176; at Tadoussac, ii. 101; the importance of, ii. 102.

GABOURY, LOUIS, ii. 82.
Galinée, Father, i. 141.
Gallican Church, the, i. 153.
Gallican (National) Party, the, i. 153; tenets of, i. 153; outflanked by the Ultramontanes, i. 154; its struggle against the Ultramontanes, i. 155.
Gannentaa, meaning of the word, i. 83.

Ganong, W. F., on the supposed site of Fort La Tour, i. 39.
Ganuntaah, meaning of the word, i. 83.
Garacontié, the famous chief, i. 245.
Garde de la Marine, the, ii. 57.
Garneau, the Canadian, i. 224; on the emigration to Canada, ii. 13.
Garnier, Julien, at the Seneca missions, ii. 116.
Garonne River, the, ii. 145.
Garrean, the Jesuit, murdered by the Mohawks, i. 85.
Gaspé, i. 187.
Gaudais-Dupont, i. 194, 195, 198, 199, 200, 201, 203, 215, 218.
General Court of Massachusetts, the, i. 43; severe law against the sale of liquor to the Indians passed by, ii. 127.
General Hospital of Paris, the, ii. 182.
General Hospital of Quebec, the, founded by Saint-Vallier, ii. 182.
Gentilhomme, the, ii. 52.
Gentry, English, ii. 52.
George, Lake, i. 248, 253.
Germanic race, the, ii. 201
Gibbons, Capt. Edward, i. 21, 25; joins La Tour against D'Aunay, i. 28, 29, 32; returns to Boston, i. 32; entertains D'Aunay's envoys, i. 42, 43.
Gibbons, Mrs. Edward, i. 21, 22, 25.
Giffard, the physician, ii. 26, 35, 43.
Giffard, Robert, i. 195.
Gloria, Jean, i. 203.
Godé, Nicolas, i. 110.
Godefroy (son), death of, i. 119.
Good Hope, Cape of, i. 234.
Gookin, Daniel, i. 248.
Government House, the, at Quebec, ii. 44.

Governor-General of Canada, the, powers of, ii. 63; his relations with the intendant, ii. 64.
"Governor's Garden," the, i. 21.
Grafton, sent to Fort St. Jean with provisions, i. 38; captured by D'Aunay, i. 38, 41.
Grande Baye, La, i. 15.
Grandet, i. 255, 263, 264, 265.
Grand voyer, the, in Canada, ii. 76.
Great Britain, the King of, ii. 44.
Great Lakes, the, ii. 59, 198.
Great Seminary, the, at Quebec, i. 220; founded by Laval, i. 220; Laval's arrangement for the support of, i. 223.
Greenland, ii. 202.
Guercheville, Madame de, grant made by Louis XIII. to, i. 4.
Guiche, the Count de, i. 230.
Guienne, the admiralty court of, i. 16.
Guimont, Louis, ii. 165.
Guion, Jean, ii. 43.
Gynecocracy, among the Indians, i. 85.

Habitant, the, ii. 51, 69, 96, 167, 202.
Harley, Archbishop of Rouen, ii. 18.
Harvard College, ii. 161.
Hawkins, Thomas, joins La Tour against D'Aunay, i. 28, 29, 32; returns to Boston, i. 32.
Hazard, i. 7.
Hazeur, ii. 92; memorial of, ii. 93.
Henriette of England, i. 230.
Henry IV., of France, grant made to De Monts by, i. 3.
"Hermitage," the, i. 145; account of, i. 146; the zealots at, i. 147; i. 204, 205, 207, 228; ii. 212-217.
Hertel, François, his letter to Le Moyne, i. 121, 122; captured by the Mohawks, i. 122; his letter to his mother, i. 123; adventures of, i. 123; death of, i. 123; letters of nobility of, i. 123; estimates of, i. 124.
Hocquart, the intendant, his view of the Canadians, ii. 191.
Holland, i. 121, 237.
Holy Family, the, attempt to found a religious colony at Montreal in honor of, i. 98.
Holy See, the, i. 160.
Holy Wars of Montreal, the, i. 96-117.
Horn, Cape, ii. 202.
Hôtel Dieu of Montreal, the, ii. 38.
Hôtel Dieu of Quebec, the, i. 104, 125; Talon's portrait at, ii. 4; ii. 36; the ruins of, ii. 98; ii. 137, 157, 158.
Houssart, i. 162.
Hubbard, i. 15, 19, 32.
Hudson's Bay, i. 234, 236; ii. 101.
Hudson River, the, Dutch heretics at the mouth of, i. 15; settlements of, i. 119; i. 248.
Huguenots, the, i. 204, 240; ii. 90, 156, 157.
Huissier, the, in Canada, ii. 67.
Hundred Associates, the, ii. 41.
Hunt, Prof. Sterry, on the evidences of the earthquake at Quebec, i. 185.
Huron Colony, the, coveted by the Iroquois, the Mohawks, and the Onondagas, i. 62.
Huron Indians, the, destruction of, i. 58; Iroquois plans to destroy, i. 62; turn to the Jesuits for aid, i. 62; attack of the Mohawks on, i. 76; abandoned to their fate by the French, i. 86; joined by Father Ragueneau, i. 86; slaughtered by the Onondagas, i. 87; take refuge in Quebec, i. 125; at

the Long Saut, i. 134; desert Daulac, i. 134, 137, 138.
Huron mission, the, i. 63.
Hutchinson, Mrs., preaching of, i. 25.

IBERVILLE, Le Moyne d', ii. 59.
Ignace, Father, the Superior of the Capucins, at Port Royal, i. 12; tribute to D'Aunay, i. 48.
Incarnation, Marie de l', on the Mohawk Iroquois attack on Du Plessis Bochart, i. 55; on the capture of Father Le Moyne by the Mohawks, i. 68; on the French colony among the Onondagas, i. 75; on the Mohawks' attack on the Hurons, i. 76; on the political influence of women among the Iroquois, i. 84; on the Medicine Feast, i. 92; on the Onondaga mission, i. 94; on the appearance of the comet above Quebec, i. 119; on the threatened attack of the Iroquois, i. 125; on the desertion of Daulac by the Hurons, i. 137; her eulogy on Laval, i. 161; on the earthquake at Quebec, i. 184, 185, 186, 187; on the appointment of the Marquis de Tracy as lieutenant-general of America, i. 238, 241; on the Holy War in Canada, i. 243; her letters home, i. 244; i. 252; on Tracy's expedition against the Mohawks, i. 254, 256; on Tracy's success, i. 257; i. 261; on Talon's zeal for the success of the colony, ii. 7; on the peopling of Canada, ii. 12; on the emigration to Canada, ii. 13, 15; on the "King's gift," ii. 21; on the premium on marriage in Canada, ii. 23; her estimate of the officers on the Richelieu, ii. 30; at the Ursuline Convent in Quebec, ii. 36; on the Canadian settler, ii. 39; on witches in Canada, ii. 157; on the education of girls in Canada, ii. 167; on the influence of the troops on Canada, ii. 171.
Indians, the, grand council held at Quebec, i. 57; conclude treaty with the French, 61; celebration of the Dream Feast, i. 72; political influence of women among, i. 84; their fur-trade with the French, ii. 103; forest-trade with, ii. 104; severe law passed by the General Court of Massachusetts against the sale of liquor to, ii. 127.
Indian women, the, reproductive qualities of, ii. 25.
Infant Jesus, the chapel of the, at Montreal, ii. 38.
Innocent XI., Pope, i. 153, 154, 156, 158, 159, 220.
Intendant of Canada, the powers of, ii. 62; his relations with the Governor-General, ii. 64; the ruling power in the colony, ii. 73.
"Ipswich Letter," the, i. 30; Governor Winthrop's reply to, i. 31; great effect of, i. 31.
"Ironsides," Cromwell's invincible, ii. 202.
Iroquois Indians, the, attack the French at Montreal, i. 55; capture Father Poncet, i. 56; at war with the Eries, i. 57; make peace with the French, i. 57; the five "nations" of, i. 57; grant life to Father Poncet, i. 59; native fickleness of, i. 62; plans to destroy the Hurons, i. 62; their friendly reception to Father Le Moyne, i. 66; desire

peace with Canada, i. 66; the capital of, i. 81; dissimulation of, i. 81; political influence of women among, i. 84; dealings of Aillebonst with, i. 88; dreams the oracles of, i. 91; their attacks on Montreal, i. 109-116; the French make a truce with, i. 110; kill Le Maitre and Vignal, i. 111, 112; their threatened attack on the French, i. 125; captured by the French, i. 127; Daulac's expedition against, i. 129; their encounter with Daulac at the Long Saut, i. 131-139; i. 244; sue for peace, i. 265; the hopes of the Jesuits for, ii. 116.

Iroquois missions, the, ii. 119.

Iroquois War, the, i. 54-57; Canada writhes under the scourge of, i. 118; at its height, i. 120; renders the fur-trade worthless, i. 175.

Isle à la Pierre, i. 112.

Isle aux Oies, i. 68; ii. 171.

Isle La Motte, i. 260.

JACOBIN convent, the, i. 205.

Jacobin monks, the, i. 205.

Jacquelin, Marie, marries Charles de la Tour, i. 17; proves a valuable ally to La Tour, i. 17; taken prisoner by D'Aunay, i. 17; released by D'Aunay, i. 17; sails for Boston, i. 20; in Boston, i. 28; returns to France, i. 36; forbidden to leave France, i. 36; escapes to England and sails to America, i. 36; arrives in Boston, i. 36; rejoins La Tour, i. 37; captured by D'Aunay, i. 40; her death, i. 40; ii. 206.

James I. of England, grant made to Sir William Alexander by, i. 4.

Jamin, Captain, i. 17.

Jansenism, i. 148, 157, 205.

Jansenists, the, their struggle with the Jesuits, i. 146; ii. 156, 212, 215, 216.

Javille, ii. 211.

Jemsec, supposed site of Fort La Tour at, i. 39.

Jerome, Saint, ii. 147.

Jesuit College, the, at Quebec, ii. 37.

Jesuit missions, the, ii. 116; importance of, ii. 117; extremities of, ii. 119; the splendid self-devotion of, ii. 145.

Jesuits, the, grant made by Louis XIII. to, i. 4; the Hurons apply for aid to, i. 62; invited by the Onondagas to plant a colony among them, i. 63; send Father Le Moyne among the Onondagas, i. 64; at Onondaga, i. 70, 80; decide to establish a colony among the Onondagas, i. 74; Governor Lauson makes a grant of land to, i. 74; fearful task essayed by, i. 84; among the Cayugas, the Senecas, and the Oneidas, i. 84; frightful position of, i. 89; admirable coolness of, i. 90; the Medicine Feast, i. 91; escape from the Indians, i. 93; arrival at Quebec, i. 94; jealousy for the Sulpitians at Montreal, i. 103; reticence and dissimulation practised by, i. 104; in despair, i. 119; torture considered a blessing in disguise by, i. 124; their struggle to obtain the bishopric of Canada, i. 142-145; animosity of Father Queylus to, i. 143, 144; conflict with the Jansenists,

i. 146; the most forcible exponents of ultramontane principles, i. 153; their struggle against the Sulpitians, i. 155; triumph over the Sulpitians, i. 160; adepts in human nature, i. 164; their sagacity in choosing Laval to be Bishop of Canada, i. 164; Avaugour desires to be on good terms with, i. 179; Mézy appeals to, i. 209; accusations against Mézy, i. 214; Mézy's charges against, i. 217; their ideas in regard to the relations of the Church and State, i. 226; victory over the Iroquois, i. 265–267; begin their ruined missions anew, ii. 116; their hopes of converting the Iroquois, ii. 116; always in the van of religious and political propagandism, ii. 119; La Mothe's hatred for, ii. 121; denounce the brandy traffic, ii. 124; enter on the work of reform, ii. 125; trade of, ii. 129–131; forbidden by the King to carry on trade, ii. 130; the recall of Mézy a defeat in disguise for, ii. 132; Courcelle's opposition to, ii. 133; Talon ordered to watch, ii. 133; Colbert plans against, ii. 136; rigorous at Quebec, ii. 152; derive great power from the confessional, ii. 153; form the Congregation of the Holy Family, ii. 154; reluctant to share their power with the Récollets, ii. 154; the ablest teachers in Canada, ii. 161; letter from Mézy to, ii. 226–228; ii. 253.
"Jesuits' Well," the, i. 79.
Jesus, the Company of, i. 69; ii. 248.

Jesus, the Island of, i. 224; ii. 139.
Jesus, the Order of, see *Order of Jesus*.
Joachim, Saint, ii. 165.
Jogues, Father Isaac, i. 257.
Joliet, Louis. ii. 92.
Joseph, Brother, ii. 130.
Joseph, Saint, the labors of Mlle. Mance in honor of, i. 98; hospital at Montreal in honor of, i. 101.
Josselyn, on the earthquake at Quebec, i. 187.
Jouaneaux, at Montreal, i. 107; devotes himself to the service of the Sisters, i. 107.
Juchereau, see *Saint-Ignace Frances Juchereau de*.
Judge, the, in Canada, ii. 68.
Jumeau, Sister, at Montreal, i. 107.

KALM, the Swedish botanist, ii. 192; his view of the Canadians, ii. 192.
Kamouraska, ii. 142, 164.
"King's gift," the, ii. 21.
"King's girls," the, ii. 20.
"Kirke," the, i. 5.
Kirke, the brothers, Sir William Alexander fits out a private expedition under, i. 7; success of the expedition, i. 7.
Kirke, Sir David, gives assistance to La Tour, i. 45.

LABADIE, Sergeant, ii. 37.
La Barre, Governor, ii. 155, 176, 177, 179, 232.
La Bouteillerie, ii. 142.
La Chaise, Père, ii. 127; his correspondence with Laval, ii. 140.
Lachenaye, i. 178.
La Chesnaye, Charles Aubert de,

memorial of, ii. 10; on the brandy quarrel, ii. 126, 127; ii. 184.
La Chine, i. 65; ii. 23, 38.
La Chine Rapids, the, ii. 38.
La Citière, vast domain of, ii. 46.
La Combe, ii. 142.
La Dauversière, Le Royer de, founder of the sisterhood of St. Joseph, i. 97; appropriates for himself the money of the sisterhood, i. 98, 102; portrait of, i. 98; visited by Mlle. Mance, i. 100; a wretched fanatic, i. 100; agent of the Association of Montreal, i. 101; death of, i. 102.
Ladies, the, in Canada, ii. 193.
La Durantaye, i. 263; ii. 59; at Michilimackinac, ii. 121.
La Fayette, Madame de, i. 230.
La Ferté, Juchereau de, appointed councillor at Quebec, i. 195, 196; i. 213.
Lafitau, on the political influence of women among the Iroquois, i. 84; on the resemblance between the Iroquois and the ancient Lycians, i. 85; ii. 168.
La Flèche, town of, i. 100, 101, 102.
La Flèche, Nuns, the, i. 102; in Canada, i. 104; extreme poverty of, i. 105.
Lafontaine, Judge, ii. 51.
Lafontaine, Sir L. H., ii. 45.
La Fredière, Major, sent to garrison Montreal, ii. 171; his tyranny, ii. 172; accusations against, ii. 173; ordered home to France, ii. 173.
La Galisonnière, Marquis de, ii. 168.
La Hontan, ii. 16, 17, 18, 20, 21, 68, 70, 83, 90, 105; complains of the clerical severity in Canada, ii. 150, 151; ii. 156, 183; his view of the Canadians, ii. 191.
Lalemant, Charles, i. 226.
Lalemant, Father Jerome, i. 166, 167, 171, 172, 179, 181, 182, 183, 184, 211, 213; ii. 123; on the trade of the Jesuits, ii. 129; ii. 219, 220.
La Lucière, La Motte de, i. 263, 265; ii. 14, 24, 229.
Lamberville, among the Onondagas, ii. 116.
Lamoignon, President of the Company of New France, i. 178.
La Mothe-Cadillac, ii. 59; at Michilimackinac, ii. 121; his hatred for the Jesuits, ii. 121; on the relations of Laval and the King, ii. 135; the founder of Detroit, ii. 151; on the clerical severity in Canada, ii. 151, 152, 254, 255.
La Motte, see *La Lucière, La Motte de*.
La Mouche, Chief, i. 134.
Langlois, Noël, ii. 54.
La Peltrie, Madame de, i. 145.
La Potherie, i. 252; ii. 70, 83; on the women of Quebec, ii. 189.
Lareau, ii. 67, 82, 101.
La Salle, ii. 10, 38, 59; on the brandy quarrel, ii. 126; on the trade of the Jesuits, ii. 130; on Father Bardy's sermon against the governor, ii. 135; on the power derived by the Jesuits from the confessional, ii. 153.
La Tesserie, appointed councillor at Quebec, i. 213.
La Tour, Abbé, i. 141, 152, 155, 181, 184, 193, 214, 218, 221, 228, 241; ii. 13, 32, 70, 97, 166, 184.
La Tour, Charles Saint-Étienne

INDEX. 281

de, brought to Acadia, i. 5; becomes attached to the service of Biencourt, i. 5; Biencourt bequeaths his property to, i. 5; becomes owner of Fort Loméron and its dependencies, i. 5; appeals to the King for a commission to command in Acadia, i. 5; attacked by Sir William Alexander, i. 5; made a baronet of Nova Scotia, i. 7; receives grants of land near Cape Sable and on the St. John River, i. 7; builds a fort on the St. John River, i. 7; his English titles to lands at Cape Sable become worthless, i. 9; returns to Paris, i. 9; extensive grants of lands made to, i. 9; made lieutenant-governor in Fort Loméron and commander at Cape Sable, i. 9; dissensions with D'Aunay, i. 9; his position and qualities compared with D'Aunay, i. 9; his little kingdom at Cape Sable, i. 10; the true surname of his family, i. 10; bitter enmity for D'Aunay, i. 14; receives a land grant on the St. John, i. 14; removes from Cape Sable to Fort St. Jean, i. 14; his feud with D'Aunay, i. 14, 15; attacks the Plymouth trading-house at Machias, i. 15; refuses to aid D'Aunay against Penobscot, i. 16; plots against D'Aunay, i. 16; marries Marie Jacquelin, i. 17; she proves a valuable ally to, i. 17; captures some of D'Aunay's soldiers; battle with D'Aunay, i. 17; taken prisoner by D'Aunay, i. 17; released by D'Aunay, i. 17; his commission revoked, i. 18; refuses to obey the King's command, i. 18; in open revolt, i. 19; sails for Boston, i. 20; arrives in Boston, i. 21; asks Governor Winthrop for aid against D'Aunay, i. 22; among the Puritans, i. 25; attends training-day in Boston, i. 26; allowed by Governor Winthrop to hire allies against D'Aunay, i. 28; sails with his allies from Boston, i. 32; D'Aunay flees before, i. 32; asks aid from Governor Endicott, i. 32; his petition not granted, i. 33; rejoined by his wife, i. 37; D'Aunay captures Fort St. Jean, i. 39; his wife captured, and her death, i. 40; entertained by Samuel Maverick, i. 45; receives assistance from Sir David Kirke, i. 45; treachery of, i. 45; death of D'Aunay, i. 48; suddenly appears as the favorite of royalty, i. 49; his fruitful visit to France, i. 50; return to Acadia, i. 50; marries Madame d'Aunay, i. 51; his share of Acadia, i. 52; obtains a grant of Acadia from Cromwell, i. 53; sells his share to Temple, i. 53; his death, i. 53; his descendants, i. 53; official report of André Certain on D'Aunay and, ii. 205-211.

La Tour, Madame Charles de, see *Jacquelin, Marie*.

La Tour, Claude de, i. 5; captured by the privateer "Kirke," i. 5; his marriage, i. 5; renounces his French allegiance, i. 6; made a baronet of Nova Scotia, i. 6; sent to Cape Sable, i. 6; early history of, i. 10.

La Tour, Fort, supposed site of, i. 39; see also *Loméron, Fort*.

Laubia, Captain, ii. 37.
Laurent, Jean, ii. 211.
Lauson, Governor, Jean de, receives the Onondaga deputation, i. 69; favors the establishment of the Onondaga colony, i. 74; makes a grant of land to the Jesuits, i. 74; not matched to the desperate crisis of the hour, i. 77; i. 116, 196; ii. 46, 88, 184.
Lauson, son of the governor, the seneschal of New France, i. 119; death of, i. 119.
Lauzon, Côte de, census of, ii. 35.
Laval-Montmorency, François Xavier de, bishop at Quebec, i. 102; allied to the Jesuits, i. 102; looks on the colonists of Montreal with more than coldness, i. 102; maxims of, i. 141; appointed bishop of Canada, i. 145; sketch of, i. 145; eulogy on, i. 151; boundless zeal of, i. 152; of one mind with the Jesuits, i. 154; sails for Canada, i. 154; Queylus puts himself in opposition to, i. 155; his dislike of divided authority, i. 155; not a man of half measures, i. 156; Queylus in conflict with, i. 158; his letter to the Pope, i. 159; reconciliation with Queylus, i. 160; his triumph complete, i. 160; an object of veneration to Catholics, i. 161; eulogies on, i. 161; his austerity of life, i. 162; sanctity of, i. 162; portraits of, i. 163; characteristics of, i. 163; Colbert the true antagonist of, i. 165; quarrels with Argenson, i. 166, 167, 168, 170, 171; Ferland's admiration for, i. 172; urges the removal of Argenson, i. 178; the brandy quarrel, i. 181; sails for France, i. 182; urges the removal of Avaugour, i. 182; his triumph, i. 193; constructs a new council, i. 194; his selection of Mézy as governor, i. 206; signs of storm, i. 207; Mézy in opposition to, i. 209, 213; accusations against Mézy, i. 214; Mézy recalled, i. 215; his threefold strength at court, i. 215; the death of Mézy, i. 216; Mézy's charges against, i. 217; his desire to obtain the title of Bishop of Quebec, i. 219; obtains his desires, i. 220; proposes to establish a seminary at Quebec, i. 220; his idea of the parish priest, i. 221; his arrangement for the support of the seminary, i. 222; acquires vast grants of land in Canada, i. 224; the father of the Canadian Church, i. 224; tribute to, i. 224; his funeral eulogy, i. 225; stories of his asceticism, i. 225; his ideas in regard to the relation of Church and State, i. 226; cared for nothing outside the Church, i. 228; receives the Marquis de Tracy, i. 239; on the peopling of Canada, ii. 12; his seigniory of Beaupré, ii. 34; his opposition to the brandy traffic, ii. 125; the King distrusts, ii. 128; his relations with the King, ii. 135; returns to France, ii. 139; asks to have a successor appointed, ii. 139; forbidden to return to Canada, ii. 140; his correspondence with Père La Chaise, ii. 140; his invectives against the luxury and vanity of women, ii. 148; de-

INDEX. 283

nounces balls in Canada, ii. 149; encourages education in Canada, ii. 162; his industrial school, ii. 166; letters between D'Argenson (brother of the governor) and, ii. 217-220; ii. 222; order received from Mézy, ii. 224; his reply, ii. 226; ii. 253, 254, 256.

Laval's Seminary, at Quebec, ii. 186; the burning of, ii. 186.

La Valterie, Lieutenant, ii. 37.

Laval University, of Quebec, i. 161, 223.

Lavater, ii. 4.

La Vérendrye, Varennes de, ii. 24, 59.

Lavigne, i. 112; nocturnal adventure of, i. 114.

Le Ber, the merchant, i. 107.

Le Ber, Jacques, ii. 53.

Le Ber, Jeanne, ii. 98; the venerated recluse of Montreal, ii. 157; sketch of, ii. 158-161.

Le Ber, Pierre, ii. 98.

Le Borgne, unscrupulous plans against Madame d'Aunay, i. 50, 51; gets a lion's share of Acadia, i. 52.

Leclerc, ii. 211.

Le Clerc, ii. 11; on the early colonists of Canada, ii. 13.

Le Jeune, Father, on the Mohawks' attack on the Hurons, i. 76; on the Iroquois attacks on Montreal, i. 115; asked by Anne of Austria to select a bishop for Canada, i. 144; sagacious choice of, i. 145.

Le Maitre, the priest, i. 96; killed by the Iroquois, i. 111.

Le Mercier, Father, on the French victory over the Iroquois at Montreal, i. 55; on the close of the Iroquois War, i. 58; on the sale of beaver-skins in Canada, i. 58; on the departure of Father Le Moyne to the Onondagas, i. 64; joins the colony among the Onondagas, i. 74; falls ill, i. 78; at Onondaga, i. 79, 80; on Chaumonot's power among the Indians, i. 83; i. 241; on Courcelle's desire for war, i. 246; on Talon's attempt to establish trade between Canada and the West Indies, ii. 7; his punishment of the brandy traffic, ii. 125; private journal of, ii. 129; ii. 153.

Le Moyne, Charles, i. 129, 245; at the head of the "Blue Coats" of Montreal, i. 254; a man of sterling qualities, ii. 60.

Le Moyne, Charles (the younger), ii. 60; his fort, ii. 60; ii. 173, 174.

Le Moyne, Father Simon, sent among the Onondagas, i. 64; his journey, i. 64; reception by the Iroquois, i. 65; his harangue, i. 66, 67; discovers the famous salt-springs of Onondaga, i. 68; returns to Quebec, i. 68; captured by the Mohawks but released, i. 68; among the Mohawks, i. 69; returns to Montreal, i. 69; goes again among the Mohawks, i. 88; letter from Hertel to, i. 122.

Le Noir, François, ii. 22, 23.

Leroles, cousin of Tracy, i. 251.

Lesdiguières, Duchesse de, letter from Charlevoix to, ii. 194.

Lesser Seminary, the, at Quebec, i. 223.

Lestang, i. 19.

Levi, Point, i. 126, 238; ii. 187.

Levite, i. 215.

Loméron, Fort, Biencourt at, i. 5;

Charles de la Tour becomes the owner of, i. 5; attacked by Sir William Alexander, i. 5, 6; Charles de la Tour made lieutenant-governor in, i. 9; his life at, i. 11.

Long Lake, i. 249.

Long Saut Rapids, the, i. 131; encounter of Daulac with the Iroquois at, i. 131-139.

Longueuil, the seigniory of, ii. 38, 43.

Longueuil, Baron de, see *Le Moyne, Charles (the younger)*.

Lorette, the mission of, ii. 118.

Lormeau, Ensign, Cariou's attack on, ii. 173, 174.

Lorraine, the regiment of, i. 243.

Lotbinière, the seigniory of, ii. 38.

Louis, Father, i. 205, 206.

Louis, M., goes to Boston as D'Aunay's envoy, i. 41; completes treaty with the Puritans, i. 44; returns to D'Aunay, i. 45.

Louis XIII., of France, grant made to Madame de Guercheville and the Jesuits by, i. 4; La Tour begs a commission to command in Acadia from, i. 5, 7; gives North America to the company of New France, i. 7; revokes La Tour's commission, i. 18; orders D'Aunay to keep peace with the Puritans, i. 33.

Louis XIV., of France, pleased with D'Aunay's capture of Fort St. Jean, i. 46; grants royal favors to D'Aunay, i. 46; reverses the decree against La Tour, i. 49; reflections on the colonial administration of, i. 50; favors Laval's wishes for the bishopric of Quebec, i. 220; his sun rising in splendor, i. 230; fortune strangely bountiful to, i. 230; formed by nature to act the part of a king, i. 231; the embodiment of the monarchical idea, i. 232; has the prosperity of Canada at heart, i. 236; resolved that a new France should be added to the old, i. 239; peoples Canada, ii. 11; alarmed by Talon's demands for more men, ii. 13; offers a bounty on children, ii. 23; the Father of New France, ii. 27; his zeal spasmodic, ii. 27; the triumph of royalty culminates in, ii. 41; preserves feudalism in Canada, ii. 41; the dispenser of charity for all Canada, ii. 57; alone supreme in Canada, ii. 65; on justice in Canada, ii. 69; letter to Duchesneau, ii. 75; ever haunted with the fear of the Devil, ii. 80; his edict against swearing, ii. 80; the excess of his benevolence, ii. 83; death of, ii. 84; Saint-Simon's portrait of, ii. 86; influence of Madame de Maintenon on, ii. 86; retains exclusive right of the fur-trade at Tadoussac, ii. 101; the *coureurs de bois* an object of horror to, ii. 109; appeal made in the brandy quarrel to, ii. 126; never at heart a prohibitionist, ii. 127; distrusts Laval, ii. 128; his attitude on the brandy quarrel, ii. 128; forbids the Jesuits from carrying on trade, ii. 130; his relations with Laval, ii. 135; his liberality to the Canadian Church, ii. 137; on education in Canada, ii. 162; contributes to the relief of the Canadian poor, ii. 182; his instructions to Talon regarding

INDEX. 285

the government and the clergy in Canada, ii. 251.
Louisburg, the capture of, ii. 203.
Louvigni, Bernières de, royal treasurer at Caen, i. 145, 151; sketch of, i. 145-147; i. 204, 206; laudatory notice of, i. 206; the maxims of, i. 228; ii. 212, 213, 215.
Louvre, the, library of, i. 178.
Loyola, Ignatius de, sage policy of, i. 144; followers of, ii. 152.
Lussaudière, the seigniory of, ii. 38.
Lycians, the ancient resemblance of the Iroquois to, i. 85.
Lyons, ii. 15.

Mace, Sister, i. 101; at Montreal, i. 107, 109.
Machias, Plymouth trading-houses at, i. 15; attacked by La Tour, i. 15.
Madeleine, Cape, ii. 129.
Madry, chosen alderman of Quebec, i. 212.
Magdelaine, Cape, ii. 248.
Maillet, Sister, i. 97, 101, 109.
Maine, State of, i. 8; ii. 59, 119.
Maintenon, Madame de, i. 227; ii. 86; influence on Louis XIV., ii. 86, 156.
Maisonneuve, Chomedey de, governor of Montreal, i. 106; forms a military fraternity at Montreal, i. 116; proclamation of, i. 116; i. 128, 130, 131, 175; removed by Mézy, i. 207; removed by Tracy, ii. 64; his death in obscurity, ii. 64.
Mal Bay, ii. 34, 92.
Malta, Knights of, i. 165.
Mance, Jeanne, returns to Canada, i. 97; her labors in honor of St. Joseph, i. 98; her hospital work at Montreal, i. 98; loses the use of her arm, i. 99; returns to France, i. 99; her miraculous cure, i. 99; her visit to Mme. de Bullion, i. 100; her visit to Dauversière, i. 100; gains recruits in La Flèche, i. 102; attacked by fever, i. 103; returns to Montreal, i. 103; description of her hospital, i. 105.
Mans, i. 17.
Manufactures, at Canada, ii. 97.
Margry, ii. 168, 192; on La Tour and D'Aunay, ii. 205-211.
Marie, M., visits the Puritans, i. 34; his reception by the magistrates, i. 34; his terms of peace from D'Aunay, i. 34; his return to Port Royal, i. 35; returns to Boston as D'Aunay's envoy, i. 41, 44; completes treaty with the Puritans, i. 44; returns to D'Aunay, i. 45.
Marie, Sieur, ii. 207, 209.
Marie Thérèse, i. 230.
Marine and Colonies, the Archives of the, ii. 85, 127.
Marot, Bernard, ii. 211.
Marquette, Father, his old mission at Michilimackinac, ii. 119.
Marriage in Canada, bounty on, ii. 21.
Martin, Henri, on Colbert, i. 233.
Martyrs, the mission of the, ii. 116; Bruyas at, ii. 116.
Massachusetts, Bay of, i. 15.
Massachusetts, State of, figures as an independent state, i. 35.
Massachusetts magistrates, the, grant aid to La Tour against D'Aunay, i. 28; letter to D'Aunay, i. 33; refuse to grant La Tour's second peti-

tion, i. 33; reception of M. Marie, i. 34; his terms of peace from D'Aunay, i. 34.

Maverick, Samuel, La Tour entertained by, i. 45.

Mazarin, Cardinal, i. 142, 154; death of, i. 231.

Mazarin library at Paris, the, i. 265.

Mazé, Péronne de, secretary to Avaugour, i. 192; appointed councillor at Quebec, i. 213.

Medicine Feast, the, i. 90-92.

Ménard, joins the colony among the Onondagas, i. 74; sets out for the Cayugas, i. 84.

Menou, Comte Jules de, i. 9, 10, 16, 17, 19, 20, 27, 50, 51.

Menou, René de (father of D'Aunay), i. 18, 50.

Mesnu, Peuvret de, appointed secretary of the council at Quebec, i. 195.

Meules, the intendant, ii. 10, 13, 54, 58, 69, 70, 71, 72, 73, 74, 78, 79, 94, 96; issues a card currency, ii. 99; ii. 139, 183, 232.

Mexico, the viceroy of, i. 44.

Mézy, Saffray de, appointed governor of Quebec, i. 194; youth of, i. 204; a military zealot, i. 205; merits of, i. 206; removes Maisonneuve, i. 207; signs of storm, i. 207; removes Bourdon, Villeray, and Auteuil from the council, i. 208; his appeal to the Jesuits, i. 209; appoints Chartier attorney-general, i. 212; banishes Bourdon and Villeray to France, i. 214; accusations of Laval and the Jesuits against, i. 214; receives a peremptory recall, i. 215; his defeat, i. 215; his death, i. 216; his letter to Marquis de Tracy, i. 216; his will, i. 216; his charges against Laval and the Jesuits, i. 217; on the right of Montreal to trade with France, ii. 88; his recall a defeat in disguise for the Jesuits, ii. 132; ii. 222; his order to Laval, ii. 224; Laval's reply, ii. 226; his letter to the Jesuits, ii. 226-228.

Michael, Saint, i. 247.

Michilimackinac, the chief resort of the coureurs de bois, ii. 113, 115; Father Marquette's old mission at, ii. 119; abuses at, ii. 119-121; difficulties in transferring trade to Montreal from, ii. 122; Jesuit beaver-skins at, ii. 120.

Micmac Indians, the, at Cape Sable, i. 11; at Port Royal, i. 12; give assistance to La Tour's outcasts, i. 46.

Milet, among the Oneidas, ii. 116.

Milton, the Blue Hill in, i. 23.

Missions, the Jesuit, ii. 116.

Mississippi River, the, ii. 59, 92, 119.

Mississippi Valley, the, posts of the coureurs de bois in, ii. 112.

Mituvemeg, Chief, i. 130.

Mohawk Iroquois Indians, the, i. 55; defeat and kill Du Plessis Bochart, i. 55; Three Rivers beset by, i. 56; make overtures of peace, i. 57; i. 59; covet the Huron colony, i. 62; pretended indignation with the Jesuits, i. 64; capture Father Le Moyne, i. 68; attacks on the French, i. 68; take no part in the Erie War, i. 68; attack on Montreal, i. 68; Father Le Moyne among, i. 69; their opposition to the French colony among the Onondagas, i. 75; attack on the Hurons, i. 76; at Onondaga, i. 81; murder the Jesuit Garreau, i. 85; make insolent demands of the French, i. 86; Father Le Moyne again goes among, i. 88; capture Hertel, i. 122; i. 138; i. 244; the French plan to chastise, i. 245; Courcelle's march against, i. 246; his failure, i. 249; sue for peace, i. 251; their treachery, i. 251; Sorel sent against, i. 251; Tracy sets out against, i. 253; the French victorious against, i. 257; sue for peace, i. 266; Frémin and Pierron ordered to, i. 266; Bruyas among, ii. 116.

Mohawk town, the lower, i. 60.

Mohawk towns, the, i. 248; Tracy attacks, i. 255; captured by the French, i. 257.

Mohegan Indians, the, i. 124.

Molin (Motin), Jeanne, marries D'Aunay, i. 11, 16; death of her husband, i. 48; in need of help, i. 50; oppressed by Le Borgne, i. 50, 51; applies to the Duc de Vendôme, i. 51; marries La Tour, i. 51; her children, i. 52.

Montagnais Indians, the, ii. 34.

Montespan, Madame de, i. 231.

Montigny, Abbé de, see *Laval-Montmorency, François Xavier de*.

Montmagny, Governor, i. 165; ii. 129.

Montmorenci, the cataract of, ii. 35.

Montmorency, Anne de, Constable of France, i. 145.

Montreal, site of, i. 4; attacked by the Iroquois, i. 54; the Onondaga Indians at, i. 56; attacked by the Mohawks, i. 68; holy wars of, i. 96-117; school for female children at, i. 97; attempt to found a religious colony in honor of the Holy Family at, i. 98; blood and blows rife at, i. 98; a government within a government, i. 103; population of, i. 105; attacks of the Iroquois on, i. 109; character of its tenants, i. 110; miracles at, i. 110-112; a year of disaster at, i. 115; Maisonneuve forms a military fraternity at, i. 116; i. 118; in danger from the Iroquois, i. 125, 133, 139; Father Souart left in spiritual charge of, i. 142; its struggle against Quebec, i. 155; the virtual independence of, i. 175; tariff of prices at, ii. 5; young women shipped to, ii. 20; the great mill at, ii. 32; local government at, ii. 64; the corporate seigniors of, ii. 68; her right to trade with France, ii. 88; a *bourse* established at, ii. 101; great annual fair established at, ii. 103; the harboring-place of the *coureurs de bois*, ii. 112; difficulties in transferring trade from Michilimackinac to, ii. 122; the Sulpitians rigorous at, ii. 152; the sisterhood at, ii. 167; the natural resort of desperadoes, ii. 175; almshouse established at, ii. 182; ii. 238.

Montreal, the Association of, i. 101, 116.

Montreal, Island of, i. 130; passes into the possession of the Sulpitian priests, i. 141; the head of the colony, ii. 28.

Montrealists, the, reticence and dissimulation practised by, i. 104; ascend the St. Lawrence, i. 104; reach their new home, i. 104; want to monopolize the fur-trade, i. 176.

Monts, De, see *De Monts*.
Morangi, M. de, i. 177.
Moras, Ensign, ii. 37.
Moreau, i. 19, 50, 51.
Morel, Ensign, ii. 173, 174.
Morel, Father, ii. 142; the charge of, ii. 142-144.
Morin, Sister, i. 106; in Montreal, i. 109; on the miracles at Montreal, i. 112; on the influence of the troops on Canada, ii. 171.
Morgan, i. 83.
Morrison, William, Jr., ii. 235.
Morton, on the earthquake at Quebec, i. 187.
Motteville, Madame de, i. 230.
Mouron, Captain, i. 20, 27.
Murray, General, ii. 44.

NATIONAL (Gallican) party, the, i. 153; tenets of, i. 153.
Nau, Michelle-Thérèse, i. 195.
New England, i. 187; the Puritan churches of, ii. 145; the colonists of, ii. 200; compared with Canada, ii. 199-203.
Newfoundland, i. 7, 45; the French fisheries of, ii. 94.
New France, La Tour becomes governor in, i. 49; incessant supernaturalism the key to the early history of, i. 61; political segregation in, ii. 200.
New France, the Company of, see *Company of New France, the*.
New Hampshire, State of, ii. 115.
New Netherlands, i. 187; passes into English hands, i. 249.
New Orleans, city of, ii. 59.
New Scotland, charter of, i. 4.
Newspaper, the first Canadian, ii. 161.
New York, site of, i. 4; i. 113; Talon urges the purchase or seizure of, ii. 10.

Nicholson, General, finally seizes Acadia for England, i. 52.
Nicole, the Jansenist, on the zealots at the "Hermitage," i. 146-151; i. 205, 206.
Nicolls, governor of New York, i. 260.
Noblesse, Canadian, ii. 51; French, ii. 52.
Noddle's Island, i. 45.
Noël, Jean, ii. 44.
Noël, Philippe, ii. 44.
Normandy, ii. 13.
Normans, the, ii. 12.
North America, contest for ownership of, i. 3; given by Louis XIII. to the Company of New France, i. 7.
Norton, John, signs the "Ipswich Letter," i. 30; Governor Winthrop's reply to, i. 31.
Notre Dame, the brethren of, i. 123.
Notre Dame, the Church of, at Montreal, i. 226.
Notre Dame, the Church of, at Quebec, ii. 36, 37.
Nova Scotia, i. 4, 8.
Nuns, the, at Montreal, i. 105; privations of, i. 106; additions to, i. 107; Jouaneaux devotes himself to the service of, i. 108.
Nuns, the, at Quebec, ii. 157, 158.

OHIO RIVER, the, ii. 59.
Olier, Jean Jacques, founder of St. Sulpice, i. 99; death of, i. 99.
Ondakont, Joachim, adventures of, i. 78.
Oneida Indians, the, i. 57, 66; at Onondaga, i. 81; the Jesuits among, i. 84; i. 244; send deputies to Tracy, i. 266; Bruyas ordered to, i. 266; Milet among, ii. 116.

INDEX.

Onondaga, the famous salt-springs of, i. 68; the Jesuits at, i. 54–95; Le Moyne at, i. 121.

Onondaga colonists, the, journey of, set out from Quebec, i. 74; i. 77–79; evil designs of the Indians upon, i. 89; the Medicine Feast, i. 91; their escape, i. 93; their arrival in Quebec, i. 94.

Onondaga Iroquois Indians, at Montreal, i. 56; covet the Huron colony, i. 62; invite the French to plant a colony among them, i. 63; Father Le Moyne sent among, i. 64; demand a French colony to be established among them, i. 69; Chaumonot and Dablon sent among, i. 70, 71; their punishment of prisoners, i. 72; celebration of the Dream Feast, i. 72; the Jesuits decide to establish a colony among, i. 74; at Onondaga, i. 82; jealousy for the Mohawks, i. 86; slaughter their Huron prisoners, i. 87; diabolical plots against the Jesuits, i. 89; send an embassy to Quebec, i. 245; sue for peace, i. 266; Lamberville among, ii. 116.

Onondaga, the Lake of, i. 67, 79, 80; France and the Faith intrenched on, i. 83.

Onondaga, the Mission of, see *Saint Mary of Gannentaa, the Mission of*.

Onondaga River, the, i. 65, 70.

"Onontio," i. 174.

Ontario, Lake, i. 65, 78.

Orange, Fort (Albany), i. 188.

Order of Jesus, the, i. 154.

Orinoco River, the, i. 234.

Orleans, the Duke of, i. 230; ii. 84.

Orleans, the Island of, census of, ii. 35; i. 62, 76; ii. 43, 82, 139, 164.

Orleans, the seigniory of, ii. 138; population of, ii. 139.

Ormeaux, Sieur des, see *Daulac, Adam*.

Oswego River, the, i. 78, 93, 94.

Ottawa River, the, i. 125, 128, 130.

Oudiette, granted monopoly in the Tadoussac trade, ii. 102; establishes a hat factory, ii. 106; becomes bankrupt, ii. 107.

Ouelle River, the, ii. 38, 93.

Palace of Justice, the, ii. 71.

Palace of the Intendant, the, ii. 71.

Papal (Ultramontane) Party, the, i. 153; tenets of, i. 153.

Paris, i. 9, 99; ii. 13.

Paris, the Archbishop of, ii. 127.

Paris, the General Hospital of, ii. 18.

Paris, the Parliament of, i. 154, 190.

Parishes, the country, ii. 189.

Pawnee Indians, the, ii. 190.

Pays d'Aunis, ii. 13.

Pemigewasset River, the, ii. 115.

Penobscot, the Pentegoet of the French, i. 15; Plymouth trading station at, i. 15; attacked by D'Aunay, i. 15; i. 17.

Penobscot River, the, i. 15.

Pentegoet of the French, the, i. 15.

Pequot Indians, the, antagonism to the whites, i. 24.

Percherons, the, ii. 12.

Pérot, Isle, ii. 38.

Perrot, Governor of Montreal, ii. 83.

Perrot, Nicolas, i. 77, 252.

Petit Cap, the, heights of, ii. 165; shrine at, ii. 166.

Petit, Father, ii. 187.

Petite Nation, the, seigniory of, i. 224.
Petraea, Bishop of, see *Laval-Montmorency, François Xavier de*.
Peuvret, Laval's secretary, ii. 226.
Philadelphia, site of, i. 4.
Philip's War, ii. 118.
Phipps, Admiral, ii. 233.
Phips, Sir William, captures Acadia for England, i. 52.
Picards, the, ii. 12.
Picardy, ii. 13.
Pierron, Father Jean, ordered to the Mohawks, i. 266.
Pijart, the Jesuit, i. 144.
Plymouth, i. 15.
Plymouth trading-houses, at Machias, i. 15; attacked by La Tour, i. 15; at Penobscot, i. 15; attacked by D'Aunay, i. 15.
Poincy, Longvilliers, ii. 211.
Point aux Trembles, ii. 38.
Poiton, ii. 13.
Poncet, Father, captured by the Iroquois, i. 56; his life spared by the Iroquois, i. 59; his adventures among the Iroquois, i. 59-61.
Ponchartrain, ii. 49, 100, 107.
Porpoise-fishing, ii. 93.
Porte St. Antoine, the, i. 242.
Portland Point, supposed site of Fort La Tour at, i. 39.
Portneuf, the seigniory of, ii. 43.
Port Royal, Razilly reaches, i. 8; D'Aunay makes his headquarters at, i. 9; D'Aunay's reign at, i. 11; description of, i. 13; i. 32, 36, 37, 38, 48; captured by Maj. Robert Sedgwick, i. 52; ii. 207, 208.
Pottawattamie Indians, the, ii. 112.
Poutrincourt, i. 5.

Pretextata, ii. 147.
Prévot, Major of Quebec, ii. 259.
Priests, the Canadian, ii. 145.
Printing-press, the, first in Canada, ii. 161.
Propaganda at Rome, the, i. 219.
Protestantism, in Canada, ii. 203.
Puritans, the, threaten to destroy the infant colony by their theological quarrels, i. 24; their ideas of religious toleration, i. 24; troubles of, i. 25; Louis XIII.'s desire to keep peace with, i. 33; D'Aunay makes overtures of friendship to, i. 33; M. Marie visits, i. 34; D'Aunay sends envoys to, i. 42.
Pyrenees, the, peace of, i. 242.

QUATRE ARTICLES of 1682, the, i. 153.
Quebec, site of, i. 4; least exposed to Indian attacks, i. 56; grand council of the Indians at, i. 57; fur-trade at, i. 58; peace concluded with the Indians at, i. 61; the Canadian Church focussed at, i. 103; i. 118; a comet appears above, i. 119; in danger, i. 125, 133, 139; its struggle against Montreal, i. 155; portents of coming evil, i. 182; the earthquake at, i. 185-187; a little hell of discord, i. 193; the new government, i. 194; plan to make a city of, i. 212; political troubles at, i. 213; Laval proposes to establish a seminary at, i. 220; tariff of prices at, ii. 5; young women shipped to, ii. 19; settlements about, ii. 29; Talon aims to concentrate the population around, ii. 32; census of, ii. 35; the superior council at, ii. 66;

INDEX. 291

chimney-sweeping neglected at, ii. 77; a *bourse* established at, ii. 101; the Jesuits rigorous at, ii. 152; the Congregation of the Holy Family in, ii. 154; almshouse established at, ii. 182; early police regulations of, ii. 185; the Lower Town burned to the ground, ii. 186; busy months at, ii. 188; the women of, ii. 189; ii. 238.
Quebec, the Château of, ii. 61.
Quebec, the Church of, i. 241.
Quebec, the College of, ii. 161.
Quebec, the Council of, created by Laval, i. 191; refuses to acknowledge the powers of Dumesnil, i. 191; the members of, i. 195; seize the papers of Dumesnil, i. 198; Mézy in opposition to, i. 208; changes made by Mézy in, i. 213.
Quebec, the Rock of, the French made a lodgment on, i. 7; i. 103; ii. 164.
Queu, De, on the Jesuits at Onondaga, i. 73.
Queylus, Abbé de, i. 141; the Sulpitian candidate for the bishopric of Canada, i. 141; made vicar-general for all Canada, i. 142; description of, i. 143; his experiences in Quebec, i. 143; his animosity to the Jesuits, i. 143, 144; opposes Laval, i. 155; shipped to France, i. 156; ordered to Rome, i. 156; receives a cold welcome, i. 156; disobeys the King's orders and returns to Canada, i. 157; in conflict with Laval, i. 157; again compelled to return to France, i. 158; his expulsion a defeat for the Sulpitians, i. 158; bulls obtained from Rome by, i. 158; finds his position untenable, i. 160; reconciliation with Laval, 160; returns to Canada as a missionary, i. 160; ii. 153.

Radisson, Pierre Esprit, remarkable narratives of, i. 94; account of Daulac's fight with the Iroquois, i. 138.
Raffeix, at the Seneca missions, ii. 116.
Ragueneau, Father, on the dissimulation of the Iroquois, i. 81; joins the Huron fugitives, i. 86; i. 172; on the earthquake at Quebec, i. 184; his trade with the Indians, ii. 126; at Quebec, ii. 152.
Raisin, Sister, i. 102.
Rameau, i. 11, 51, 53.
Rattlesnake Hill, i. 23.
Raudin, Ensign, ii. 37.
Raudot, the intendant, ii. 49, 77, 93, 97, 178, 241.
Razilly, Claude de, takes possession of the French settlements in Acadia and Canada for France, i. 8; reaches Port Royal, i. 8; grants of Acadian lands made to, i. 8; death of, i. 9; succeeded by D'Aunay, i. 9; i. 11.
Récollet Friars, the, in Fort St. Jean, i. 37; join D'Aunay, i. 38; complain that D'Aunay ill-used them, i. 49; cherished hope of, i. 141; missions of, ii. 118; sent to Canada by Colbert, ii. 136; Talon favors, ii. 137; the Jesuits reluctant to share their power with, ii. 154; in dispute with the bishop, ii. 155; ii. 206, 207, 208, 253.
"Redoubt of the Infant Jesus," the, i. 116.

Rémy, Daniel de, Sieur de Courcelle, i. 236; appointed governor of Canada, i. 236; his arrival at Quebec, i. 239; breathed nothing but war, i. 246; his march against the Mohawks, i. 246; his "Blue Coats," i. 247; failure of his expedition, i. 249; his second expedition against the Mohawks, i. 253; characteristics of, ii. 133; Talon complains to Colbert of, ii. 133; Colbert's letter to, ii. 133; his opposition to the Jesuits, ii. 133; his episode with Father Châtelain, ii. 152; ii. 250.

Repentigny, i. 195; chosen mayor of Quebec, i. 212; joins Tracy against the Mohawks, i. 254, 256; asks aid from the King, ii. 55.

Repentigny, Madame de, ii. 97.

Richelieu, Cardinal, at the head of the Company of New France, i. 7; supports the Capuchin friars, i. 13; first plants feudalism in Canada, ii. 41.

Richelieu River, the, i. 133, 244, 247, 261; ii. 28, 29, 30, 33, 37, 38.

Riverin, ii. 92; memorial on the establishment of commerce in Canada presented by, ii. 93, 237, 238.

Rivière du Loup, ii. 142.

Rivière du Sud, ii. 142.

Robert, appointed intendant of Canada, i. 218.

Robineau, René, ii. 43, 60.

Rochefort, ii. 92.

Rochelle, Huguenot city of, i. 18, 96, 99, 101, 102; ii. 12, 90, 196.

Rochet, i. 19.

Rocky Mountains, the, discovery of, ii. 24, 59.

Roman Catholic Church, the, ii. 158; stands out conspicuous in the history of Canada, ii. 203.

Romans, the, ii. 29.

Rome, i. 156, 158.

Rome, the Court of, i. 159.

Rosiers, Cape, i. 52.

Rouen, ii. 18.

Rouen, the Archbishop of, i. 142, 154, 155, 159, 160, 220; ii. 18.

Rouen, the Parliament of, i. 154.

Royalty, the triumph of, ii. 41.

Ryswick, the treaty of, restores Acadia to France, i. 52.

Sable, Cape, i. 5, 6, 7; Charles de la Tour made commander at, i. 9; La Tour's little kingdom at, i. 10; La Tour removes to Fort St. Jean from, i. 14; La Tour returns to, i. 45.

Saguenay River, the, ii. 34.

"St. André," the ship, i. 96; the company on board, i. 96.

St. Anne, Fort, i. 260, 261; Dollier sent to, i. 262; the garrison at, i. 264.

St. Anne, heights of, ii. 164.

St. Anne, settlement of, i. 126.

St. Anne de la Pocatière, ii. 38.

St. Anne du Petit Cap, ii. 166.

St. Anne River, the, i. 130.

Saint-Augustin, Mother Catherine de, i. 183, 240.

Saint-Castin, ii. 59.

St. Charles River, the, ii. 71, 187.

"St. Clement," the, i. 19, 20; in Boston Harbor, i. 21; sails for France, i. 36.

St. Croix Bay, i. 8.

St. Croix, Point, i. 76.

St. Croix River, the, i. 8.

St. Denis, the seigniory of, ii. 142.

Saint-Denis, Mother Juchereau de, Superior of the Hôtel-Dieu, i.

INDEX. 293

161; her eulogy on Laval, i. 161.

St. Étienne, Charles de, son of La Tour, i. 51.

Saint Francis Xavier, the mission of, ii. 116; Milet at, ii. 116.

St. Gabriel, the fortified house of, i. 110, 111.

St. Germain, the treaty of, restores the French settlements in Acadia and Canada to France, i. 8.

Saint-Ignace, Frances Juchereau de, i. 126; on the earthquake at Quebec, i. 184, 185; on the merits of Mézy, i. 206; on the Marquis de Tracy, i. 238; on the arrival of the Marquis de Tracy at Quebec, i. 239; on Talon's zeal for the success of the colony, ii. 8; on the population of Quebec, ii. 35; on the condition of the ornamental arts in Canada, ii. 98; on the miracles in Canada, ii. 161; on Paul Dupuy, ii. 171; on extravagance in Canada, ii. 183.

St. Jean, Fort, La Tour removes from Cape Sable to, i. 14; location of, i. 14; i. 16, 17, 18, 20, 36; attacked and captured by D'Aunay, i. 39; site of, i. 39; i. 41, 46; its value as a trading-station, i. 47; La Tour regains possession of, i. 51, 52; captured by Maj. Robert Sedgwick, i. 52.

St. Joachim, the parish of, seminary at, i. 223; ii. 164, 165.

St. John, city of, i. 7, 39.

St. John River, the, Charles de la Tour, receives grants of land on, i. 7, 14; Charles de la Tour builds a fort on, i. 7; i. 29, 36, 38; ii. 205, 206, 207, 208, 210.

Saint John the Baptist, the mission of, ii. 116; Lamberville at, ii. 116.

Saint Joseph, the mission of, ii. 116; Carheil at, ii. 116.

St. Joseph, the Sisterhood of, founded by Danversière, i. 97; left penniless, i. 98.

St. Laurent, the seigniory of, ii. 43, 60.

St. Lawrence, the Gulf of, i. 52.

St. Lawrence River, the, i. 4, 7, 46, 56, 59, 64, 73, 78, 88, 94, 103, 104, 119, 165, 179, 185, 187, 224, 236, 238, 246; ii. 8, 29, 33, 34, 37, 39, 95, 101, 141, 164, 196, 198.

St. Louis, the castle of, i. 239.

St. Louis, Château, i. 120; ii. 32, 36, 70, 80, 126; history of, ii. 232-235.

St. Louis, city of, ii. 59.

St. Louis, Fort, at Quebec, ii. 224.

St. Louis, Fort of, i. 56, 73, 77, 86, 103, 250.

St. Louis, the Lake of, i. 65; ii. 38.

Saint-Lusson, takes possession of the country of the Upper Lakes, ii. 10.

St. Malo, i. 94.

St. Martin's Day, ii. 47, 50.

Saint Mary of Gannentaa, the mission of, the beginnings of, i. 83; crisis drawing near at, i. 88; a miserable failure, i. 94.

St. Michel, ii. 187.

Saint-Ouen, the parish of, ii. 215.

Saint-Ours, Monsieur de, ii. 56.

Saint Ours, town of, ii. 30.

St. Paul, the Bay of, ii. 34, 92, 101.

Saint-Père, Jean, i. 110.

St. Peter, Lake, ii. 29.

Saint-Quentin, M. de, i. 123.

Saint-Simon, Duc de, his portrait of Louis XIV., ii. 86, 87.

St. Sacrament, Lake (Lake George), i. 253.

INDEX.

St. Sulpice, the Seminary of, i. 99; founded by Olier, i. 99; i. 141, 159; ii. 38, 137; attacked by Saint-Vallier. ii. 140; the citadel of the Canadian Church, ii. 140.

St. Valérien, Mont, i. 143.

Saint-Vallier, Bishop of Quebec, succeeds Laval, ii. 128; letter from the King to, ii. 128; ii. 137; attacks the Seminary of Quebec, ii. 140; estimates of, ii. 141; ii. 144; his directions to Denonville, ii. 146; his invectives against the vanity of women, ii. 147; ii. 164, 179; overwhelmed with beggars. ii. 182; founds the General Hospital of Quebec, ii. 182.

Ste. Claire d'Argentan, the abbey of, i. 149, 150.

Sainte-Hélène, Mother du Plessis de, ii. 18.

Ste. Marie, the fortified house of, i. 110; the scene of hot and bloody fights, i. 114.

Ste. Thérèse, Fort, i. 247, 249, 250.

Salem, La Tour in, i. 32; M. Marie, in, i. 35.

Salières, Colonel de, i. 242, 243, 245.

Salina, the salt-springs of, i. 80.

Salmon Falls, fort and settlement of, i. 123.

Saltonstall, signs the "Ipswich Letter," i. 30; Governor Winthrop's reply to, i. 31.

Sangrado of Montreal, the, i. 261.

Saratoga Lake, i. 249.

Sarrazin, Michel, the physician, ii. 168; sketch of, ii. 169.

Savoy, i. 242.

Schenectady, i. 249.

Schools, in Canada, ii. 162.

Sedgwick, Major Robert, conquers Acadia for England, i. 52.

Seignelay, the minister, memorial on the establishment of commerce in Canada, presented by Chalons and Riverin to, ii. 94, 95, 237, 238.

Seignior, the, in Canada, ii. 42, 67, 79.

Seigniorial tenure, in Canada, ii. 33, 51.

Seigniories, in Canada, ii. 33, 42.

Seneca Indians, the, i. 57, 66, 75; at Onondagas, i. 82; the Jesuits among, i. 84; i. 133; send an embassy to Quebec, i. 245; sue for peace, i. 251, 266.

Seneca missions, the, i. 94; ii. 116; Raffeix and Garnier at, ii. 116.

Seven Years' War, the, i. 39.

Sevestre, Charles, i. 196.

Sévigné, Madame de, i. 230.

Shawmut, the peninsula of, i. 15.

Shea, J. G., ii. 4.

Sheldon, ii. 121.

Ship-building in Canada, ii. 98.

Sillery, i. 68, 75, 246; Jesuit eel-pots at, ii. 131; the heights of, ii. 196.

Sillery, the mission of, ii. 118, 122.

Sioux Indians, the, ii. 112.

Slavery in Canada, ii. 190.

"Soldiers of the Holy Family of Jesus, Mary, and Joseph," i. 116.

Sorbonne, the, the Fathers of, ii. 126; the scholastic duels of, ii. 162.

Sorel, i. 245; sent against the Mohawks, i. 251; ii. 30.

Sorel, Fort of, ii. 38.

Sorel, town of, i. 245; new forts at, i. 247; ii. 30.

Souart, Father, i. 141; left in spiritual charge of Montreal, i. 142.

South America, i. 234.

Spain, ii. 150.

Stuarts, the, i. 164.

INDEX. 295

Sulpitians, the, i. 100; efforts to strengthen the colony at Montreal, i. 102; jealousy of the Jesuits for, i. 103; assume entire spiritual charge of Montreal, i. 110; the Island of Montreal passes into the possession of, i. 141; their plans to obtain the bishopric of Canada, i. 141; despair of obtaining the bishopric, i. 142; their struggle against the Jesuits, i. 155; the expulsion of Queylus a defeat for, i. 158; their plan of land-grants, ii. 29; claim the right to name their own local governor, ii. 64; missions of, ii. 118; rigorous at Montreal, ii. 152.

Sulte, Benjamin, ii. 184.

Superior, Lake, i. 138; the copper of, ii. 7; posts of the *coureurs de bois* on, ii. 112.

Susane, on the regiment of Carignan-Salières, i. 243.

Swearing, Louis XIV.'s famous edict against, ii. 80.

Syndic, the, in Canada, ii. 79.

TADOUSSAC, i. 186, 236; ii. 34; fur-trade at, ii. 101.

Talon, Jean Baptiste, i. 188, 215; appointed intendant of Canada, i. 236; his arrival at Quebec, i. 239; the chosen agent of paternal royalty, ii. 3; his personal appearance, ii. 3; his portrait, ii. 4; a true disciple of Colbert, ii. 4; sets himself to galvanize Canada, ii. 5; Colbert's instructions to, ii. 5; his zeal for the colony, ii. 6-10; his policy, ii. 9; urges the purchase or seizure of New York, ii. 10; his fidelity to his trust, ii. 10; failing health, ii. 10; asks for his recall, ii. 10; resumes the intendancy, ii. 10; his property, ii. 10; his efforts to people Canada, ii. 13, 15, 16; places a premium on marriage, ii. 22; satisfactory results, ii. 25; his plan of dividing the lands into seigniorial grants, ii. 29; on the Canadian settler, ii. 31; aims to concentrate the population around Quebec, ii. 32; his model seigniory, ii. 33; his villages, ii. 33; grants of land made by, ii. 37; his plan of administration, ii. 42; asks for patents of nobility, ii. 53; the old brewery of, ii. 71; his attempt to establish trade with the West Indies, ii. 91, 98; ii. 129, 133; complains of Courcelle, ii. 133; ordered to watch the Jesuits, ii. 133; favors the Récollets, ii. 137; orders La Fredière home to France, ii. 171; tries to control the inns, ii. 185; his correspondence with Colbert regarding marriage and population in Canada, ii. 229-232; ii. 236; his memorial of the present condition of Canada, ii. 248; his letter from Colbert on the government and the clergy in Canada, ii. 250; instructions received from the King regarding the government and the clergy in Canada, ii. 251; ii. 254.

Tellier, i. 227.

Temple, Thomas, obtains a grant of Acadia from Cromwell, i. 53.

Terron, i. 201.

Theresa, Saint, the day of, i. 255.

Thousand Islands, the, i. 87.

Three Rivers, settlement of, i. 55, 56; beset by the Mohawks, i. 56; fur-trade at, i. 58; i. 118,

121, 122, 125, 127, 130, 133, 247, 250; tariff of prices at, ii. 5; ii. 24, 37; local governor at, ii. 64; ii. 83; annual fair established at, ii. 104; ii. 129, 179; almshouse established at, ii. 182; ii. 238.
Tilly, the seigniory of, ii. 44.
Tilly, Le Gardeur de, appointed councillor at Quebec, i. 195, 213; asks aid from the King, ii. 55.
Tilly (son), ii. 73.
Torture, considered by the Jesuits to be a blessing in disguise, i. 124.
Tourmente, Cape, i. 238; ii. 34, 164, 196.
Tracy, Marquis Prouville de, i. 179, 188, 216, 236; appointed lieutenant-general of America, i. 237; description of, i. 238; his arrival at Quebec, i. 238; received by Laval, i. 239; sets out against the Mohawks, i. 253; success of his expedition, i. 257; trouble with the English, i. 260; his return to Quebec, i. 260; the Iroquois sue for peace, i. 265; his expedition against the Iroquois the most productive of good, i. 267; leaves Canada, ii. 3; his tariff of prices, ii. 5; the fruit of his chastisement of the Mohawks, ii. 37; his plan of administration, ii. 42; asks for patents of nobility, ii. 53; removes Maisonneuve, ii. 64; ii. 133; escapes clerical attacks, ii. 135; ii. 254.
Trade in Canada, restrictions upon, ii. 89.
Tremblay, M., i. 162.
Tremont, i. 23.
Trimount, i. 23.
Troyes, town of, i. 102.
Turenne, i. 263.

Turgis, the true surname of La Tour's family, i. 10; the arms of, i. 10.
Turkish Wars, the, ii. 171.
Turks, the, i. 188, 242.
Two Mountains, the Lake of, i. 130.

ULTRAMONTANE (Papal) Party, the, i. 153; tenets of, i. 153; outflank the King and the Gallicans, i. 154; its struggle against the Gallicans, i. 155.
United Colonies, the, commissioners of, i. 34, 35, 42, 44.
Upper Lakes, the, Saint-Lusson takes possession of the country of, ii. 10.
Ursuline Convent at Quebec, the, i. 171; ii. 36; engraving of, ii. 36; burned, ii. 36.
Ursulines, the, of Caen, ii. 215.
Ursulines, the, of Quebec, i. 125, 145, 243; ii. 7, 36, 83, 137, 158, 167.
Utrecht, the Peace of, ii. 98.

VALOIS, i. 229.
Varennes, town of, ii. 30, 38.
Varennes, René Gaultier de, ii. 24, 259.
Vasseur, describes the burning of Laval's seminary, ii. 186.
Vaudreuil, ii. 242.
Vendôme, Duc de, Madame d'Aunay applies for help to, i. 51.
Verchères, town of, ii. 30, 38.
Verd, Cape, i. 234.
Verrazzano, voyage of, i. 3.
Versailles, ii. 61, 84, 141.
Viger, J., i. 144, 255.
Vignal, Guillaume de, the priest, i. 96; killed by the Iroquois, i. 112, 113.

INDEX. 297

Villemarie, see *Montreal*.
Villeray, Rouer de, appointed councillor at Quebec, i. 195; Argenson's opinion of, i. 196; becomes the richest man in Canada, i. 197; i. 203; removed from the council by Mézy, i. 208; i. 213; banished to France, i. 214; ii. 221, 222.
Vimont, Father, ii. 129.
Virginia, English heretics in, i. 15; i. 46, 234.
Vismes, Dubreuil, ii. 211.
Vitry, Sieur, ii. 93.

WALCKENAER, i. 230.
Ward, Nathaniel, signs the "Ipswich letter," i. 30; Governor Winthrop's reply to, i. 31.
Washington, site of, i. 4.
West, the Company of, the, i. 234.
West India Company, the, ii. 65; its charter revoked, ii. 89; extinguished, ii. 102; revived, ii. 109; given a monopoly of exporting beaver-skins, ii. 109.
West Indies, the, i. 44, 237, 241; Talon's efforts to establish trade between Canada and, ii. 7, 91, 96; ii. 106; slaves imported into Canada from, ii. 190.
William Henry, Fort, i. 253.

Williamson, i. 7.
Winthrop, Fort, i. 21.
Winthrop, Governor, i. 19; La Tour asks aid against D'Aunay from, i. 22; entertains La Tour, i. 23-27; allows La Tour to hire allies, i. 28, 29; sharply criticised for giving assistance to La Tour, i. 29; his action approved by the majority, i. 30; the "Ipswich letter," i. 30; his reply to, i. 31; letter from Bradstreet to, i. 31; entertains D'Aunay's envoys, i. 42; arranges a treaty with D'Aunay, i. 43, 44; deceived in La Tour, i. 46.
Witches, Canada never troubled by, ii. 157.
Wolf Indians, the, i. 124.
Wolfe, ii. 44.
Women, political influence among the Iroquois of, i. 84.
Wood, i. 22, 23.
Wooster River, i. 123.

XAVIER, Saint Francis, fête of, i. 166; i. 225.

YORK, the Duke of, i. 249.

ZRIN, the fortress of, i. 188.

www.ingramcontent.com/pod-product-compliance
Lightning Source LLC
Chambersburg PA
CBHW030729230426
43667CB00007B/642